Jewish Influences

in

American Life

Volume III
of
The International Jew

The World's Foremost Problem

Being a Reprint of a Series of Articles
Appearing in THE DEARBORN INDEPENDENT

November, 1921

Reprinted 2004 by
Liberty Bell Publications
PO Box 890
York, SC 29745
www.libertybellpublications.com
803.684.4408

ISBN: 1-59364-019-6

FOREWARD
To the Bi-Centennial Edition

In the year1920 Henry Sr. published *The International Jew,* a comprehensive survey of Jewish Power in the United States and throughout the world. This four-volume work was originally serialized in the *Dearborn Independent,* the house organ of the Ford Motor Company.

These books have been best-sellers in many parts of the world, and have been translated into the languages of most civilized countries. Sadly, there are many countries today where possession of these books has been made punishable by confiscation or worse. In Germany, for example, a person who wants to borrow *The International Jew* from a library must first prove that he needs it for historical research. In other words, an ordinary tax-paying member of the public who supports the public library with his hard-earned money is unable to further his knowledge or satisfy his curiosity in this regard.

It is therefore in the interest of spreading truth that we republish these books in full so that new generations shall see for themselves how our problems of today are the same problems which have "mysteriously" occurred since the turn of the century. The fact that even the wealthy Henry Ford, Sr. could be forced to withdraw these books, starkly illuminates the power of the Jews, even in the 1920's. To reprint *The International Jew* now, when the Jews are so much more powerful, is some indication of the tremendous courage of the publisher.

Every American who loves his country should make it his duty to buy sufficient copies for donation to libraries, universities, business associations, etc. Most important, every American parent should have at least one set at home to pass on to his children.

In further support of the findings and conclusions of *The International Jew,* an excellent companion book, *The Dispossessed Majority,* by Wilmot Robertson, exposes the rapid increase of Jewish power since the first publication of Henry Ford's great work. No conscientious, thinking American should be without these amazing, fact-filled books.

Preface

THE present volume, third in the series, is compiled for the same purpose as its predecessors—to enable new readers of THE DEARBORN INDEPENDENT to commence their reading with the earlier articles in the series of studies in The Jewish Question.

It was inevitable that the publication first to open the discussion of this Question would be compelled to meet the degrading charge of "anti-semitism" and kindred falsehoods; but it was also inevitable that if the work of such a publication should prove to be valid, the way would be cleared for discussion by other publications which had not and need not bring upon themselves the charge of racial hatred.

This is precisely what has occurred. An undreamed of publicity for the essentials of the Jewish Question has been achieved in this country. It is noteworthy that whether the publicity be in agreement with or against THE DEARBORN INDEPENDENT the essential facts are the same, and these facts were first set forth in this paper.

That, indeed, constitutes the strength of the articles. The facts are provable; they are not disprovable. The reader can confirm the facts from his own observation. With regard to the matters discussed in these volumes, there are too many observers of the Jew to permit misstatements to pass. This also constitutes the dilemma of the self-appointed defenders of the Jews: they may abuse THE DEARBORN INDEPENDENT, but they cannot disprove the facts. They do not make even an impressive denial of them. The whole situation would be much clarified if Jewish spokesmen would use frankness, instead of a fusillade of cheap and irrelevant abuse.

The year has witnessed much notable discussion of The Jewish Question in magazines of quality. A few have descended to white-washing, fewer still to sheer pro-Jewish propaganda; but such articles as those in the September *Century;* those in the *Atlantic* for February, May and July; *The Nineteenth Century and After* for April; the true and admirable accounts by Lieut. Commander Hugo W. Koehler, of the U. S. Navy, in the *World's Work* for July, August, September and October—these testify to the reality of the matter. The more serious religious press, as represented by publications like the *Christian Standard, the Christian Century, The Moody Monthly* which is published by The Moody Bible Institute, Chicago, have also added materially to the literature of the question. In editorial vision and liberty of discussion, the religious press has shown itself to be freer of control than has the secular press.

This volume contains information dealing with the influence of the Jewish idea on American life. The departments of life here studied do not by any means exhaust the list. The studies are more and more centering on the actual operations of the Jewish program upon the American people, and the effect of Jewish conceptions on our common life. These studies are appearing in THE DEARBORN INDEPENDENT now. They will be gathered into future volumes as 'may be required.

November, 1921.

Contents

The Writer of the Following Letter Is a Jew:

"Gentlemen:

> *'Because you believe in a good cause,' said Dr. Johnson, 'is no reason why you should feel called upon to defend it, for by your manner of defense you may do your cause much harm.'*

"The above applying to me I will only say that I have received the books you sent me and read both with much interest.

"You are rendering the Jews a very great service, that of saving them from themselves.

"It takes courage, and nerve, and intelligence to do it and pursue such a work, and I admire you for it."

XLIII.

The Jews and the "Religious Persecution" Cry

W E CHEERFULLY give the Jews of the United States credit for knowing when they are getting their money's worth. In the defense that has been set up for them they know that they have not had their money's worth, neither from Jewish money collectors nor from the "Gentile fronts" to whom the money has been paid. The Louis Marshall line of defense has broken down. The boycott has dribbled into nothingness. Speeches in Congress and editorials in newspapers have sounded too hollow to carry conviction. The Question has proved itself far too big for those who have entered the defense for gain, to satisfy personal grudges, or to win what they feel to be the favor of the stronger side. The Jews long ago quit the course which some of the "gentile fronts" still continue; the Jews recognized the futility of it.

No intelligent Jew in the United States ever was asinine enough to declare that the Jewish Question is a religious question and that THE DEARBORN INDEPENDENT'S investigation of that question constituted "religious persecution." No Jew known beyond the next street has ever ventured such a silly charge. But it is apparently all that remains for the "Gentile fronts" to shout about. From what can be learned of them they are for the most part men of no religion themselves and they use the term "religious persecution" as a red rag which they think will stir people into action. It is rather curious

how the cry of "religious persecution" is used to evoke the
spirit of persecution against alleged persecutors.

THE DEARBORN INDEPENDENT this week goes out of its
course to squelch once and for all this cry of religious
persecutions.

Three statements are sufficient to outline the situation:

First, neither directly nor by implication has THE
DEARBORN INDEPENDENT held that the Jewish Question is a
religious question. On the contrary, supported by the highest
Jewish authority, this paper has held that the Jewish
Question is one of race and nationality. (See issues of October
9 and 16, 1920; reprinted in the new book, volume two of "The
International Jew.")

Second, there is no religious persecution of the Jew in the
United States, unless the agitation of various humane societies
for the abolition of "kosher killing" may be considered such.
The Massachusetts Society for the Prevention of Cruelty to
Animals has published a valuable study of the Jewish method
of slaughtering animals for food, in which is adduced much
scientific evidence to support the conclusion that the Jewish
method is "needlessly cruel." But even this can only with
difficulty be stretched into an interference with "the religion of
the Jews." The Jewish method of slaughter as now practiced is
not commanded in the Old Testament but in the Talmud, and
is, therefore, not religious in the authoritative sense, but
traditional. Moreover, there is positive evidence that modern
methods achieve the Jewish purpose (the disposal of the blood
of the carcass) much better than does the Jewish method. This
is the only instance where even remotely the religion of the
Jews has been touched.

Third, the fact is that while there is no "religious
persecution" of the Jews, there is very much real religious
persecution *by* the Jews. That is one of the outstanding
characteristics of organized Jewish life in the United States,
its active, unceasing, powerful and virulent attacks upon any

and all forms of Christianity which may chance to come to public notice. Now and again we hear of outbreaks of sectarian bigotry between Catholics and Protestants, but these are not to be compared with the steady, relentless, alert, anti-Christian activity of the Jewish organizations. There are doctrinal disputes within the Christian churches, but none that challenge the basis of Christianity itself; organized Judaism, however, is not content with doctrinal disputation, but enlists its vast commercial and political power against everything that it regards as, in its own words, "Christological manifestations."

Now, these are facts, and being facts, they are important, and they ought to be publicly known.

No President of the United States has yet dared to take his inaugural oath on the open pages of the New Testament—the Jews would denounce him. When General Pershing announced that he considered the morale of the American soldier due to the interest of the Christian men and women at home, the Jews had him cut out the word "Christian." Various governors of American states, having used the word "Christian" in their Thanksgiving proclamations, have been obliged to excise it on demand of the Jews. The word "Christian" was compelled to be cut out of the officers' training manual at the Plattsburg training camp. Everything that would remind the child in school that he is living in the midst of a Christian civilization, in a nation declared by its Supreme Court to be founded on Christian principles, has been ordered out of the public schools on Jewish demand.

People sometimes ask why 3,000,000 Jews can control the affairs of 100,000,000 Americans. In the same way that ten Jewish student can abolish the mention of Christmas and Easter out of schools containing 3,000 Christian pupils.

In a nation and at a time when a minority of Jews can print every year a record of the apologies they have extorted form public officials for "having inadvertently used the term 'Christian,' " it is desirable that this charge of "religious persecution" should be placed where it belongs. In the *Daily American Tribune,* a Catholic daily published at Dubuque, Iowa, appeared a recent headline which said a great deal—*Not Persecution of The Jews, But Protection of The Christians.*

It is now proposed to let the Jews speak for themselves on this question. The Jewish press has been searched for an authoritative expression charging that the study of the Jewish Question constitutes "religious persecution," and none has been found. That cry has been reserved for "Gentile fronts" for use among Christians. All the attacks from the Jewish camp are against the doctrines and institutions of the Christians. They have carried on an insistent and successful persecution, and the details of it have filled the Jewish press for years past.

Upon reading the following selections, the remark of Dean Swift will probably come to mind: "We are fully convinced that we shall always tolerate them, but not that they will tolerate us."

The Red Cross is objectionable to the Jew. H. Lissauer, in *The Jewish Times,* proposed that the Magen David be substituted for "the red cross" on the Red Cross Society badges worn by Jews.

"We should not let our sensitiveness to charges of intolerance overcome our conscientious religious objections to the cross," says Mr. Lissauer. The editor of *The Jewish Independent* thinks the suggestion "is worthy of serious consideration."

The Gideons are objectionable to the Jew. The Gideons is the name given to the Christian Commercial Travelers' Association of America, whose efforts are responsible for the Bibles which are to be found in most hotel rooms. This is from the Cleveland *Jewish Independent*:

"It is quite evident that the Gideons do not know a typically Jewish name when they see or hear one. The Gideons' object, according to their letterheads, is 'winning commercial traveling men for Christ' and the way this is done is by placing a Christian Bible in each guest room of every hotel.

"The Gideons have been at it a long time, long enough to know better, but the other day they sent a letter to Max Cohen of this city, who is a traveling man but the kind the Gideons have no right to ask for funds, and the person who selected him for an 'easy mark' certainly should have had better sense.

"Mr. Cohen utterly failed to 'fall' for the invitation and instead of sending his little donation he wrote a letter to the secretary, C. A. Johnson, in which he bluntly said: 'Don't you think you ought to use better judgment than to ask me to contribute to a strictly religious work opposite to my own belief?'

"If the Gideons insist upon filling up hotels with Bibles that have no business there they should go to the right persons for contributions."

The Jews do not like the Salvation Army nor the Y. M. C. A. Many thousands of printed lines expressed the fury with which they regarded attempts to "Christianize the Army and Navy" during the war, and the wild arguments with which they sought to make "Y" work and Salvation Army work appear to be a violation of the principle of no union of Church and State. The same objection was made to religious welfare work during the building of the Panama Canal. If there is any challenge of this on the part of uninformed "Gentile fronts" (the Jews themselves will not challenge it) the evidence can be produced. It is only a matter of space.

The Jews did not like Theodore Roosevelt's choice of a hymn for the Progressive party:

"With Hon. Oscar S. Strauss as the nominee for the governorship of New York on the Progressive ticket, this question rises: Will the voters on the East Side of New York march to the Progressive battle hymn, 'Onward, Christian Soldiers,' or will the song have to be changed to fit the candidate?"— *American Israelite.*

The Jews hate with a malice beyond expression what they call "mission holes," that is, a place of instruction maintained by Christian churches where inquiring Jews may learn what Christianity is and, in many instances, where destitute and neglected Jews may receive assistance and counsel. The boast of how "The Jew cares for his own" is given a jolt by the dire need which has called Christian welfare work into Jewish settlements.

This hatred overrode good judgment so completely that in 1911 Assemblyman Heyman introduced into the New York State legislature a bill making it an offense punishable by fine or imprisonment to entice or tempt a minor under sixteen years of age into a religious mission, Sunday school or church without the written consent of the parents or guardian of the minor! The language indicates a part of the contempt in which the welfare work undertaken by Christian institutions for the neediest class of children in America is held by the leaders among the Jews; not by the masses of the Jews themselves, however, except when they are terrified by their leaders.

In St. Louis, application for a charter of the Jewish Christian Association was opposed. The converted Jews wanted an association of their own. They represented that they had been ostracized by the Jews and were desirous of organizing and owning their own meeting place. A referee advised against the charter on the ground that "it would be contrary to the broad spirit of religious freedom guaranteed under the constitution of Missouri." The referee was, of course, coached by Jews. In the name of religious freedom these Jews opposed giving an association freedom enough to preach the gospel.

In Toronto the Jewish leaders issued a proclamation throughout all Toronto Jewry forbidding the use of reading rooms, baths, dispensaries, motion picture shows or anything else which they described as "the petty bribery of conversionist tricksters who seek for their wealthy donators to open the gates of heaven and find salvation for their sins by converting a weak-minded Jew."

By the way, all converted Jews are weak-minded or criminal, if we are to believe the hundreds of statements to that effect in the Jewish papers. The Jews are, without exception, superior people until they become Christians; *then* learn what they are from the Jewish leaders!

Among the nice names for this welfare work are "Jesus holes," "mission traps," "Jew-snatchers," "child stealers."

It happened that one of the helpers in the Chicago Gospel Mission was principal of a Chicago public school. The Jews raised a great outcry against him, denounced him as unfit to teach children, and guilty of the "the moral turpitude of eating food provided by taxes of which a large share is received from Jews, whose children they seek to entice from their parental religion and whose men and women they are seeking to degrade into liars and hypocrites." All because a competent man was willing to meet Jewish inquirers, or perhaps bring a few of the benefits of civilization into the neglected ghetto. If this school teacher were Christian enough to have a conscience, he would resign, said the Jewish thunderers, and with that never-failing tinge of dark-mindedness they added: "What is done in secret in these haunts can, of course, only be guessed at."

Talk about bigotry! This from a people who encourage the cry that THE DEARBORN INDEPENDENT is engaged in "religious persecution," though THE DEARBORN INDEPENDENT has not yet carried even one of the scores of sensational and important stories which show the Federal Government discovering synagogues and rabbis as agents of the illicit liquor traffic. "These *haunts*" and hints of the things that may go on there, is the only way the *American Israelite* can find to refer to welfare works in which some of the best people, from no motive but the goodness of their hearts, engage.

A book of 500 pages could be filled with the unreasonable and in many cases positively vicious statements of leading Jews on any of the subjects touched here.

The Jews do not like the Christian Sabbath. The literature of attack against this institution is voluminous and the arguments extreme. Sunday is Christian, therefore to the Jew it is taboo. Court records in every state bear testimony to the fight of the Jews against Sunday. Few legislatures have escaped being pestered with bills on the subject. The latest fight has been the strongest yet waged, to destroy Sunday by throwing it wide open to Jewish exploitation. Yet the Jews are most chary of their own Sabbath. When recent college examinations fell on Jewish holy days, the Jews had the examinations changed. When primary elections last year fell on Jewish days, every power was moved to change them. There are Jewish records of a western governor being remonstrated with because a condemned criminal was sentenced to be hanged on Saturday—did the governor mean to "offend 3.000,000 Jews?" The St. Louis Charity Fair in 1908 planned to remain open on Friday evening; a great outcry; did the managers of that fair mean to insult the Jews; didn't they know that the Jewish Sabbath began on Friday night?

But when it is a question of maintaining the integrity of Sunday—pooh! pooh! "Don't the Christians know that Sunday perpetuates the silliest superstition, that their god Jesus rose from the dead?" When certain people aid the post office employes in an attempt to close the post offices on Sunday, the Jews regard it as a step back toward the dark ages.

Here is a Jewish editorial relating to Governor Cox. It appears that Governor Cox in 1914 stood for a decent Sunday and liquor law enforcement, and this is the threat held out to him:

"At the 59th Jackson Day banquet of the Wayne County (Ohio) Democracy, which was held at Wooster, Governor Cox made the principal address in which he defended laws passed at his instigation. The governor laid particular stress on the fact that for the first time in her history, Ohio now enjoys a 'Christian Sabbath.'

14

" 'I stand or fall by the Christian Sabbath in the next campaign,' the governor is reported to have said . . .

"There are many who construe the declaration to mean that Governor Cox has bid defiance to the liberal element of the state and will rely upon the religious and class prejudices which he is arousing and keeping alive in the rural districts, to re-elect him to his present office, or, what is clearly plain from his entire attitude, boost him into the nomination for United States Senatorship. The *Israelite* will take great pleasure about the time the leaves begin to turn in reminding Governor Cox of his statement that he 'will stand or fall by a Christian Sabbath' in the coming campaign. "—*American Israelite.*

The literature of Jewish thought toward Sunday presents complete evidence of the leaders' antagonism to this distinctly Christian and Anglo-Saxon institution. Sunday has never been regarded as set apart, in those countries where the Jewish idea has most infiltrated. The decline of Sunday in the United States is directly along the line of those invasions for the Sunday spirit which are mostly aligned with Jewish commercial interests. In Great Britain and her colonies where the Jew is not permitted to usurp a superior place as chief censor of morals and religion and education, Sunday is decently observed. The situation is this country is that, instead of enjoying its liberty, the Jewish leaders have taken liberties. The student who wished to know how deep and hard-set is the anti-Sunday program will find all the material he wants in Jewish sources.

The theme of this article is "religious prejudice." You will not find it anywhere within the whole range of the Jewish Question, except on the Jewish side. There is, in the United States, a religious prejudice, but it is strictly Yiddish. If the Christian population bothered one one-hundred thousandth part as much about Jewish religion as the Jews bother about Christian observances, the whole fabric of Talmudical teaching would be consumed in the bright light to which general attention would bring it, the bright light from which it has always been concealed. Sheer analysis in the interest of mental health, if undertaken by fifty men, would compel the Jewish people by their own decision to abandon the darkness which holds them now. Jewish Talmudism owes its existence today to the indifference with which it is regarded. This is the far opposite extreme of "religious persecution."

The list of headlines describing the various angles of Jewish anti-Christian religious prejudice is not, however, exhausted.

The Jew is prejudiced against the Bible. When he uses that term, he does not mean what the ordinary person means. Therefore, he does what he can to destroy public honor of the Book, unless it be an occasion where a President has been inaugurated, when it will run through the Jewish press like a strong breeze that once more has a Christian statesman ignored the Christian Bible and turned to the Jewish Bible. It is rather a trifling matter to mention; its significance comes solely from the light it throws on the Jewish attitude. It is not a trifling thing in Jewry, as the country will probably be made aware if any future President should be sworn in with, say, the Sermon on the Mount open before him.

And yet, even here, we observe a strange paradox. A Jewish authority says: "The Jew is a paradox. He is at once an idealist and a materialist. He is parsimonious and extravagant. He is courageous and cowardly. He is modest and vulgar. He is persistent and yielding. He is peaceful and warlike"—and so on. And though the Jew opposes the Bible in the schools, he never misses a chance to put it there, with the Jewish trade-mark. He quotes the Psalms—"We wrote them." He quotes Isaiah—"We Jews did that."

Most people sit open-mouthed at these glorious authors of Scripture and do not know how to answer. It is time the Churches began to learn what to say to the Jewish taunts— "We gave you your god;" "We gave you your Bible." "We gave you your savior." Perhaps it is also time that the Jews themselves considered how long the boast will stand the usage they are giving it.

In any case the literature which the Jews wrongfully claim as their own production, is rather far distant in time to justify its being used as a mantle of glory for the political rabbis, the discredited theatrical and movie magnates, and the violent penmen of the Jewish press. Rather too distant in time! We, the race that confronts the Jews, have done somewhat more recent work; for example, the Declaration of Independence and the Emancipation Proclamation, not to mention the psalms and pronouncements of the great American prophets that have lifted up the world.

So, the Jew is very willing that the Bible should be in the schools, provided it is not what he calls "the Christian Bible." Listen to this:

"Hebrew is to be taught in the Chicago high schools. Students who include this language in their course are to receive the credit now allowed for the study of other classical languages. Of infinite value in the training of the mind are the wonderful narratives of Genesis, and boys and girls will find the history of Israel under the Judges much more appealing than Caesar's bridge over the Rhine."

The people of New Jersey thought so, too; they believed that a reading from this ancient book every day would mean much to the general culture of the pupils. But what did the paper just quoted say about it? It called the cultivated Bible appreciators of New Jersey "soul-snatching enthusiasts" and raised a mighty yell about the "forcible conversion of Jewish children," although it was provided that Jewish or any other children should be excused from the reading if desired. Another mighty yell about excusing the children all on account of the tyranny of reading the Christian Bible in the schools—regardless of the fact, which every public school teacher knows, that no class of children is oftener out of school for religious reasons than are the Jews.

Truly, these people are a paradox. They are not fair. They are constituted so that they cannot see the other side of anything. For a time they actually do convince the secularists that everything public should be secularized down to the last notch of atheistic demand. Non-Jews are fair. They are willing to see the other people's point of view. When it was said to us that the "Merchant of Venice" was a cruelty upon Jewish school pupils, we said, without investigation, "Out goes the Merchant, then!" We discovered later that the Jewish children liked and appreciated that play better than any other group. Brander Matthews helped us discover that.

And so when they said, "Reading the Bible is sheer proselytizing; it isn't fair," the non-Jew, who wanted to prove that he is fair and unprejudiced above all things else (a weakness the Jews know how to manipulate), said, "Well, then, out goes the Bible!" And it went out. Very well! What next? "You must abolish Christmas, too." "You must not keep Easter—the Jews don't like it." "It is anti-Semitic to observe Good Friday." In other words, to please the sensitive Jewish natures we must eradicate from Christian civilization all that is Christian in it.

In the meantime what transpires? Having induced "fair-minded" non-Jews to do all these things—and every one above enumerated has been done over and over again at Jewish demand—the Jews then proceeded to sow Judaism on the fields thus denuded of Christianity. "No religion in the institutions of the State"—yet in every state university last year there were, and in every state university this year there probably will be, courses of lectures delivered by Jewish rabbis—the lectures delivered in the colleges themselves—propagandizing the youth of the non-Jews with Judaistic religion, ethics, and economics. That is what the so-called Jewish "Chautauqua" exists for. It is not a Jewish "Chautauqua"; it is Jewish propaganda in public educational institutions.

That is the repayment the Jews have made for our "fair-mindedness." Their demand for complete secularization is merely their preparation of the soil for their carefully organized sowing of the seed of Judaism. And non-Jews permit it to continue, for there is nothing they fear so much as that their opposition will be regarded as "religious prejudice."

The Jew glories in religious prejudice, as the American glories in patriotism. Religious prejudice *is* the Jews' chief expression of their own true patriotism. It is the only well-organized, active and successful form of religious prejudice in the country because they have succeeded in pulling off the gigantic trick of making not their own attitude, but any opposition to it, bear the stigma of "prejudice" and "persecution." That is why the Jew uses these terms so frequently. He wants to label the other fellow first. That is why any investigation of the Jewish Question is so quickly advertised as anti-Semitism—the Jew knows the advantage of labeling the other man; wrong labels are most useful.

This does not by any means exhaust the list of headlines describing the various avenues in which the expression of virulent Jewish religious prejudice and persecution is found. But it exhausts the space allotted to these articles each week. Therefore, the subject will be concluded next week.

It is not a pleasant subject. Religious prejudice is just as unpleasant to write about as it is to experience in any other way. It is totally contrary to the genius of the American and the Anglo-Saxon. We have always regarded religion as a matter of conscience. To believe as he will is part of every man's fundamental liberty. To interfere with force to change anyone's belief is exceedingly stupid.

Holding these hereditary principles, one chooses to study that active stream of influence in American life which is known as the Jewish stream, and immediately upon doing so, one finds himself classed with the bigots and torturers of other times.

It is now time to show that the cry of "bigot!" is raised mostly by bigots. There is a religious prejudice in this country, there *is*, indeed, a religious persecution, there *is* a forcible shoving aside of the religious liberties of a majority of the people, and this prejudice and persecution and use of force is Jewish and nothing but Jewish.

This is the answer to the cry of "religious persecution," and we shall make it so complete and definite that a repetition of the cry against students of the Jewish Question will automatically mark the criers as either too ignorant or too vicious for consideration.

Issue of June 4. 1921.

XLIV

Are the Jews Victims
or Persecutors?

Half of Christendom worships a Jew; the other half worships a Jewess."—Jewish editorial.

"If the gospel story is correct, Judas was a pretty decent sort of a fellow. It was only *after he had become a convert to Christianity that he became that which has made his memory an accursed thing for nineteen hundred years.*"—Jewish editorial.

"Our land is frequently called a Christian nation. No doubt the majority of our citizens believe this. No less an authority than Justice Brewer of the Supreme Court so expressed himself in 1892. But the statement is clearly false. ....*This is not a Christian nation. In inspiration, at least, it is a Hebrew nation,* for the Constitution which we now enjoy traces back to the Hebrew Commonwealth."—Jewish editorial.

(From the minutes of a meeting of the Committee on Families of the New York Board of Child Welfare.)

Mr. Hebbard: "That is one of the things I have in mind, that a widow brings deliberately into her home a nameless child and the inevitable consequence of that is that her legitimate children are always thereafter pointed out."

Miss Sophie Irene Loeb: "As far as nameless children are concerned, *Christ himself was a nameless child.* Let us get away from nameless children."

21

Dr. Dirvoch: "I think where there are three or four children in a home and a little stranger enters that home without a father, you are corrupting the morals of those legitimate children by permitting them to remain in such surroundings."

Miss Loeb: "I say to you that this committee, if it takes such an attitude as that, is one hundred years behind the times."

Mr. Cunnion: "Anything against purity is immoral."

Miss Loeb; "*What has that to do with the question of purity? Was the mother of Christ pure?*"

Mr. Cunnion: "*Certainly.*"

Miss Loeb: "*He had no name!*"

Mr. Cunnion: "*You can't bring that in here. We believe he was conceived without sin.*"

Mr. Menehan (to Miss Loeb) : "*That is very wrong to make that statement.*"—Cited in letter of complaint to Mayor Hylan.

"The intimate relation of church and state in the great non-sectarian United States of America received direct demonstration on August 12 (1913), when a deputy sergeant-at-arms of the Senate was hurriedly sent out to get a preacher of any old denomination to open the Senate with prayer. The session opening an hour earlier than usual, the regular chaplain was not at hand, but with still two minutes to spare the deputy returned in an automobile, hurried to the Vice President's office and introduced the Rev. Dr. C. Albert Homas, of Canonsburg, Pennsylvania, to Mr. Marshall just in time for the Vice President to lead the way into the Senate chamber to open the session at 11 o'clock, and once again the Union was saved. We shudder to think what might have happened if no preacher had been captured in time to open the session with prayer!"—Jewish editorial.

"President Wilson in his inaugural address said: 'The firm basis of the Government is justice, not pity.' This is sound

Jewish doctrine as laid down by Moses and the Prophets in contradistinction to the doctrine of love, as attributed to Jesus. This coming from so good a churchman as President Wilson might be a little surprising were it not that it is a well-known fact that whenever our Christian brethren want to talk to reasoning men they go to the Old Testament for their inspiration."—Jewish editorial.

"President Wilson at his inaugural gave another instance of the well-known fact that in solemn moments when they need comfort and inspiration, Christians turn to the Old Testament and not to the New. So President Wilson, when he kissed the bible after taking the inaugural oath, selected the passage, Psalm 46."—Jewish editorial.

"Reference has frequently been made in these columns to a number of addresses made by the late Isaac M. Wise at the celebration in honor of his 80th birthday anniversary in the course of which he predicted *that in a quarter of a century from that date (1899) there would be practically nothing left in Protestant Christianity of a belief in the divinity of Jesus Christ* of the distinctive dogmas of Christianity, and that all Protestant Christians by whatever name they called themselves, *would be substantially Jews in belief.* To any one who notes the signs of the times it is apparent that this prophecy is being rapidly fulfilled . . . .*The Jesus superstition* and the *fantastic dogmas built upon his supposed divine origin,* die slowly, but that they are dying is nevertheless apparent."—Jewish editorial.

T HE subject of this article is "Religious Prejudice and Persecution—Are the Jews Victims or Persecutors?" A study of history and of contemporary Jewish journalism shows that Jewish prejudice and persecution is a continuous phenomenon wherever the Jews have attained power, and that in neither action nor word has any disability placed upon the Jew equaled the disabilities he has placed and still contemplates placing upon non-Jews. It is a rather startling reversal of all that we have learned from our Judaized histories, but nevertheless it seems to be the truth.

Attention is once more called to the fact that the Jews themselves are not raising the cry of "religious persecution" here or elsewhere, but they are allowing their Gentile fronts" to do it for them—just as they have not denied the statements made in this series (among themselves they freely admit most of them) but let "Gentile fronts" do it for them. The Jews would not be averse to raising the cry of "religious persecution" perhaps, (provided they could make it stand) were they not afraid that it would call attention to their own persecuting activities. But their "Gentile fronts" have brought that upon them.

There is no Christian church that the Jews have not repeatedly attacked.

They have attacked the Catholic Church. This is of special interest just now when Jewish agents are doing their utmost to arouse Catholic sentiment in their favor by circulating charges which these agents personally know to be false. THE DEARBORN INDEPENDENT has perfect confidence in the information which Catholic leaders may have on the Jewish Question. On this subject the Catholic priesthood is not misled.

Examples of this attack are numerous. "Half of Christendom worships a Jewess," is not a statement but a slur, flung by Jewish men who say in their ritual of morning prayer: "Blessed art thou, O Lord our God, King of the Universe, *who hast not made me a woman."* The Talmudists' discussions of the Virgin Mother are often vile. The Christian festivals, whose preservation is due to the Catholic custom and conscience, are all attacked by Jews.

The American Israelite, whose great prestige in American Jewry is due to its having been founded by Rabbi Isaac M. Wise, *opposed the establishment of Columbus Day* and berated Governor Hughes for signing the law making it a holiday in New York. The act that established it deserved "the contempt of thinking men." Why? Is not the discovery of America a memorable event? Yes, but Columbus was a Catholic! However, in recent months the Jews are proving him to have been a Jew, so we may expect some day to see Columbus Day insisted upon with Jewish rites.

The *Catholic Columbian* made editorial reference to the increasing Jewish influence on the American press, in these words: "Jewry is getting its grip on the news of this country as it is on Reuter's and the Havas agency in Europe."—A perfectly polite and true observation.

But the Jewish editorial thunderer came back—"The *Columbian*, in its sneaking Jesuitical way, does not mention the fact that these (the Jewish) papers are the very cleanest in the country. The *Columbian* cannot point to a single daily owned by one of its co-religionists that begins to compare with the above papers."

The sweet spirit here evidenced is very significant today when an appeal is being made to create a strong pro-Jewish Catholic sentiment.

If there is in the world any extra-ecclesiastical undertaking by Catholics which has won the undivided approval of the Christian world as *the Passion Play of Oberammergau* has done, the present writer does not know what it is. Yet in a volume entitled "*A Rabbi's Impressions of the Oberammergau Passion Play,*" Rabbi Joseph Krauskopf, D.D., of Philadelphia, has stigmatized that notable production as reeking with falsehoods and vicious anti-Semitism. In the rabbi's eyes, of course, it is, for him the entire Christian tradition is a poisonous lie. The whole fabric of Christian truth, especially as it concerns the person of Christ, are "the hallucinations of emotional men and hysterical women."

"Thus," says the rabbi (p. 127) "was invented that cruel story, that has caused more misery, more innocent suffering, than any other work of fiction in the range of the whole world's literature." And thus the simple peasants of Oberammergau, presenting the Catholic faith in reverent pageant, are labeled anti-Semites.

These are not isolated instances. Antagonism to the Catholic Church runs throughout Jewish literature. The Jewish attitude was summed up in an editorial in the *Jewish Sentinel* of November 26, 1920, as follows: *"Our only great historical enemy, our most dangerous enemy, is Rome in all its shapes and forms, and in all its ramifications. Whenever the sun of Rome begins to set, that of Jerusalem rises."* These, however, are matters well known to Catholic leaders.

In their turn the other Christian denominations have been attacked. When *the Methodist Church* put on the great pageant entitled *"The Wayfarer,"* Rabbi Stephen S. Wise played critic and made the solemn and silly statement that had he been a South Sea Islander (instead of the itinerant platform performer which he is) his first impulse, after seeing "The Wayfarer," would have been to rush out into the street and kill at least three Jews. It says a great deal, perhaps, for the channel in which Rabbi Wise's impulses run, but the tens of thousands of Methodists who say "The Wayfarer" will not be inclined to attribute such a criticism to the spirit of tolerance which Rabbi Wise so zealously counsels the Christians to observe.

The Episcopal Church also has felt the attack of the Jews. Recently the Jewish press raised a clamor that the Episcopal Church was not competent to teach Americanism in our cities because it held that Christianity and good citizenship were synonymous. And when the Episcopal Church made provision for mission work among the Jews, the torrent of abuse that was poured out gave a very vivid picture of what the Jewish mind naturally turns to when aroused. This abuse is not reproduced here because of its excessive violence and disrespect. It is similar to that which is heaped upon all attempts to explain Christianity to the Jews. "What would the

Gentiles do if we sent Jewish missionaries to them?" ask the violent editors. Any Gentile can answer that—nay, even the Jews themselves can answer that. In the first place, the Jews do not want to teach their religion to Gentiles because there is a Talmudical restriction against it; Talmudically the Gentiles are not good enough to mingle with the religious matters of the Jews. In the second place, the Jews do send missionaries everywhere, not to spread Jewish religious principles, but propaganda favoring the Jews as a race and people, as is done in our colleges through the so-called "Jewish Chautauqua." In the third place, let there be produced one Jewish missionary, who has ever received anything but a considerate reception wherever he has appeared.

The Jews are bitter against all Christian denominations because of the conversion of numerous Jews to them. A large number of Jews have become Catholics; one of the *Knights of Columbus'* most useful lecturers against the menace of radical socialism is a converted Jew. It is so also with the *Presbyterian Church* which has been the most recent victim of Jewish vituperation. But only upon the Catholic Church has the Jew poured more wrath and malediction than he has poured upon *Christian Science.* The Christian Science church has attracted large numbers of Jewish converts. Some of them have become very active, devoted members of that form of faith. Scores of columns and pages have been devoted to their denunciation in Jewish newspapers, magazines and books. Christian Science is a peculiar anathema to the Jew.

Where then is the religious prejudice? Search through the publications of all the churches named, and you cannot find in all their history so much of the spirit of prejudice and persecution as you can find expressed in the Jewish press in one single day. Jewry reeks with such prejudice. In politics, education, social functions, public holidays, literature and newspapers, they see everywhere traces of "Christological manifestations" and cry them down.

No public man has ever given public evidence of his Christian faith without rebuke from the Jews. Mr. Bryan, Mr. Marshall, Mr. Taft, Mr. Wilson, two of them Presidents, one of them Vice President, and the other Secretary of State, have all been called to task from time to time for their sins in this respect. Mr. Marshall is a devout man, whose faith is real to him, and he speaks very naturally about it at times. He has, therefore, been attacked oftener in the Jewish press than has any other public man of recent times. Nothing is more ludicrous to the Jewish press than a Vice President of the United States openly confessing that he is an "idolator," that is, a worshipper of the dead Jewish imposter whom the Christians ignorantly call "Christ." To Mr. Marshall's honor, be it said, he never apologized, he never begged to withdraw his public statements. Neither did William J. Bryan, whose lecture "The Prince of Peace" contained statements in honor of Christ which brought him into conflict with Jewish spokesmen everywhere, and whose remarks about missions after a trip around the world were savagely attacked by Jews. Mr. Bryan did not apologize either. Mr. Taft was promptly called down on several occasions for using forms of the word "Christian," which were particularly offensive to the Jewish press because they had advertised far and wide during the Taft campaign that Mr. Taft was practically a Jew in his belief in that he had abandoned all the distinctive Christian doctrines pertaining to Christ. After his lapses in which he used the term "Christian" approvingly, it was explained on his behalf (1) that he was accommodating himself to the audience, and (2) that he used the term as a synonym for civilization! But isn't it significant that the name of Christ should be an integral part of the very name of the highest civilization? Mr. Taft was a true liberal, liberal enough to tolerate Christian orthodoxy. And that was a rather weak spot, as far as the Jews' estimate of him went.

Mr. Wilson, while President, was very close to the Jews. His administration, as everyone knows, was predominantly Jewish. As a Presbyterian elder, Mr. Wilson had occasional lapses into the Christian mode of thought during his public utterances, and was always checked up tight by his Jewish censors. In 1914, speaking before the American University at Washington, he said:

"That is the reason why scholarship has usually been most fruitful when associated with religion, and *scholarship has never been, so far as I can at this moment recall, associated with any religion except the religion of Jesus Christ.*"

That was terrible. So terrible that Herman Bernstein was chosen to administer the castigation.

And Mr. Wilson made proper reparation:

"My dear Mr. Bernstein: I am sorry that there should have been any unfair implication in what I said at the opening of the American University. You may be sure that there was nothing of the kind in my mind, or very certainly nothing in my thoughts that would discriminate in the important matter you speak of against Judaism. I find that one of the risks and penalties of extemporaneous speaking is that you do not stop to consider the whole field, but address yourself merely to the matter in hand. With sincere respects and appreciation,

Cordially yours,

Woodrow Wilson."

The heading given this notice in the Jewish press was, "He Did Not Mean It."

All of the President's offending took place in 1914. The second offense he gave was by taking the position of honorary chairman of the International Lord's Day Congress, which was to be held the next year in connection with the Panama

Exposition. It was, however, the Christian Sunday which received the bulk of the abuse on that occasion.

The subject is "religious prejudice." Where does it exist in this country in more continuous and virulent character than among the Jews? Read these items selected at random from Jewish papers:

"District Grand Lodge No. 4, Independent Order B'nai B'rith, voted at the annual election held in San Francisco, March 2 (1911) to exclude from the order Jews who join *the Christian Science Church.* The body after earnest discussion decided that the portals of the order shall be closed against the Christian Scientist Jews on the ground that such Jews have abjured Judaism. The vote upon the question was almost unanimous."

"The Jewish Community at Philadelphia has found it necessary to publish a warning to the Jewish people against *the Daily Vacation Bible Schools* which are being established in various parts of the city, also against certain missions and settlement houses, all of which are *traps into which Jewish children are decoyed for the purpose of seducing them from the religion of their parents.* These institutions belong to that class of conversionist agencies which wage a campaign for the seeking of converts through *workers . . . (who) are a class of criminals that keep just within the law and deserve no better treatment than is usually accorded to people of that kind."*

When a bishop of the Episcopal Church said, "We must make the United States indisputably a Christian nation," the Jewish press retorted that such a thing could not be done until the Constitution of the United States had been "abolished." "Christian America" is a persecuting term according to the professional Jewish spokesmen, and the most laborious efforts have been put forth by them to prove on paper that the United States is not and cannot be Christian.

Not only do the Jews *disagree* with Christian teaching— which is their perfect right, and no one dare question it—but they seek to *interfere* with it. It is not religious tolerance in the midst of religious difference, but religious attack that they preach and practice. The whole record of the Jewish opposition to Christmas, Easter and certain patriotic songs shows that.

When Cleveland and Lakewood arranged for a community Christmas, the Cleveland Jewish press said: "The writer of this has no idea how many Jews there are in Lakewood, but if there is only one, there should be no community Christmas, no community religion of any kind." That is not a counsel of tolerance, it is a counsel of attack. The Christmas literature of American Judaism is fiercer than the flames of the Inquisition. In the month of January, the Jewish press has urged its readers to begin an early campaign against Christmas celebrations the next Christmas—"Only three hundred and sixty days before Christmas. So let us do our Christmas arguing early and take plenty of time to do it."

If anything, Easter is attacked yet more bitterly. But we refrain, for good reasons, from repeating what Jews commonly say on such occasions. The strange inconsistency of it all is to see the great department stores of the Levys and the Isaacs and the Goldsteins and the Silvermans filled with brilliant Christmas cheer and at Easter with the goods appropriate to the time. The festivals of the "heathen" are very profitable. Jewish merchants have been chided for this—not over-severely—by certain rabbis. But on the whole the rabbis had better remain content, for there are no forces more rapidly secularizing the two festival days than are the merchandising and profiteering forces.

Even religious intolerance has its gleesome moments, and the Jews' come whenever the signs appear of the greater secularization of the church. One parallel between the Protocols and the real hopes of the Jews is written in *the common Jewish prophecy that Christianity is doomed to perish.* It will perish by becoming, to all intents and purposes, Judaism. And it will become Judaism, first, by ousting all the

31

doctrines pertaining to the person of Christ, excising from the Gospels the great "I Ams" which are His distinctive teaching concerning Himself; and second, by devitalizing Christianity of all the spiritual content which flows from a union by faith with a Person believed to be divine. That is the only way it can be done. There may be a union of all the churches of the Christian faith because the fundamentals are the same: no union of Christianity and Judaism can occur unless Judaism takes in Jesus as the Messiah, or unless Christianity ejects Him as the Messiah. Judaism sees the union coming by the ejection of the Lord and the Messiah, and rejoices at every sign of it.

Dr. Charles R. Aked, who has since blossomed out as a Jewish spokesman, delivered a sermon in which he cast aside all the "supernatural" elements in the life of Christ, from His birth, to the significance of His death, and was hailed by the Jewish press as *"the fulfillment of the prophecy that within fifty years the religion of all the American people, outside the Catholic Church, would be Judaism in principle even though not in name."*

"No Jew," says the *American Israelite*, "will conceal his gratification when he finds Christians virtually admitting that liberal Christianity is practically an acceptance of the doctrine of liberal Judaism."

Unfortunately, this is true. Liberal Christianity and Liberal Judaism meet, but only by the surrender of all that is distinctively Christian in doctrine. A liberal Christian is more Jewish than Christian. The statement may sound harsh and arouse resentment, but it is a very simple matter for any liberal Christian to convince himself of this by reading the volume of liberal Jewish doctrine put out by Kaufman Kohler, president of the Hebrew Union College. Liberalism is the funnel by which Christianity is expected to run into Judaism, just as liberalism so-called in other departments of life is expected to bring about certain other Jewish aims.

"Liberalism" in Jewish thought means a wide-open country in every way. Judaism has opposed every significant reform that has come to the country; prohibition, Sunday decency, movie and stage regeneration, and community reverence for sacred things. Judaism has been the prop of the liquor traffic, Sunday desecration, movie and stage excesses, and public contempt for the sacred things of the prevailing religion; and it is all too evident that the Jewish propaganda has made serious inroads everywhere.

A Congregational Church in New Jersey decided to abandon the Bible in some of its classes and substitute sociology, politics, municipal government and kindred subjects for study, and the Jewish press hailed it as another sign that the church was "in a fair way to adopt what is in substance American Judaism." In St. Louis a clergyman, instead of preaching sermons, began to act out moralistic dramas which he himself had written, and the Jewish press again hailed it as a sign of the dissatisfaction of the Christian with his church. Everything done in every branch of the Christian church has been closely watched, and wherever a departure occurred from the distinctly Christian position it was extravagantly applauded; and wherever loyalty to the landmarks appeared, it was just as extravagantly condemned. Judaism does not wish the Christian church to remain Christian. This accounts for destructive Higher Criticism being almost exclusively the work of Jews, although the world has long known them under the guise of "German critics."

Jewish intolerance today, yesterday and in every age of history where Jews were able to exert influence of power, is indisputable except among people who do not know the record. Jewish intolerance in the past is a matter of history; for the future it is a matter of Jewish prophecy. One of the strongest causes militating against the full Americanization of several millions of Jews in this country is their belief—instilled in them by their religious authorities—that they are "chosen," that this land is theirs, that the inhabitants are idolators, that the day is coming when the Jews will be supreme. How can they otherwise act than in agreement with such declarations? You can see what is meant if you read Jewish articles describing the shoving aside of the New England people by the Jews; the supercilious attitude adopted toward the stock that made America is merely a foreshadowing of what would be the complete attitude if power and influence made it possible. Bolshevism, which began with the destruction of the class that contained all the promise of a better Russia, is an exact parallel for the attitude that is adopted in this country regarding the original stock.

We are not permitted by the Jews to sing the "Battle Hymn of the Republic" in our schools because one of the stanzas has a Christian flavor. The Jews claim that the presence of one Jewish child in an assembly of children ought in "fairness" to prevent the singing of that historic song.

Norman Hapgood, writing in a Jewish publication, said: "I need hardly explain that I do not think Jews ought to insist overmuch on their rights or nationality in a negative sense. They ought to be as much Jews as they can, but ought to be as little as possible of what is merely anti-Christian. For the Jews to try to get a song out of the public schools because it praises Jesus is perhaps natural but hardly wise." Mr. Hapgood received a lot of abuse for his well-conceived counsel.

Again we come to the end of our space with the record hardly scratched. Sufficient has been presented to show the strong, unceasing anti-Christian activity of the Jews in the United States. Had the Jewish press been read extensively by non-Jews during the past 15 years, this present series of articles would have been unnecessary—the people would have known the facts. It is to present some of the facts that are illustrated in the Jewish press along the line of religious intolerance that these two articles have been written.

Jewish spokesmen plead for suppression of facts in the name of "religious tolerance," and they denounce exposure of the facts as being "religious persecution." Read the whole non-Jewish religious and secular publications and you will not find one one-hundred thousandth part of the animosity against the Jewish religion which is found in the Jewish press—continuously found week after week for long years— against the Christian religion. The present writer has never seen nor heard of an article attacking the Jews' religion.

So, once for all, in spiking the cry of "religious persecution," we show that it exists in quantity and strength among the Jews—nowhere else. No one imbued with the American spirit would or could condemn, hinder, or even remonstrate with any person on account of the faith he holds.

As to "religious prejudice" or "persecution" entering into the present series of articles—there they are, reprinted in booklet form for permanent examination: where is the prejudice or persecution? *Cite the page!*

Jewish spokesmen would use their energy to better advantage, and more to the honor of the Jewish people, if they would address themselves to *what is in the articles*, rather than to what is not in them. The statements made by THE DEARBORN INDEPENDENT have been voluminously *discussed*; but they are still awaiting an *answer*.

Issue of June 11, 1921

"This clannishness would eventually break down were it not for the deliberate efforts of Jewish leaders who are determined that Israel shall remain an imperium in imperio. If the Jews persist in maintaining a distinct ethnic consciousness and an exclusive community life, anti-Semitism will thrive in America as it has thrived in Europe. The American nation, itself the result of fusion, will not tolerate without protest a foreign element in it."
—Herbert Adams Gibbons
in the Century, September, Page 789.

XLV

Jewish Gamblers Corrupt
American Baseball

T HERE are men in the United States who say that
baseball has received its death wound and is slowly
dying out of the list of respectable sports. There are other
men who say that American baseball can be saved if a clean
sweep is made of the Jewish influence which has dragged it
through a period of bitter shame and demoralization.

Whether baseball as a first-class sport is killed and will
survive only as a cheap-jack entertainment; or whether
baseball possesses sufficient intrinsic character to rise in
righteous wrath and cast out the danger that menaces it, will
remain a matter of various opinion. But there is one
certainty, namely, that the last and most dangerous blow
dealt baseball was curiously notable for its Jewish character.

Yet only lesser Jews were indicted. Inevitably the names
of other Jews appeared in the press accounts, and the people
wondered who they were. A Jewish judge presided. Jewish
lawyers were prominent on both sides of the cases. Numerous
strange things occurred.

But the strangest of all is the fact that although American
fans felt something epochal had happened in baseball, few
really know what it is.

There had been enough time for others to tell the truth if
they were so disposed. Many sport editors have come as near
telling it as their newspapers would permit them. But it

becomes daily more evident that if the matter is to be laid bare, so that Americans may know where to look for danger THE DEARBORN INDEPENDENT will have to do it.

And this is not of our own choosing. Baseball is a trivial matter compared with some of the facts that are awaiting publication. Yet it is possible to see the operation of the Jewish Idea in baseball as clearly as in any other field. The process is the same, whether in war or in politics, in finance or in sports.

To begin with, Jews are not sportsmen. This is not set down in complaint against them, but merely as analysis. It may be a defect in their character, or it may not; it is nevertheless a fact which discriminating Jews unhesitatingly acknowledge. Whether this is due to their physical lethargy, their dislike of unnecessary physical action, or their serious cast of mind, others may decide; the Jew is not naturally an out-of-door sportsman; if he takes up golf it is because his station in society calls for it, not that he really likes it; and if he goes in for collegiate athletics, as some of the younger Jews are doing, it is because so much attention has been called to their neglect of the sports that the younger generation thinks it necessary to remove that occasion of remark.

And yet, the bane of American sports today is the presence of a certain type of Jew, not as a participant but as an exploiter and corrupter. If he had been a sportsman for the love of sport he might have been saved from becoming an exploiter and corrupter, for there is no mind to which the corrupting of a sport is more illogical and even unexplainable than the mind of the man who participates in it.

There will be a very full case made out in justification of the use of the above terms "exploiter" and "corrupter" with regard to baseball. But it would be just as easy to make out the same sort of case with regard to wrestling and horse-racing. Wrestling is so completely ruled by Jews as to have become an outlawed sport. The story of wrestling is not only the story of the demoralization of a sport, but also the story of the wholesale bunkoing of the public.

The same is true of horse-racing. The whole atmosphere of this sport has been tinged with dishonesty. The horses remain almost the only well-bred creatures connected with it. Yet why should the art of breeding and training and testing fine horses be debasing? Only because a certain class saw in it a chance to play upon the weaknesses of men for the sake of gain.

That, indeed, explains the presence of the Jew in modern sports and it also explains why the Jewish Idea in sport, instead of being preservative, is corruptive. The Jew saw money where the sportsman saw fun and skill. The Jew set out to capitalize rivalry and to commercialize contestant zeal.

This is not necessarily the only course the Jew could have taken with regard to sports, but it is the course that he most notably has taken, and as scandal follows scandal it would seem to be high time that organized Jewry should undertake to control or repudiate those Jews who have been most instrumental in corrupting and nearly destroying our cleanest, most manly public sports.

It is worth noting that in Chicago, where the Jewish Anti-Defamation League has its headquarters, there was not a word of reproof sent out from Jews to the Jewish culprits, chiding them for their activities. Not a word. But at the same time the pressure of the Anti-Defamation League was heavy on the whole American newspaper press to prevent the public statement that the whole baseball scandal was a Jewish performance from end to end.

Baseball had a close call for its life back in 1875. Rowdyism, gambling, drinking and general disorderliness on the baseball fields brought the sport very low in public estimation, so low that attendance at the games fell heavily.

In this year 1921 there is another public rebuke being administered baseball by the same means—a very heavy reduction of public support in attendance at the games.

39

The storm began to be heard as far back as 1919. The Cincinnati Nationals had defeated the Chicago Americans in the World Series of that year, and immediately thereafter the country became a whispering gallery wherein were heard mysterious rumors of crooked dealing. The names of Jews were heard then, but it meant nothing to the average man. The rumors dealt with shady financial gains for a number of Jew gamblers of decidedly shady reputation.

But "they got away with it," in the parlance of the field. There was not enough public indignation to force a show-down, and too many interests were involved to prevent baseball being given a black eye in full view of an adoring public.

However, not everyone forgot the incident. Some who had the interest of honest sport at heart, and a regard for facts as well, kept on the trail—long after the trail grew cold, long after the principal wrongdoers forgot their early caution. Where money had once been taken successfully, the gang would be sure to return.

Time went on until the 1920 season began to wane. One day when the Chicago and Philadelphia National League teams were engaged in a series at Chicago, strange messages began to reach the office of the Chicago club. The messages were dated from Detroit and informed the Chicago club and management that several "well-known" Jews were betting heavily on Philadelphia. The bets involved large sums of money, and as the contest was only the ordinary run of daily game, not an important contest at all, the unusual interest of Jewish plungers attracted attention. At the same time it was observed that money began rolling into the pool rooms on Philadelphia.

Chicago club officials called a hasty conference on receipt of the messages. They called in Grover Cleveland Alexander, explained the situation to him, and told him it was up to him to save the game. It was not Alexander's turn to pitch, Claude R. Hendryx having been chosen for that day; neither was Alexander in training to pitch that day. However, he did go to the box, and although he hurled his heart out to beat Philadelphia and thwart the Jew gamblers, he failed.

Then came the big scandal. A Cook County grand jury was called into session at Chicago and asked to investigate. When this grand jury had completed its labors, eight members of the Chicago American League team were under indictment for throwing the World Series of 1919, the previous year, to the Cincinnati Reds. And all along the line of the investigation the names of Jews were plentifully sprinkled.

It was discovered that the indictments brought by the first grand jury were faulty; a second one was called and it was under the second group of indictments that the famous trial at Chicago was held.

One difference in the work of the two grand juries was that the second indicted five Jews who had escaped the first one. Two of these men were Carl Zork and Benny Franklin, who were just as much implicated at the time of the first grand jury as the second, but the prosecutor's office did not try to secure their indictment. Why? Because Replogle, the attorney representing the prosecution, said there were enough men indicted without Zork and Franklin. These two St. Louis Jews were represented by Alfred S. Austrian, a Jewish lawyer, of Chicago

This second grand jury also indicted Ben and Louis Levi and their brother-in-law, D. A. Zelser, gamblers from Des Moines. Their indictment was not secured at the first grand jury investigation directed by Replogle, assistant to Hoyne, who was then acting for the state of Illinois. Between the first and second grand juries a political change had occurred, and the public interests in the second grand jury were in the care of a new prosecuting attorney, Robert Crowe, a former judge.

It becomes necessary at this point in the narrative to give a brief "Who's Who" of the baseball scandal, omitting from the list the names of the baseball players, who are sufficiently known to the public. This list will comprise only those who have been in the background of baseball and whom it is

41

necessary to know in order to understand what has been happening behind the scenes in recent years.

For the first name let us take Albert D. Lasker. He is a member of the American Jewish Committee, was recently appointed by President Harding to be chairman of the United States Shipping Board, and is known as the author of the "Lasker Plan," a widely heralded plan for the reorganization of baseball, which practically took the sport out of non-Jewish control. He is reputed to be the second richest Jew in Chicago and was head of the advertising agency which became famous under the Gentile names of Lord & Thomas. Moreover he is a heavy stockholder in the Chicago Cubs—the Chicago Nationals.

The so-called "Lasker Plan" has been attributed to Mr. Lasker, although it is not here intimated that he has specifically claimed to be its originator. The intimation is not made for the reason that to do so might be putting Mr. Lasker in the position of claiming what is not true. Until he makes the claim, the term "Lasker Plan" must remain merely a designation, and not a description of its origin.

This matter brings us to the name of Alfred S. Austrian, a Jewish lawyer of Chicago, who is a warm friend both of Mr. Lasker and of the Replogle aforementioned. It is said that Mr. Austrian was really the originator of the "Lasker Plan" which for certain reasons was handed to Mr. Lasker, who was not averse to publicity and who knew the art of self-advertising. Now, it appears that Austrian was also the legal representative of Charles A. Comiskey, owner of the Chicago Americans, and that he was also, if he is not now, the legal adviser of William Veeck, president of the Chicago National League Club, in which it has just been said that Lasker is a heavy stockholder. It was this club which was touched by the questionable game of August, 1920, and which afterward released Hendryx, the pitcher chosen for and withdrawn from that game. The Chicago National League Club has never

42

explained why it released Hendryx and he has never demanded redress.

Mr. Austrian's further activities will appear when the narrative of the investigation and trial is resumed.

Then there is Arnold Rothstein, a Jew, who describes himself as being in the real estate business but who is known to be a wealthy gambler, owner of a notorious gambling house at Saratoga, a race track owner, and is reputed to be financially interested in the New York National League Club.

Rothstein was usually referred to during the baseball scandal as "the man higher up." It is stated that in some manner unknown he received the secret testimony given before the grand jury and offered it to a New York newspaper. However, the fact is this: the grand jury testimony disappeared from the prosecuting attorney's safe-keeping. It is stated that, when Rothstein found out it did not incriminate him, he then offered it for publicity purposes. The price which it is said to have cost is also stated. It is further stated that the New York paper to whom the secret stolen testimony was offered, in turn offered its use for a larger sum to a Chicago newspaper, and that the Chicago newspaper, to protect itself, called up Robert Crowe, the new prosecutor, who advised that, in printing it, the newspaper would incur an unpleasant risk. Other Chicago editors were warned, and the testimony was not printed. Even the New York newspaper thought better of it, and did not print it.

In this connection, Rothstein threatened suit against Ban Johnson, of the National Commission, the big-bodied, big-minded, honest director and protector of straight baseball—but the suit, like others of the kind, has not been brought.

Rothstein is known on Broadway as "a slick Jew." That he is powerful with the authorities has been often demonstrated. His operations on the turf have led to suggestions that he be ruled off.

Alfred S. Austrian, hereinbefore mentioned, was the legal adviser of Rothstein during the baseball scandal.

Hugh S. Fullerton, the able sport writer of the New York *Evening Mail,* writing on July 28, 1921, made a plea that "a person guilty of crooked work on a race track should be expelled not only from the race track but from ball parks, tennis courts, football fields and every place else where sport is promoted. These sport spoilers must be barred from every sport."

And in the same paper, referring specifically to Rothstein, Mr. Fullerton writes:

"There is in New York a gambler named Rothstein who is much feared and much accused. His name has been used in connection with almost every big thieving, crooked deal on the race track, and he is openly named in this baseball scandal. There has been no legal proof advanced against him beyond the fact that he is the only man in the entire crowd who had money enough to handle such a deal. At least $200,000 was used in actual cash, and no one concerned could command that much money excepting Rothstein, who is either the vilest crook or the most abused man in America.

"Rothstein sits in the box with the owner of the New York Giants. He has the entree to the exclusive clubhouses on race tracks; he is prominent at fights."

Then, after naming Abe Attell and Bennie Kauff, who also enjoy exceptional privileges around the New York club, Mr. Fullerton makes his plea for the exclusion of "sport spoilers" from every ground where sport is promoted.

Then there is Charles A. Comiskey, who is one of the most impressive examples in the country today of a good Irishman being entirely eclipsed by a Jew. Comiskey was one of the staunchest supporters of honest baseball in this country and he gave great assistance in erecting the major league game to the position it occupied just before the scandal. He used his best endeavors, also, to get the truth about the "throwing" of the World Series by his men. But his efforts were thwarted and even he, perhaps, has not the ghost of a suspicion how it was done.

44

So that, instead of Mr. Comiskey, we look at the Jew behind him who is Harry Grabiner. With Comiskey in failing health, Grabiner is in charge at Comiskey Park. More than that, he appears to be in charge of Comiskey himself, preventing him from making public statements and otherwise dictating to him—pushing himself forward in a manner that has indelibly and unpleasantly impressed nearly every sport writer in America.

Chicago's support of the White Sox began to slump even before the scandal and it was helped on by the unpopularity of Grabiner's methods which were wholly characteristic of what the Americanized Jew calls the "kikes." As secretary of the club, Grabiner has grabbed the headship, and if Comiskey had power enough to unseat him he would do more than the courts have done to purge the White Sox from its most serious remaining blemish.

There are shady spots at Chicago that neither the grand jury nor the court trial brought out, one of which is now related:

At all ball parks in the American League, and in the National, for that matter, officials of the "home club"—that is, of the club in whose home city the game is being played—"take the gate." To "take the gate" is to collect the tickets and render a report of the attendance. Tickets are designed and numbered for the different gates—box gate, pass gate, grand stand gate, bleacher gate, and the rest. The accounts are made up showing the number of people who passed through each gate. When all the reports are in, it can be seen at a glance what the paid attendance is, and the shares of the contesting clubs.

In former times it was the custom for the visiting club to assign a secretary to watch the gates and thus insure an honest count, but years ago the "honor system" was adopted, leaving the entire accounting to the "home club," and this "honor system" was strictly observed. No one suspected cheating. The count was made during the sixth and seventh innings of each day's game, the officials of the home club visiting all the gates, taking the turnstile count, and making the record. Three slips were then prepared showing the home club's share, the visiting club's share and the grand total.

Under Grabiner's regime the "honor system" as practiced at the Chicago park began to be suspected. It began to be mysteriously suggested that visiting teams were not getting their full share. Through a system of false accounting, it was said, money was being held out. Naturally, with all the other secret investigations that were proceeding in baseball, this clue was not left untouched. Detectives were hired. Watchers were stationed. Secret counts were made. Not only one club nor only two clubs adopted secret methods of finding out what was occurring under Grabiner's secretaryship. They discovered that the "honor system" was not in vogue at that park. Their suspicions were confirmed, the mysterious rumors were verified. It would probably be highly objectionable to pro-Jewish persons to mention the Jewish management with these methods—but there are the facts.

The White Sox of Comiskey's palmy days have certainly ridden to a sorry finish under the Jewish control that has been foisted upon it. And it is typical; for there is no surer clue by which to trace a certain type of Jew than by the near certainty that even with honest money rolling in upon him, he will try to increase the flow by petty dishonesty which, once discovered, declasses him forever. It is typical. There is a lure in trickery that appeals to some men more than sound and satisfying achievement does. Think of a world-famous baseball club allowing a system that cheated the guest club of a few hundred admissions fees!

Then next in this gallery of notables in the background of baseball is the Jew gambler, Abe Attell, whose connection with sports has been of a questionable character ever since his dethronement from his pugilistic pedestal. Attell is known as the "king bee" of the scheme to "throw the games" in the World Series. He knows all about underhanded "throwing" of contests, because he has "thrown" his own fights, now feigning to be beaten when it involved gambling bets and easily winning when the same reasons prompted. Attell is of such a character that he ought to be barred from the grounds of any sport, as Mr. Fullerton suggests. He is the Morris Gest of sport, without Gest's success. All the players named Attell as the "fixer." Even Rothstein named Attell as the "fixer". It seemed unanimous—with perhaps Axtell's own consent—that he should be regarded as the "fixer": it made it so much more comfortable for others. Attell went so far as to say that he approached Rothstein with the proposition to raise a pool to bribe the players to "throw the games," but Rothstein declined. And yet Maharg, another Jew, whose name spelled backward is "Graham," says that a telegram came through signed "A. R." which promised $20,000. The "A. R." was supposed by some to mean Arnold Rothstein, but others say he is too shrewd even to sign his initials. However, it was asserted that 10 gamblers, all Jews, cleaned up $250,000 on the games and that nearly as much money was used to manage it.

Attell was the "goat," the unanimity being rather startling. It has been known, of course, that men have been so deep in sin that they have been chosen to bear the sins also of their friends on promise that "influence" would be exerted, or on threat that if they didn't stand as "goat" certain past indiscretions would be advertised. Whatever Attell's case might have been, he stood the gaff.

Attell told the ball players that Rothstein was putting up the money.

And Attell was never brought to book. It was even testified that Abe Attell was not Abe Attell at all. Certain moneys lost in a bet had been repaid and the expected testimony in a certain matter turned out to be other than was expected. Attell was held in New York for an extradition hearing. Sammy Pass, a Jew, was one of the witnesses. So was Johnny Seys. The hearing resulted in New York refusing the extradition of Abe Attell.

Then came the Dempsey-Carpentier fight, in Jersey, which Abe Attell attended. Chicago officers were in attendance, too, with extradition papers signed by the governor of New Jersey. They intended to take Attell back with them, though without passing through New York. Attell attended the fight, but the underground wires, so active in this entire case, were working, and Attell eluded the western officers.

The next name in the roster will be that of Barney Dreyfuss, a Jew, owner of the Pittsburgh National League Club. Mr. Dreyfuss appeared in the public eye during the conduct of the grand jury inquiry into the shady games, with an insistent demand that the National Commission, the ruling body in baseball, of which Ban B. Johnson is the acknowledged leader, should be abolished, and another plan, the "Lasker Plan," substituted. It was intended to discredit the National Commission under cover of the rottenness that had been discovered between the Jew gamblers and the venial Chicago players. It was primarily an anti-Johnson move and nothing else, and it was led by a Jew whose principal followers were the rapidly increasing group of Jewish controllers of American baseball. What they have against Ban B. Johnson, impartial investigators have been unable to discover. Mr. Johnson's chief characteristic, with reference to the Jewish side, has been his implacable enmity to crookedness of any kind. That ought not to be a disqualification if baseball is to be saved. Yet the Jew-conceived, Jew-named and Jew-advocated "Lasker Plan" won out.

Carl Zork, the St. Louis Jew who was indicted, is variously described as a shirt-maker and a silk-broker. There are no variations, however, in his description as a gambler. He is part of the Jewish national net of gamblers which acts nationally and makes "killings" on a national scale.

It should be observed that the principal Jewish abuses are nation-wide. This was shown in the United States Government's investigation of the white slave traffic; the bootlegging business is nation-wide; so is race-track gambling; baseball pools also are a national network for the catching of "suckers." There is, therefore, nothing unusual that a shirt-maker from St. Louis and a horse-trader from East St. Louis, and a bootlegger from Albany—together with clever high-ups and hopelessly declassed low-downs—should all be involved in a baseball scandal that breaks in Chicago. They are all really part of a national group.

Carl Zork, for example, staged the fight between Attell and a third-class boxer in which Attell welched in the sixth round in order to "throw" the fight, because his friends had all bet on the third-rate man, getting tremendous odds. His friends would never have made the bet, or having made it could never have won it, without Attell's deliberate quitting and feigned whimpering. It was one of the rawest of many raw deals witnessed in Jew-controlled sports, but Attell is that kind of man. He is a servant for that kind of scheme. It was not by accident that Zork, the silk-broker, and Attell, an ex-prize fighter, should be linked in the baseball scandal. They had been linked in crooked work before. They are part of the national machinery organized and operated for the purpose of separating "Gentile boobs" from their money.

If there were no "Gentile boobs," or if the "Gentile boob" would only take a square look at the man behind the nation-wide spider web, the gamblers and the Jewish sport purveyors would be in another kind of business, with perhaps less money to flaunt in the faces of honest people.

If fans wish to know the trouble with American baseball, they have it in three words—too much Jew. Gentiles may rant out their parrot-like pro-Jewish propaganda, the fact is that a sport is clean and helpful until it begins to attract Jewish investors and exploiters and then it goes bad. The two facts have occurred in pairs too frequently and under too many dissimilar circumstances to have their relationship doubted.

When you contrast the grand stands full of Americans supposing they are witnessing "the only clean sport," with the sinister groups playing with the players and the managers to introduce a serpent's trail of unnecessary crookedness, you get a contrast that is rather startling. And the sinister influence is Jewish. So patent was this that even newspapers could not cover the facts this time.

49

Years before this public scandal broke, involving a whole team, it was noticed that certain Jewish gamblers formed the habit of rooming with certain baseball players. It worried the managers. The fact that the gamblers coddled in among the players was fraught with a suggestion of disturbing unusualness. Managers tried the experiment of trading such players— getting them out of their teams as quickly as possible. However, the snuggling game was continued until it honeycombed the whole of baseball, with the result that it was with no trepidation at all that the Jewish gamblers could walk up and suggest to players that a game be thrown for a price. The occurrence which formed the basis for the investigation was not the first of the kind—far from it; the approach of the gamblers was too easy, the reception given them by the players was too casual, to warrant that view. Nor were the men whose names were given to the public the only men involved.

The only fact of value brought out of all the trouble is that American baseball has passed into the hands of the Jews. If it is to be saved, it must be taken out of their hands until they have shown themselves capable of promoting sports for sports' sake. If it is not taken out of their hands, let it be widely announced that baseball is another Jewish monopoly, and that its patrons may know what to expect.

Issue of September 3, 1921.

XLVI.

Jewish Degradation of American Baseball

E VERY non-Jewish baseball manager in the United States lives between two fears, and they are both describable in the Biblical term "the fear of the Jews." The first fear concerns what the Jews are doing to baseball; the second fear concerns what the Jew would do to the manager if he complained about it. Hence, in spite of the fact that the rowdyism that has afflicted baseball, especially in the East, is all of Jewish origin—the razzing of umpires, hurling of bottles, ceaseless shouting of profane insults; in spite of the fact that the loyalty of players had to be constantly guarded because of the tendency of individual Jewish gamblers to snuggle up to individual players; in spite of the evidence that even the gate receipts have been tampered with—the managers and secretaries of baseball clubs have been obliged to keep their mouths closed. Through fear they have not dared say what they know. As one manager said, "Good God, man, they'd boycott my park if I told you!"

This is in free America, and in the "cleanest game"! It is time for baseball fans to begin to look round.

Incidentally, the fans have been looking round. The fans *know.* If managers only knew how much the fans have observed, they might feel more certain of support in the event of a move toward a clean-up.

All that a Jew needs to make him eligible to baseball or any other sport on the same terms with other people, is to develop a sportsman's spirit. The Jew has crowded into all

51

the lucrative sports, but only on the commercial side of them, seldom if ever in sympathy with the sport as a real sportsman. The Jews referred to as gamblers in these articles are not really gamblers: they take no chances; they are not sportsmen enough to gamble; they are "sure thing" men. The "Gentile boobs" who walk into their traps are the people who provide the money. Even in the field of money, the Jew is not a sport—he is a gangster, ringing a gang of his ilk around his victims with as much system as a storekeeper supplies clerks and delivery boys.

Lately the Jews have been endeavoring to prove that they are sports. Venial sport editors are sometimes induced to write certain laudatory articles along that line, and frequently the name of Benny Leonard is used—Benny Leonard, the light-weight fighter. Benny forms an instructive illustration just along this line. Benny declares that he went into the ring without a scar and that he will leave the ring without a scar. Why? Because he will let no one hit him. He will go a long way to avoid pain.

The true wrestler risks and often suffers physical pain. So does the true ring fighter. But it is a Jewish characteristic to avoid, if possible, the pain of contest, just as it is a characteristic to avoid unnecessary effort.

Look at the other light-weight champions and fighters. Kid Lavinge carries scars; his hearing is affected by the blows he took. Battling Nelson was so badly shattered by his fights that operations were necessary. Ad Wolgast, as a result of the honest straight fighting he endured, went into a sanatorium. Imagine Willie Ritchie and Freddie Welsh boasting that they never took a blow! But Benny Leonard is still unscarred. It may be boxing, but it is not fighting.

Wrestling is so tightly controlled by Jewish managers, that a real wrestler is absolutely barred out, for fear he will be able to show that the handful of wrestlers hired by the Jewish trust are not wrestlers at all, but only impositions on the good nature of the public. In order that the statement just made may not be misunderstand, it is repeated: the wrestling game at present is like the chariot race in a circus—the performers are hired men and the race is only a sham. The Jewish controllers of wrestling will not permit a real wrestler to appear—indeed, they go to infinite pains to bar him out—because a real wrestler would immediately show up the game. Wrestling is as much a Jewish *business*, controlled in its every part, as the manufacture of clothing, and its hirelings are mostly Gentiles.

That is what baseball was coming to. The whole sport was getting down to an "exhibition game" status. The overtone of "money, money, money" grew louder and louder. The sport aspect of the game was beginning to give way to the "show" aspect. There were numerous signs that an attempt was being made to "star" certain persons, to run "headliners," and to pull off a game with a sensational ending—just like a ballet is staged, or a pageant. Thrills were being offered—not as the give and take of the game, the accident of tensest action, but as practiced acting.

That is, baseball was slowly being brought under the level of the box-office idea.

There were forces against this metamorphosis of the game. Certain men saw what was coming. There were also forces favoring the change, and wanting it to come. Curiously enough, the forces that favored turning baseball into afternoon vaudeville were Jews, and those who favored keeping the game as part of American outdoor sports were non-Jews.

There was more involved in that Chicago trial—that curious medley of Jewish defendants, witnesses, lawyers and judge—than the mere trial of baseball players accused of unlawfully taking money.

The players were the "Gentile boobs." The players were not a whit different than a candidate for the United States Senate who plays the game according to the Jewish method. Every player on trial was there because he had listened to the suggestions of a Jew. The Jews who made the suggestions were not on trial. Some of them were not even indicted. Some who were called before the grand jury were not required to testify. Others who were indicted were acquitted. The spotlight of the whole scandal was centered on the non-Jewish players who were pushed out in front to do the job and who were known to any number of Jewish witnesses as having been mixed up in whatever shady work there may have been. The "Gentile boobs" had no witnesses; the Jews had all of them.

This is not a whitewash for the players. They deserved all they got for mixing up with the low hangers-on; but they did not deserve it alone. Had they been half men there would have been a few Jewish gamblers cured for life of the little habit of approaching ball players with a shady proposition. The players are Jewish dupes. To be such a dupe is punishment enough.

It would be erroneous, however, to hold the opinion that corruption in baseball began with the matter which was aired in court. Reference was made at the beginning of this article to the fear which the managers feel. This fear is of long standing. The managers had observed certain manifestations of evil years before. They had heard rumors which they did not repeat to their closest friends. They had started quiet investigations, the results of which they did not reveal even to their partners in the clubs. Everybody acquainted with the true situation lived in deathly fear of emitting a whisper that might give a clue to the truth. But the truth is stronger than walls and doors and steel vaults—the truth was known at every stage of the game, by somebody.

Fans may recall that several years ago one of the eastern teams began to get rid of most of its men. It was a strange proceeding and occasioned much discussion. The sport pages speculated about it and the "wise" ones doped out plausible or fantastic explanations. The true explanation has never yet been given, and it is this: the manager of that club had seen certain things in the World Series of that year which turned him cold. He knew that he saw them; morally he was convinced that something was wrong; he exhausted every available method to get at the truth, and failed; so, unable to bring the men to public punishment, he simply got rid of them one by one, and the next season he had practically "rebuilt" his team. That was not more than ten and not less than five years before the 1919 World Series which formed the basis of the Chicago scandal.

It may be stated also that this which follows is the consensus of Jewish opinion as regards baseball: You can't kill baseball as a *business*. It will always draw a gang on an afternoon, particularly a Sunday afternoon. It can be 'pepped' up and 'jazzed' up in a way that will make it quite a show."

The Jews are probably right, that baseball cannot be killed as a business. But it can be killed as a sport. And the American baseball fans who value the game as a sport should wish its utter destruction rather than consent that it become a rendezvous for the gangs that now fill the Jew-controlled burlesque houses. Baseball as a business will become a danger in American life, a mob-center, a hang-out of the disorderly and criminal classes.

There is another peculiar Jewish story regarding baseball which has not been told and it necessarily brings in the name of Judge Landis, of Chicago, an upright man with a wise head, whom the Jews would better not try to fool.

When the story is told, however, even the Jews will agree that Judge Landis is too shrewd for them.

Before the baseball scandal the situation was this: Ban Johnson was the head of organized baseball, through the National Commission. He had brought the sport from a minor place to its position as the national game. Ban Johnson was something of an autocrat, as all leaders must be, because as old General Booth of the Salvation Army said: "If the Children of Israel had been managed by a committee, they never could have crossed the Red Sea." Autocracy has its uses, especially in striking out new lines. Ban Johnson used his power for baseball, not for personal aggrandizement. He saw the game grow great, he wanted it kept clean. In his efforts to keep it clean, he made certain enemies. One of those enemies, the Jewish owner of a baseball club, threatened to "get Johnson." As far as the National Commission as the head of organized baseball is concerned, they did "get" him. But so far as his prestige is concerned, so far as his character and reputation are concerned, they did not "get" him.

Judge Landis was a fan. That is, he was a fan, besides being a learned and rather strict judge. Judge Landis was one of the few judges who did not quail before Chicago meat packers and Jewish bootleggers. Judge Landis always went the limit on the numerous cases of Jewish business crookedness that came before him—"blue sky" investment companies, and the like. He was at least one judge who tried Jew and Gentile alike and whose impartiality and fearless righteousness no one doubted.

Judge Landis was a rather uncomfortable man to have on the bench in Chicago.

Moreover he was a comparatively poor man. The United States pays its judges only $7,500 a year. That is less than $150 a week, comparatively little on which to live as a Federal judge must live. Yet Judge Landis lived in a modest house and within his income. And no one ever dared tamper with him. An honest judge on the bench, a frugal man outside.

And he was a fan!

Now, while Ban Johnson was doing his best for baseball, and while Judge Landis was seeing a game as often as his duties permitted, certain others were viewing the situation. One of them was Alfred S. Austrian, the Jewish lawyer referred to in the last article, attorney for several ball clubs, friend of Replogle and Lasker, attorney for Rothstein the gambler and several others. Barney Dreyfuss, the Jewish owner of the Pittsburgh Club, was on the trail of Johnson, on persistent enmity. The Jewish coterie in Chicago and the

Jewish influence throughout American baseball looked at Johnson and they looked at Judge Landis.

Then the great idea broke! If at one stroke they could rid baseball of Johnson and rid the bench of Landis, what a good job that would be.

Both these men were dangerous to Jews—not that they intended to be, not that they were consciously so—and it would be desirable to remove both from the spheres of their activity.

Then it was that the Jew lawyer, Austrian, came forth with the "Lasker Plan," named for his Jewish friend Lasker, member of the American Jewish Committee, head of Lord & Thomas (Gentile names) and Chairman of the United States Shipping Board.

The "Lasker Plan" proposed that the National Commission with Ban Johnson be superseded by a one-man government, that one man to be selected from outside both leagues.

The proposal was not an immediate success. Even the National League was in no hurry to obey this suggestion against Johnson. Indeed, there was so much hesitancy on the part of the Nationals in which the Jewish colleagues expected to find their best support, that the trump card was played.

What was that trump card? It is said to be the secret testimony of the grand jury before which Ban Johnson was glad to appear as a witness to tell the jury everything it would need for a proper prosecution of its inquiry, and before which Alfred S. Austrian also appeared to save some of his clients from the consequences of such testimony. The report is that Austrian was able to reproduce at the National League meeting the secret testimony which Ban Johnson had given before the grand jury, and by that means swing the Nationals against Johnson and in favor of the "Lasker Plan," because in the grand jury room Johnson told the truth about certain elements in baseball, which was held to reflect on National League members. What those elements are may be gathered from a survey of the people who were interested in "getting" Johnson. Johnson is anything but anti-Semitic. He probably has never stopped to think about such a thing. He has never been known to attack Jews as Jews. But he has stood for straight baseball, and for so standing he has won the enmity of the Jews in baseball. These facts are sufficient to justify a conclusion.

So, with Johnson left to head only the American League and not both leagues, the next task was to select the new autocrat of baseball. Not a commission this time, but one man! With all his power, Johnson was never more than one of a commission; but the "Lasker Plan" disposes of such safeguards and leaves the whole authority in one man's hands. It will be interesting to see who becomes the second incumbent of that office, if indeed the "Lasker Plan" lasts long enough to warrant a second autocrat.

Gentle reader, do you suppose for a moment that the Jews who opposed Johnson did not know who the new leader would be? Ah, well they knew! He was to be a man outside both leagues. And he was to be a man whom the Jews would just as soon have off the bench as on it. He was, indeed, none other than Judge Landis, who can be trusted to see through a trick as far as any other living man.

Of course, he would accept a $42,500 job, he who was receiving only $7,500 a year! And, of course, he would resign from the bench!—thus the coterie reasoned.

They trooped over to the court to interview the judge. They made so much commotion on their entry that the gavel was banged for order. The interview was held. Judge Landis agreed to accept. This news was widely heralded. The judge tied them down to a seven-year contract. It was assumed in all the interviews in all the newspapers that the judge would resign. It was assumed he would devote the rest of his life to baseball.

The baseball magnates signed up under the "Lasker Plan" put across by Austrian.

Judge Landis also signed.

And then he remained on the bench!

The reader no doubt remembers how quickly enthusiasm for Judge Landis died down in certain quarters; remembers, too, no doubt, that *a fight was started immediately afterward in the United States Congress to force Judge Landis off the bench*—not to make him give up the dictatorship of baseball, but to make him quit the bench.

And be this said: in spite of all the collusion and conspiracy and trickery, of which Judge Landis was the unconscious object, baseball fell into the hands of a man who will be just as jealous for its good name as Ban Johnson was. The Austrian-Lasker-Dreyfuss plan has so far failed. And Judge Landis has rendered several decisions which show that on the bench or off the bench he has the same shrewd eye for the detection of a fallacy.

Judge Landis is safeguarded by a seven-year contract. He is free to be absolutely fearless and fair. What his accession means to baseball will be anxiously awaited.

Judge Landis is probably not empowered to stop the steady falling of baseball clubs into Jewish hands, and if this cannot be stopped, his position as supreme dictator becomes little better than that of a police court judge settling disputes relating to the rules and offenses against them. The peril of baseball goes deeper than that.

A few years ago the owners of the American League entered into a gentlemen's agreement not to sell their holdings at any time without first consulting all the other owners. The name of a prospective purchaser was to be submitted and considered, and the deal was to wait upon the approval of all the owners in the league.

In the face of that fact many people wonder how Harry Frazee became owner of the Boston American club. It is very simply explained: the agreement was not observed in Boston's case, and thus another club was placed under the smothering influences of the "chosen race." The story is worth telling:

Frazee, like so many of his kind, was in the "show business," a manager of burlesque companies. Then he saw a chance in sport. In partnership with Jack Curley, another Jew, he put on the notoriously crooked fight between Jack Johnson and Jess Willard at Havana. Curley has been the principal influence in killing wrestling, by precisely the kind of Jewish policy here described.

Jack Johnson, the Negro, was a fugitive from justice, yet he was champion prize fighter of the world. He was spending money like a wild sailor, and his funds were running low. He was getting into precisely the condition where Jews like to find a man, to use him. Unable to fight in the United States, but still possessing the championship, he was in need of a way out. At this time Frazee and Curley made a proposition to Johnson, said to involve the sum of $35,000, if he would "lay down" before Jess Willard. And thus Jess Willard, "probably the worst fighter that ever held a title," was made world champion. Frazee and Curley then exhibited Willard on the stage and in circuses, and drew rich dividends. The crooked fight at Havana did not involve Willard, he was too poor a fighter to need "fixing." Only Johnson had to be "fixed" not to knock Willard out, which he could easily have done. But between the time when Curley and Frazee gave Willard the title, and the time when Dempsey took it away from him, the Jewish syndicate made a very rich killing out of the gullible American public.

But Curley is not the subject here, he deserves a separate story. Frazee concerns this article because he became owner of the Boston baseball team. He bought a new show—the Boston club, in the best baseball city of the American League. John J. Lannin, former owner, was a real baseball man, so much so indeed that the excitement of the games told on his health and it became necessary for him to relieve himself of the strain. Frazee was waiting to cut in, and whether Lannin feared that the proposal of Frazee's name to the American League would result in disapproval, or whether Frazee himself, knowing it, contrived to make it worth while that the agreement between the American League owners should be ignored, remains an open question.

However that may be, the American League woke up one morning to find the little burlesque manager and promoter of a crooked prize fight in their midst. It was a sad shock to the dignity of "the cleanest sport."

What could they do about it? Nothing. Frazee had bought and paid for what he held.

Baseball was about as much of a sport to Frazee as selling tickets to a merry-go-round would be. He wanted to put his team across as if they were May Watson's girly girly burlesquers. Baseball was to be "promoted" as Jewish managers promote Coney Island.

The American League owners rebelled, but let them rebel! What could they do about it?

Frazee began his next inside work almost immediately. Ban Johnson was unalterably opposed to the Frazee idea of sport, and Frazee set out to "get" Johnson. A split occurred in the American League, with Frazee, Til Huston and Jake Ruppert of the New York Club, and Charles A. Comiskey and Grabiner, of the Chicago Club, on one side against Johnson, and the other American owners comprising the other party supporting Johnson.

Frazee got money out of Chicago—the home of Lasker, Austrian, Replogle and Grabiner—to put through his Boston deal. A bank loaned him a quarter of a million dollars—one of Frazee's friends was a director of the bank. Frazee's friend died and Frazee had difficulty with the bank about remaking the notes. He finally was enabled to pay $125,000. Frazee secured this money from the New York American Club by selling "Babe" Ruth. Thus the New York and the Boston clubs have become financially interwoven. Boston is referred to as "New York's farm" in baseball circles.

In the meantime, the fans of Boston feel toward Frazee as the fans of Chicago feel toward Grabiner. The "class" of Boston no longer flows through the gates. The attendance at Boston park is smaller than at any other time in the last 15 years.

Now, it is unlikely that Judge Landis could tackle that question. Has he power, or lacking power, has he daring enough to assume power to drive the peril away from the ownership and fringes of baseball? It is probably not his field, but it pertains to the future character of baseball.

The Chicago American League Club is the most recent to attract the desire of Jewish capital. The Ascher brothers of that city have offered $1,500,000 for the club franchise. The Ascher brothers comprise a Jewish family, Max, Nathan and Harry, who conduct a string of motion picture theaters in Chicago. They have erected their own theatrical circuit. Like Frazee, they wish to add baseball to their string of "show businesses," and are willing to pay the price. At the time of this writing, their offer has not been turned down.

But a significant development—and in Chicago also—is the announcements made by the Chicago *Tribune* that it will curtail the space heretofore devoted to baseball on its sport pages. This, more than anything which has occurred, indicates the new scrutiny with which the game is being viewed. For a long time many observers have wondered where the "sport" was found in sitting on a bleacher watching a few men earn their salaries. Hours thus spent in a ball park "do not take anything off the waistline of the spectators nor add anything to chest measurement," says the *Tribune;* "the majority of spectators get only eye and mouth exercise." "Journalism has overfed it with space," the *Tribune* rightly says, referring to professional baseball. In ruining baseball and securing control, the Jews may be just in time to take a loss. Better no baseball than every park an afternoon midway filled with the alien and Red elements of the country.

There is, however, a baseball duty devolving upon the police of every city, and that is the abolition of the Jew-controlled baseball pool. Gambling has grown up round the "cleanest game" to the extent of $20,000,000 a year. It flourishes in 150 cities in the country, and in many small towns. The "boobs," of course, are mostly non-Jews, the owners and profit-takers are Jews. It is as much a part of the national network of the Jewish gambling fraternity as are booze-running and horse-racing. The baseball pool runs more openly than the "books" because the very name "baseball" has seemed to give it the protection of "the cleanest sport." However, it has turned cigar-stores, barber shops, pool rooms, near-beer saloons, and newspaper stands into agencies for the national and international Jewish gambling forces. The bettor is entirely at the mercy of the managers of these pools.

These dishonest money-collecting devices are in violation of the law everywhere. The police could put them out of business easily if they should decide to give their attention to it. And thereby they would be taking the hands of a most undesirable alien class out of the pockets of the American people.

If baseball is to be saved, and there are those who seriously doubt it ever can be restored, the remedy is plain. The disease is caused by the Jewish characteristic which spoils everything by ruthless commercial exploitation. The disease may be too far gone for any cure. There are those who, like the Chicago *Tribune,* deny that professional baseball ever was a sport, and who are glad that Jewish exploiters, like scavengers, have come along to reduce it to garbage. But there is no doubt anywhere, among either friends or critics of baseball, that the root cause of the present condition is due to Jewish influence.

Issue of September 10, 1921.

XLVII.

Jewish Jazz Becomes Our National Music

A BOUT a year ago the following article appeared in the New York *Times*, a newspaper that has never been accused of anti-Semitism, and whose proprietor is one of the best-known Jews in the United States:

"Irving Berlin, Leo Feist and other officers of seven music publishing corporations in this city were charged with violating the Sherman anti-trust law in an equity suit begun yesterday in the Federal District Court by the United States Government. The defendants, it was alleged, controlled 80 per cent of the available copyrighted songs used by manufacturers of phonographs, player piano rolls and other musical reproducing instruments, and fixed prices at which the records or rolls were to be sold to the public. . . .

"The corporations involved in the action were the Consolidated Music Corporation, 144 West Thirty-seventh street; Irving Berlin, Inc., 1567 Broadway; Leo Feist, Inc., 231 West Fortieth street; T. B. Harms, Francis, Day and Hunter, Inc., 62 West Forty-fifth street; Shapiro, Bernstein & Company, 218 West Forty-seventh street; Watterson, Berlin & Snyder, Inc., 1571 Broadway, and M. Witmark & Sons, Inc., 144 West Thirty-seventh street.

"The agreement which the government seeks to dissolve is alleged to provide that the defendants would make contracts only through the Consolidated Music Corporation which they had organized . . . ."

Many people have wondered whence come the waves upon waves of musical slush that invade decent parlors and set the young people of this generation imitating the drivel of morons. A clue to the answer is in the above clipping. *Popular Music is a Jewish monopoly.* Jazz is a Jewish creation. The mush, the slush, the sly suggestion, the abandoned sensuousness of sliding notes, are of Jewish origin.

Monkey talk, jungle squeals, grunts and squeaks and gasps suggestive of cave love are camouflaged by a few feverish notes and admitted to homes where the thing itself, unaided by the piano, would be stamped our in horror. Girls and boys a little while ago were inquiring who paid Mr. Rip Van Winkle's rent while Mr. Rip Van Winkle was away. In decent parlors the fluttering music sheets disclosed expressions taken directly from the cesspools of modern capitals, to be made the daily slang, the thoughtlessly hummed remarks of high school boys and girls.

The United States Government alleged, in the above complaint, that 80 per cent of these popular songs was under the control of the seven Jewish houses named above; and the other 20 per cent controlled by other Jewish music houses not included in that special group.

It is rather surprising, is it not, that whichever way you turn to trace the harmful streams of influence that flow through society, you come upon a group of Jews? In baseball corruption—a group of Jews. In exploitive finance—a group of Jews. In liquor propaganda—a group of Jews. In control of national war policies—a group of Jews. Absolutely dominating the wireless communications of the world—a group of Jews. In the menace of the Movies—a group of Jews. In control of the Press through business and financial pressure—a group of Jews. War profiteers, 80 percent of them—Jews. Organizers of active opposition to Christian laws and customs—Jews. And now, in this miasma of so-called popular music, which combines weak-mindedness with every suggestion of lewdness—again Jews.

The Jewish influence on American music is, without doubt, regarded as serious by those who know anything about it. Not only is there a growing protest against the Judaization of our few great orchestras, but there is a strong reaction from the racial collusion which fills the concert stage and popular platform with Jewish artists to the exclusion of all others.

The American people have been urged and chided and shamed into the beginning of a rather generous popular support of music in this country, and the first thing they see for their money is that Jewish artists supplant the non-Jewish artists, and use the prestige of their membership in symphony orchestras to work various small business schemes of their own. If they were superior artists, nothing against it could be said, but they are not superior artists; they are only better known and racially favored in Jewish musical circles.

That, however, is a big subject. It will receive attention in its turn. Just now it is the "popular song" that is being considered. However, as something which true lovers and knowers of music may meditate upon in view of future studies of Jewish influence in music, this observation is offered (the italics are ours):

"Meanwhile the Oriental, especially the Jewish, infection in our music, seemingly less widespread than the German was or the French is, *may prove even more virulent.* Those not temperamentally immune to it catch it less severely, like Mr. Leo Ornstein; and if they ever throw it off, as he has given some signs of doing, seem to be left devoid of energy and, as it were, permanently anemic.

"The insidiousness of the Jewish menace to our artistic integrity is due partly to the speciousness, the superficial charm and persuasiveness of Hebrew art, its brilliance, its violently juxtaposed extremes of passion, its poignant eroticism and pessimism, and partly to the

fact that the strain in us which might make head against it, the deepest, most fundamental strain perhaps in our mixed nature, is diluted and confused by a hundred other tendencies.

"The *Anglo-Saxon group of qualities,* the Anglo-Saxon point of view, even though they are so thoroughly disguised, in a people descended from every race, that we easily forget them, and it is not safe to predicate them of any individual American, *are nevertheless the vital nucleus of the American temper. And the Jewish domination of our music,* even more than the Teutonic and the Gallic, *threatens to submerge and stultify them at every point.* "

"Let me make a nation's songs and I care not who makes the laws," said one; in this country the Jews have had a very large hand in making both.

It is the purpose of this and the succeeding article to put Americans in full possession of the truth concerning the moron music which they habitually hum and sing and shout day by day, and if possible to help them to see the invisible Jewish baton which is waved above them for financial and propaganda purposes.

Just as the American stage and the American motion picture have fallen under the influence and control of the Jews and their art-destroying commercialism, so the business of handling "popular songs" has become a Yiddish industry.

Its leaders are for the most part Russian-born Jews, some of whom have personal pasts which are just as unsavory as THE DEARBORN INDEPENDENT has shown the pasts of certain Jewish theatrical and movie leaders to be.

The country does not sing what it likes, but what the vaudeville "song pluggers" popularize by repeated renditions on the stage, until the flabby mind of the "ten-twent'-thirt' " audiences begin to repeat it on the streets. These "song pluggers" are the paid agents of the Yiddish song agencies. Money, and not merit, dominates the spread of the moron music which is styled "Jewish Jazz." Of the business details, however, more later.

Tin Pan Alley, so-called because it constitutes a group of "song shops," is populated by the "Abies" and "Izzies" and "Moes" who make up the composing staffs of the various institutions.

In this business of making the people's songs, the Jews have shown, as usual, no originality but very much adaptability—which is a charitable term used to cover plagiarism, which in its turn politely covers the crime of mental pocket-picking. The Jews do not create; they take what others have done, give it a clever twist, and exploit it. They have bought up all the old hymn books, opera scores and collections of folk songs, and if you stop to analyze some of the biggest "hits" of the Yiddish song manufacturers, you will find they are woven on the motif and the melody of the clean songs of the last generation; the music jazzed a little, the sentiment sensualized very much, and set upon their smutty road, across the country.

Because of absolute Jewish control of the song market, both in publishing and in theatrical performance, it is next to impossible for anything but a Jewish song to be published in the United States or, if published, to get a hearing. The proof of this is in the fact that the Yiddish trust owns the business and the so-called "song hits" all bear Jewish names.

A typical incident occurred in New York recently. A non-Jewish song composer had produced work of such commanding merit that musical sentiment demanded its public rendition. Jewish manager after Jewish manager was approached, but the combination was unbreakable. Finally, one New Yorker talked out and said something about "Jewish combine," which had its effect. A Jewish manager protested that he would be glad to give the work to the public. Rehearsals were held and the night of presentation arrived. The first number was a solo and a Jew appeared to sing it. He could not pronounce English words. He sang through his nose. He was most Yiddish in appearance, the long nose, with narrow, sloping forehead, curly hair. The second number was a duet, and behold two Jews appeared, whose pronunciations differed between themselves. The performance was a most hilarious tragedy. The purpose was to kill a non-Jewish product by a poor Jewish rendition. But—the Jewish manager overdid it. It needed just that to bring non-Jewish musical consciousness to the surface and to explode the advertised and money-bought notion that the Jew has predominant artistic genius. Say that he predominates in music—yes; he has paid for and organized that predominance; do not, however, say anything about his predominance in musical genius or art.

Non-Jewish music has been stigmatized as "high brow." It is purveyable only in expensively good society. The people, the masses, are fed from day to day on the moron suggestiveness that flows in a hurtful flood out of Tin Pan Alley.

Tin Pan Alley is the name given to the region in Twenty-eighth street, between Broadway and Sixth avenue, where the first Yiddish song manufacturers began business. Flocks of young girls who thought they could sing, and others who thought they could write song poems, came to the neighborhood allured by dishonest advertisements that promised more than the budding Yiddish exploiters were able to fulfill. Needless to say, scandal became rampant, as it always does where so-called "Gentile" girls are reduced to the necessity of seeking favors from the eastern type of Jew. It was the constant shouting of voices, the hilarity of "parties," the banging of pianos and the blatting of trombones that gave the district the name of Tin Pan Alley.

The first attempt to popularize and commercialize the so-called "popular" type of music was made by Julius Witmark, who had been a ballad singer on the minstrel stage. He ceased performing to become a publisher, and was soon followed by East Side Jews, many of whom have become wealthy through their success in pandering to a public taste which they first debased.

Irving Berlin, whose real name is Ignatz or Isadore Baline, is one of the most successful of these Jewish song controllers. He was born in Russia and early became a singer and entertainer. With the rise of "rag-time," which was the predecessor of "jazz," he found a new field for his nimble talents, and his first big success was "Alexander's Rag-Time Band"—a popular piece which by comparison with what has followed it, is a blushing, modest thing.

It was worth noting, in view of the organized eagerness of the Jew to make an alliance with the Negro, that it was Jewish "jazz" that rode in upon the wave of Negro "rag-time" popularity, and eventually displaced the "rag-time."

Berlin has steadily gone the road from mere interestingness to unashamed erotic suggestion. He is the "headliner" in homes as well as in the not-too-particular music halls, but his stuff without its music sometimes savors of vile suggestion.

The motif of this business can be clearly seen in the "Berlin Big Hits." There are the so-called "vamp" songs, such as "Harem Life," and "You Cannot Make Your Shimmy Shake on Tea."

Among the "successes" is the song entitled, "I Like It." It is a "vamp" song which has been sung everywhere, even by myriads of children who could not appreciate the full suggestion of the words, but were hypnotized by the atmosphere which the words created when sung; and by older folks who would not under any circumstances *speak* the words of the song, but who are victims of the modern delusion that a little flashy music covers a multitude of sins. "I Like It" deals with a girl, "Mary Green, seventeen," whose mother reproves her for flirting with the boys. (In the writing of this paragraph it was debated whether THE DEARBORN INDEPENDENT should print what Mary replies to her mother. It was argued that printing the words might give a salutary shock to skeptical readers. It was also argued that the pages of this paper never yet had been defiled by obscenity. Mary's words, sung broadcast through the country, are therefore not given here.)

Readers should reserve comment until they search the piles of moron music rubbish in their own parlors. Readers have listened to much worse stuff than Mary's words, but covered by Yiddish "jazz." It takes cold type to show what a song really is. A good test for a song is to try to read it aloud. Few normal people can.

"O-Hi-O," as sung by Yiddish comedians, has a stench of its own. It may be commented on more extensively later as an example of the Yiddish practice of having three grades of the same song, to suit different degrees of degenerate appetites.

Such songs are not the worst, by any means. Jewish purveyors to degenerate appetites have a peculiarly devilish system of presenting the same song in two or three grades. There will be the song as it is sold at the music store to addle-pated young men and women who fill their leisure with hearing or humming this syncopated senility—young men and women who pitiably imagine they are keeping up with the times. The songs thus sold and sung are rotten enough. But there is the same song, Class 2. The theme and the melody are the same, but it goes "a little further." There is a line or two in each stanza which dips below even the low standard which Jewish "jazz" has permitted in some of our parlors. And then there is Class 3—same theme, same melody—but "going the limit."

Young men about town usually know Class 2 and Class 3. The instance has been known that young women have become acquainted with these lower grades also. Forgetfulness by young men while singing at the piano evenings has given hints of the filthier version. And even where version 1 has been strictly adhered to, the mutual knowledge, politely concealed, has created an atmosphere far from wholesome.

The diabolical cunning with which an unclean atmosphere is created and sustained through all classes of society and by the same influence, will not be overlooked by any observer. There is something Satanic about it, something calculated with demonic shrewdness. And the stream flows on and on, growing worse and worse, to the degradation of the non-Jewish public and the increase of Jewish fortunes.

If THE DEARBORN INDEPENDENT were to print on this page the bare words of the popular songs that are to be found in the parlors of the most respectable section of every city, the reader's sense of decency would cry out against it. The same words when drawn out by numerous hyphens and covered up with nervous music, insinuate their way into the hummed tones of age and into the lilts of innocent childhood. Between the movies and the popular songs the Jewish groups dictate the intellectual life of the masses.

Among the latest Jewish "song hits" may be included these titles: "I'll Say She Does"; "You Cannot Shake That Shimmy Here"; "Sugar Baby"; "In Room 202"; "Can You Tame Wild Wimmen?"; and an almost endless list of the same nature, some of which titles are too suggestive for print. Yet they have free course everywhere—as everything Jewish does, in this country.

Ministers, educators, reformers, parents, citizens who are amazed at the growth of looseness among the people, rail at the evil results. They see the evil product and they attack the product. They rail at the young people who go in for all this eroticism and suggestiveness.

But all this has a source! Why not attack the source? When a population is bathed in sights, sounds and ideas of a certain character, drenched in them and drowned in them, by systematic, deliberate, organized intent, the point of attack should be the cause, not the effect. Yet that is precisely where the point of attack has not been made, presumably because of lack of knowledge.

It is of little use blaming the people. The people are what they are made. Give the liquor business full sway and you have a population that drinks and carouses. After preaching abstinence to the victims for a century, the country turned its attention to the victimizers and the abuse was greatly curtailed. The traffic is still illicitly carried on, but even so, the best way to abolish the illicit traffic is to identify the groups that carry it on.

The entire population of the United States could be turned into narcotic addicts if the same freedom was given the illicit narcotic ring as is now given the Yiddish popular song manufacturers. But in such a condition it would be stupid to attack the addicts; common sense would urge the exposure of the panderers.

A dreadful narcotizing of moral modesty and the application of powerful aphrodisiacs have been involved in the present craze for popular songs—a stimulated craze. The victims are everywhere. But ministers, educators, reformers, parents, and public-spirited citizens are beginning to see the futility of scolding the young people thus diseased. Common sense dictates a cleaning out of the source of disease. The source is in the Yiddish group of song manufacturers who control the whole output and who are responsible for the whole matter from poetry to profits.

Next to the moral indictment against the so-called "popular" song is the indictment that *it is not popular.* Everybody hears it, perhaps the majority sing it; it makes its way from coast to coast; it is flung into the people's minds at every movie and from every stage; it is advertised in flaring posters; phonograph records shriek it forth day and night, dance orchestras seem enamored of it, player pianos roll it out by the yard. And by sheer dint of repetition and suggestion the song catches on—as a burr thistle catches on; until it is displaced by another. There is no spontaneous popularity.

It is a mere mechanical drumming on the minds of the public. There is often not a single atom of sentiment or spiritual appeal in the whole loudly trumpeted "success"; men and women, boys and girls have simply taken to humming words and tunes which they cannot escape, night or day.

The deadly anxiety of "keeping up with the times" drives the army of piano-owners to the music stores to see what is "going" now, and of course it is the Yiddish moron music that is going, and so another home and eventually another neighborhood is inoculated.

But there is no *popularity*. Take any moron music addict you know and ask him what was the "popular" song three weeks ago, and he will not be able to tell. These songs are so lacking in all that the term "popular" means as regards their acceptableness, that they die overnight, unregretted. Directly the Yiddish manufacturers have another "hit" to make (it is always the public that is "hit") a new song is crammed down the public gullet, and because it is the "latest," and because the Yiddish advertisements say that it is a "hit," and because the hired "pluggers" say that every-body is singing it, that song too becomes "popular" for its brief period, and so on through the year. It is the old game of "changing the styles" to speed up business and make the people buy. Nothing lasts in the Yiddish game—styles of clothing, movies nor songs; it is always something new, to stimulate the flow of money from the popular pocket into the moron music makers' coffers.

There hasn't been a real "popular" song of Yiddish origin since the Jewish whistlers and back-alley songsters of New York's East Side undertook to handle musical America—not one, unless we except in genuine gratitude George Cohan's "Over There," a song which came out of a period of strain and went straight to the people's heart.

Two facts about the "popular song" are known to all: first, that for the most part it is indecent and the most active agent of moral miasma in the country, or if not the most active, then neck and neck with the "movies"; second, that the "popular song" industry is an exclusively Jewish industry. But the inside story of the operation of this control of the people's music presents other facts which the people ought to know, and these additional facts will appear in another article.

Issue of August 6, 1921

XLVIII.

How the Jewish Song Trust
Makes You Sing

J EWS did not create the popular song; they debased it. The time of the entry of Jews into control of the popular song is the exact time when the morality of popular songs began to decline. It is not a pleasant statement to make, but it is a fact. It would seem to be a fact of which American Jews ought to take solemn cognizance, not to anathematize those who do service by exposing the fact, but to curb that group of Jews who, in this instance, as do other groups of Jews in other instances, bring a stain upon the Jewish name.

The "popular" song, before it became a Jewish industry, was really popular. The people sang it and had no reason to conceal it. The popular song of today is often so questionable a composition that performers with a vestige of delicacy must appraise their audience before they sing. There are songs and choruses that can be purchased in any reputable music store and found in many reputable parlors which cannot be printed in this column of THE DEARBORN INDEPENDENT. If they were printed here, "Gentile fronts" would be the first to complain that this paper was using obscenity to give interest to these articles. Yet, if those songs were printed, this paper would be doing nothing more than following its policy of going to Jewish sources for its material.

Americans of adult age will remember the stages through which the popular song has passed during the past three or four decades. War songs persisted after the Civil War and were gradually intermingled with songs of a later time, picturesque, romantic, clean.

These latter were not the product of song factories, but the creation of individuals whose gifts were given natural expression. These individuals did not work for publishers but for the satisfaction of their work. There were no great fortunes made out of songs, but there were many satisfactions in having pleased the public taste.

The public taste, like every other taste, craves what is given it most to feed upon. Public taste is public habit. The public is blind to the source of that upon which it lives, and it adjusts itself to the supply. Public taste is raised or lowered as the quality of its pabulum improves or degenerates. In a quarter of a century, given all the avenues of publicity like theater, movie, popular song, saloon and newspaper—in the meantime having thrown the mantle of contempt over all counteractive moral agencies—you can turn out nearly the kind of public you want. It takes just about a quarter of a century to do a good job.

In other days the people sang as they do now, but not in such doped fashion nor with such bewildering continuity. They sang songs nonsensical, sentimental and heroic, but the "shady" songs were outlawed. If sung at all, the "shady" songs were kept far from the society of decent people. Like the styles of the demimonde that formerly were seen only in the abandoned sections of cities, the songs of smut had their geographical confinement, but like the fashions of the demimonde they broke out of their confines to spread among polite society.

The old songs come readily back to memory. Though years have intervened since they were the fashion, yet their quality was such that they do not die. The popular song of last month—who knows its name? But there are songs of long ago whose titles are familiar even to those who have not sung them.

Recall their names—"Listen to the Mocking Bird" —what song today has been boosted to general acceptance on such a simple theme? The only "birds" the people are encouraged to sing about today are "flappers" and "chickens."

And there were "Ben Bolt"; "Nellie Gray"; "Juanita"; "The Old Folks at Home"; "The Hazel Dell"; "When You and I Were Young, Maggie"; "Silver Threads Among the Gold." What margin did these songs leave for the suggestive, for the unwholesomely emotional?

In those days the people sang; they sang together; they sang wherever they met: it was the days of that now extinct institution known as "the singing school." People could sing together. The songs were common property, known to everybody, proper to everybody.

Is there such singing today? Hardly. At a recent meeting of young men in a church the chorus, "Hail, Hail, the Gang's All Here" was called for, and the chairman in agreeing called out "Mustn't say the naughty word!" With that warning the chorus was given. In calling for public singing there is an immediate uneasiness about possible indecency. There was not this uneasiness before the days of Jewish jazz.

In course of time the fashion of public song underwent a change. An entirely new crop of titles appeared, dealing with an entirely different series of subjects than the songs they displaced.

It was the period of "Annie Rooney"; "Down Went McGinty to the Bottom of the Sea"; "She's Only a Bird in a Gilded Cage"; "After the Ball is Over"—all of them clean, lighter than the preceding fashion in songs, but just as clean, and also giving a true touch to life.

Sentiment was not lacking, but it was the unobjectionable sentiment of "My Wild Irish Rose" or "In the Baggage Coach Ahead."

The non-Jewish period was marked by songs like these: "On the Banks of the Wabash," by Paul Dresser; "In the Shade of the Old Apple Tree"; "When the Sunset Turns the Ocean's Blue to Gold"; "Down by the Old Mill Stream"; "My Sweetheart's the Man in the Moon," by Jim Thornton; "The Sidewalks of New York," by Charles Lawlor.

There was also the "western" and "Indian" strain of songs, represented by "Cheyenne, Cheyenne, Hop on My Pony"; "Arawanna"; "Trail of the Lonesome Pine."

Then came the African period, being the entrance of the jungle motif, the so-called "Congo" stuff into popular pieces. "High Up in the Cocoanut Tree," "Under the Bamboo Tree," and other compositions which swiftly degenerated into a rather more bestial type than the beasts themselves arrive at.

Running alongside all this was the "ragtime" style of music which was a legitimate development of Negro minstrelsy. Lyrics practically disappeared before the numerous "cake walk" songs that deluged the public ear. "There'll Be a Hot Time in the Old Town Tonight"—the marching song of the Spanish-American War, belongs to that period. The "black and tan" resorts of the South began to reign over the nation's music both North and South. Seductive syncopation captured the public ear. The term, "ma baby," brought in on the flood of Negro melody has remained in uncultivated musical speech ever since. Minstrelsy took on new life. "Piano acts" made their appearance. "Jazz bands" were the rage.

By insensible gradations, now easily traceable through the litter of songs with which recent decades are strewn, we have been able to see the gradual decline in the popular song supply. Sentiment has been turned into sensuous suggestion. Romance has been turned into eroticism. The popular lilt slid into ragtime, and ragtime has been superseded by jazz. Song topics became lower and lower until at last they were dredges of the slimy bottom of the underworld.

The first self-styled "King of Jazz" was a Jew named "Frisco." The general directors of the whole downward trend have been Jews. It needed just their touch of cleverness to camouflage the moral filth and raise it half a degree above that natural stage where it begets nothing but disgust. They cannot gild the lily, but they can veil the skunk-cabbage, and that is exactly what has been done. The modern popular song is a whited sepulcher, sparkling without, but within full of the dead bones of all the old disgusting indecencies. Plain print returns them to their rightful status of disgust.

We are now in the period of "The Vamp"--that great modern goddess upon whom tens of thousands of silly girls are modeling themselves—"The Vamp." The original "vamp" is to be found in a forbidden French novel upon which Morris Gest founded his grossly immoral spectacle called "Aphrodite." In the Jewish popular song and the Jewish motion picture film a unity has at last been reached in "The Vamp." The vamp heroine and the harem scene—a fitting climax!

There is work here for the Anti-Defamation League. That league knows how to put the screws on anyone who disparages the Jews. From important New York publishers, down to inconsequential country newspapers, the Anti-Defamation League makes its power felt. There is work for it in the movies and the popular song industry. Why does not the league put the screws on those Jews who have degenerated the movies and debauched the popular song movement and thus brought shame upon the racial name? Why not? Is it possible that only the non-Jews are to be controlled, and Jews let to run loose? Is it possible that "Gentiles" can be curbed as by bridle and bit and that Jews cannot?

It is repeated: there is work for the Anti-Defamation League among the Jews.

More than that: there are Jews who have begged the Anti-Defamation League to purge the name of Jewry of the shame the liquor Jews, the movie Jews, the popular song Jews, the theatrical Jews, and the others are bringing on that name, and the Anti-Defamation League has not done so. It dare not.

American Jewry is desperately afraid of opening a single seam in its armor by means of a single investigation or reform. They are afraid of how far the fire of self-correction may spread.

It was the intention of THE DEARBORN INDEPENDENT to give in this article a sample of the manner in which Jewish jazz is written in three classes—No. 1 for general consumption; No. 2 for stage consumption; No. 3 for the lowest resorts. On searching through the songs for the least offensive example it is found that even the least offensive cannot be printed here. The fact is greatly regretted, for certainly some method must be found by which the public can be put into possession of full information as to what is transpiring in this hideous traffic.

The Jewish art of "camouflage" (the reader may not be aware that wartime camouflage was a Jewish invention) has always been operative. "Cover names" "cover nationalities" (these are Jewish terms) have long been known. It is quite common for Jews of the higher type to band themselves together into societies for political and racial purposes, the purposes being camouflaged by a name, such as Geological Society, or Scientific Society, or something of that sort. And thus in the vilest versification, which only a few years ago would have been refused the mails, they have flung broadcast among the youth of the world dangerous ideas under the camouflage of catchy tunes.

The tunes themselves carry a tale with them. There have been cases in the courts dealing with the "adaptation," or stealing, of tunes for "popular song" purposes. If you observe carefully you will catch reminiscent strains in many of the popular songs which you sing. If you sing, "Rocked in the Cradle of the Deep," and then sing, "I'm Always Chasing Rainbows," you will notice a basic resemblance; but that does not prove that "Rocked in the Cradle of the Deep" is itself original, its melody was originally taken from an Opus of Chopin. This is a practice which has been greatly extended of recent years.

The reason for the spread of this peculiar kind of dishonesty is to be found in the Jewish policy of "speeding up business." Ordinarily one play a week, and one or two new songs a season, was the limit of indulgence. But with the coming of the movies the "one play a week" plan has been smashed to smithereens. To get the people to pay their money every day, the programs are changed every day; and to get new plays every day, something must be cheapened. So with songs. The output is rushed to increase the income of money, and quality is sacrificed all round. There are not enough good songs in the world to supply a new one every week; not enough good plays in the world to supply a new movie every day; and so, what the songs and plays lack in worth, they make up in nastiness. In brief, nastiness is the constant quality on which the producers depend to "put across" mediocre songs and otherwise pointless plays. Nastiness is the condiment that goes with cheapness in songs and movies.

Plagiarism is the result of mediocre artists being spurred on by non-artistic promoters to produce something that can be dressed up with sufficient attractiveness to draw the public's money. But even plagiarism requires a little brains mixed with it, and when the rush of demand overwhelms the available brains, the lack is covered up by an elaborate covering of sensualism.

Men who are on the inside of the popular song business, and certain court records, all testify to the exact truth of these statements.

"But how do the Jews do it? is a question often asked. The answer is, not public demand, nor artistic merit, nor musical ingenuity, nor poetic worth—no; the answer is simple salesmanship. The public doesn't choose, the public simply takes what is persistently thrust upon it. It is a system impossible to any other race but the Jews, for there is no other race that centers its whole interest on the sale. There is no other race that makes so startling a choice in favor of "getting" money to the exclusion of "making" money. Who for a moment would think seriously of using the terms "production" and "service" with reference to popular songs or motion pictures? Motion Pictures in their higher reaches might have some claim on those terms—not the typical Jewish pictures, however; but the modern crop of popular songs, never! The terms "production" and "service" do not belong to the popular song

81

industry at all, but the term "salesman-ship" does, as the reader will presently see. It is well to remember that where there is only "salesmanship" without the other two qualities, the public is always the sufferer.

"Popularity," when interpreted by the Jews who manufacture jazz for the United States, means "familiarity," that's all. The theory is that a song need not possess merit as regards words or music to be successful. *It can be "popularized" artificially by constant repetition,* until it becomes familiarized to the public ear, and thus familiarized it becomes "successful."

The principle is expressed in the words of the song, "Everybody's Doin' It." You go to the theater and hear a song. Next day at lunch the cafe singer is singing the same song. Blaring phonographs used for advertising purposes blat out the same song at you as you pass on the street. You walk past an afternoon band concert in the park—the band is playing the same song. If you are a normal person you have a feeling that perhaps something has been going on in the world while you were engaged with your own affairs. The song—you say to yourself frankly—is silly and the music trivial; but you keep your opinion a secret, because, after all, "everybody's singin' it." Not long after you find yourself humming it. You go home, and your daughter is "practicing up" on the piece. It yells its way through your home and through your neighborhood and through your city and through your state until in sheer disgust, and in one day, the people pitch it bodily out-of-doors. But, behold, another song is waiting to take its place—a song fresh from Yiddish Tin Pan Alley. And the agony is repeated. *This occurs from 30 to 50 times a year.*

That is the principle—repeat it until it becomes familiar; that gives it the veneer of popularity.

Now, there is a method by which all this is done. Nothing "happens." It is like the "mob risings" which have been practiced in some of our cities—there is always a well-organized center that knows the technology of riot and knows exactly what it is doing. There is a way of making "revolution" as common and as familiar a thought as the movies and popular songs have made "vamps" and "harems" and "hooch" and "Hula Hula." The principle is the same—constant repetition for the purpose of familiarization.

More than one tune has been deliberately rejected by the public, has not been "liked," but the song-tinkers did not allow that little fact to intimidate them: they simply hammered it into the ears and memories of the public, knowing that "familiarization" was obtainable some time. "Whispering," for example, did not catch on for a long time. Long ago it used to be known as "Johnnies Melody": because John Schoenberger wrote it—but finally it was driven home to its present popularity. There is this to say about it, it is far more deserving of its popularity than is 98 per cent of the so-called "popular" music.

Having the principle, then, that *any song can be popularized by constant repetition,* the Yiddish music purveyors go about their business very systematically.

The song is procured—by what means, it is not always possible to say. Perhaps one of the "staff" originates a catchy tune, or a girl who plays the church organ in a distant village sends in a pretty little melody. The girl's melody is, of course, sent back as unsuitable, but if it really had a heart of melody in it, a copy is kept and "adapted." In such ways are "ideas" procured.

Then there are plenty of Jewish musical comedies and vaudeville teams. A study of the vaudeville and musical comedy business will show it to be as distinctively Yiddish as are the movies and the popular song industry. So, the Jewish song publisher makes an arrangement with the Jewish manager of the musical comedy show. This arrangement provides that one or more of the song publisher's songs should be sung several times at every performance, in response to the applause and encores of a professional song boosters' claque which is always on hand for such purposes. This claque is paid for just as any other service might be paid for.

The night comes. The song is sung. Persistent applause. Sung again. More applause. Apparently the song is a "hit." As the audience files out the lobby is echoing with the cries of Yiddish song vendors proclaiming the song of the evening to be "the big hit of the season," hundreds of copies being sold in the meanwhile.

That is the usual Broadway introduction.

The next step is to capture the "provinces"—the musical comedies and vaudeville acts playing within 100 miles of the metropolitan centers. Actors called "song pluggers" are engaged. The arrangement with them is that they will sing a particular song exclusively—give no other song a chance. The public pays to hear the actor sing; the manager pays to have him sing; the song publisher pays him to sing a certain song.

From theater to theater, from company to company, from artist to artist, the publishers' agents wend their way, making what terms they can to single artists, vaudeville team or comedy companies for boosting a new song by giving it prominent place in the program.

There are also the "stag entertainers," the young men who go about to; "parties" of one kind or another, offering amusement to the guests. This is a class of entertainers known only to the rich, but numerous enough. For instance, when the Prince of Wales toured America he was accompanied by a young man nicknamed "Rosie," of whose racial origin there need be no doubt. "Rosie" played the piano and by songs and antics beguiled the tedium of the royal journey. Well, young men of "Rosie's" sort are quite useful in advertising to select circles the latest product of the Yiddish song factories and they are, of course, regularly utilized for that purpose.

Orchestras, especially those of restaurants and dance halls, are worked in the same way.

Get as many people singing and playing introductory renditions as you can: that is the method of gaining an *artificial popularity by constant repetition.*

The chances are that the song you are humming today is being hummed by you simply because you have perforce heard it so often that it beats unconsciously within your brain.

These methods are subject to variation, of course. There was a great deal of "cutting" until the right Hebrew group survived, and then there was a great deal of "trust" method adopted. The Music Publishers' Association was organized by "Sime" Silberman and Maurice Goodman, and now all the Jewish song manufacturers are included in it. The organization has not changed any of the methods before used but has curtailed the expense. Moreover, it has served to relieve the public to this extent, that, instead of clinging to the one song paid for until the public positively gags on it, the vaudeville or movie performers now sing impartially the various songs of the various publishers forming the trust. More variety has been introduced, that is all. The same old commercialization continues.

As readers of the studies of Jewish theatrical control, which appeared in this paper, will readily understand, the Jewish control of the popular song field means that all non-Jews are barred out. It would be next to impossible for the song of a non-Jew, however meritorious, to reach the public by the usual channels. The musical magazines, the musical critics, the musical managers, the music publishers, the music-hall owners, the majority of the performers are not only all Jews, but are Jews consciously banded together to keep out all others.

The dishonest methods practiced by the Yiddish controllers of this field have been such as to move the *Billboard*, the leading vaudeville publication, to refuse to print advertisements calling for song-poems. Perhaps the reader has seen such advertisements, suggesting that someone has a tune or a song-poem that will probably make a fortune if only sent to an address on Broadway or in the region of Tin Pan Alley. The *Billboard* says:

"No more Song Poem Ads Accepted.

"After investigating the business methods practiced by some Song Poem advertisers, the *Billboard* believes it to be to the best interest of its readers to eliminate the heading, 'Music and Words' under which Song Poem advertisements appeared, and hereafter, or until existing conditions are changed, the *Billboard* will not accept any more Song Poem advertising from any concern or person. . . ."

Everywhere the "popular song" has been attacked by keen observers of social tendencies—but the attack has not been made intelligently. No public menace like this can be abolished without showing the public the source of it. Newspapers are now beginning to attack "jazz," "the vicious movies," "the disgraceful dance." Others attack the young folk who sing jazz, the people who patronize the objectionable movies, the throngs who indulge in indecent dancing. But all the time a small group of men are deliberately and systematically forcing jazz and movies and dances upon the country, spending hundreds of thousands in the effort and reaping millions of profits.

If these men were non-Jews, a multitude of fingers would be pointed toward them in identification and denunciation.

Because these men are Jews, they are allowed to go free.

You will stop these abuses when you point out the Jewish group behind them!

People sometimes say, "Well, if you went after any other nationality, you could find just as much fault as with the Jews." Is there any other nationality on which you can fasten the responsibility for vile movies? Is there any other on which you can fasten the responsibility for the illicit liquor traffic? Has any other nationality control of the theater? In the beginning action against the popular song trust, could the United States find anyone to indict besides Jewish song publishers, and could the United States Government lay less than 80 per cent of song control to one New York group alone?

If these things were not strictly Jewish in their origin, method and purpose, how could such statements be made?

Jews say, "Clean up among the Gentiles first, and then turn attention to us." Will the Jews charge Gentile control of movies, popular songs, horse racing, baseball gambling, theaters, the illicit liquor traffic—will the Jews charge Gentile predominance in any line recognized by moralists today as dangerously menacing the public welfare?

The question is too big to be explained by prejudice. The facts are too challenging to be thrust aside as universal. It is a Jewish question, made such by a series of Jewish facts.

Not content with hedging life about on every side, from the gold that is used in business to the grain that is used in bread, Jewish influence enters your parlor and determines what you shall sing at your piano or hear upon your music reproducing machine. If you could put a tag marked "Jewish" on every part of your life that is Jew-controlled, you would be astonished at the showing.

Issue of August 13, 1921

87

XLIX.

Jewish Hot-Beds of Bolshevism in the U. S.

B OLSHEVISM is working in the United States through precisely the same channels it used in Russia and through the same agents—Revolutionary and Predatory Unionism, as distinct from Business and Uplift Unionism, and Jewish agitators. When Martens, the so-called Soviet ambassador, "left" the United States after being deported, he appointed as the representative of Bolshevik sovietism in the United States one Charles Recht, a Jew, a lawyer by profession, who maintained an office in New York. This office is the rendezvous of all the Jewish union leaders in New York, some of the labor leaders throughout the country, and occasionally of one or two American government officials known to be henchmen of Jewish aspirations in the United States and sympathizers with predatory radicalism.

The situation in New York is important because from that center lines of authority and action radiate to all the cities of the United States. New York is the laboratory in which the emissaries of the revolution learn their lesson, and their knowledge is being daily increased by the counsel and experience of traveling delegates straight out of Russia.

The American does not realize that all the public disturbances of which he reads are not mere sudden outbreaks, but the deliberately planned movements of leaders who know exactly what they are doing. Mobs are methodical; there is always an intelligent core which gets done under the appearance of excitement what had been planned beforehand.

Up through the German revolution, up through the French revolution, up through the Russian revolution came the previously chosen men, and to this day in all three countries the groups thus raised to power have not lessened their hold—and they are Jewish groups. Russia is not more Jew-controlled that is France; and Germany, with all her so-called anti-Semitism, tries in vain to loosen the grip of Judah from her throat.

It is this fact of prepared disorder which makes the New York situation of interest today, because its lines of influence and authority reach everywhere throughout the country.

For that reason, and before showing how the Jewish organizations advance Bolshevism and revolution in the United States, the first step will be to describe the condition and extent of the Hebrew labor movement.

Most New Yorkers remember the "Save Fifth Avenue" movement. That avenue, from Fourteenth to Thirty-fourth street, with sections of Broadway, is historic ground. It is wrought into the history of America in a peculiarly intimate way. A little more than 15 years ago it contained the homes of the older families, the establishments of famous publishers, the stores of art dealers, and the famous shopping center. It was a district known throughout the United States as typifying American substance and good taste.

But presently, Americans who thought they were secure in their own city, were aware of an advancing shadow. A subtle atmosphere of deterioration became evident. In the top lofts of buildings, sweatshops had been installed, which noon and night poured into the streets an alien stream—not a glad, hopeful-eyed immigrant rejoicing to be in America and at work, but something darker.

It was the Russian and Polish Jew. He swarmed into this district, the most typically American of any outside of Boston and Philadelphia, from the first. Nowhere else would the sweatshops go except in the very heart of Goy respectability. There were protests and organizations; Jews were appealed to in the name of the city; they smiled and promised, but like a tide coming in, the invasion swept farther and stronger every week. New Yorkers hesitated to go down into the district to trade, and merchants lost their business. Real estate values dropped in consequence, the Jews bought valuable properties at low figures.

Today, at noontime, Fifth Avenue is packed from wall to curb with dark, squat figures in masses of thousands. They parade in dense throngs and make the street impassable. They make a strange, un-American atmosphere, Slavonic with some Oriental admixture. Their tongue is alien, their attitude is one of sullenness mingled with a sense of power. You leave the New York of American meaning whenever you approach that alien throng. They have taken over the district as completely as if they had invaded it with the bayonet.

All this would be very hopeful, of course, if we could take and sustain the attitude of the unsophisticated young reader of fiction, and regard these people as "new Americans." There is a mass of moving stories (mostly written by Jews, by the way) pretending to describe the glowing hearts with which these throngs look out upon America, their intense longing to be American, their love of our people and our institutions. Most unfortunately, the actions of these people and the utterances of their leaders give the lie to this fair picture which, as Americans, we would fain believe. The resistance offered to Americanization, consisting in the limitations put upon the Americanization program, has been sufficient to convince all observers that, so far as the Jewish invasion is concerned, it is not their desire to go the way America is going, but to influence America to go the way they are going. They talk a great deal of what they bring to America, hardly anything at all of what they found here. America is presented to them as a big piece of putty to be molded as they desire, not as a benign mother who is able and willing to make these aliens to be like her own children. The doctrine that the United States is nothing definite as yet, that it is only a free-for-all opportunity to make it what you will, is one of the most distinctive of Jewish political teachings. If it be provincialism to insist that our alien guests become American and cease their endeavors to make America something alien, then there are hundreds of thousands of Americans to plead guilty to provincialism.

"The Melting Pot," a term to which Mr. Zangwill gave currency, is not a very dignified name for our Republic, but aside from that, it is being more and more challenged as descriptive of the process that goes on here. There are some substances in the pot that will not melt. But more significant still, there are rapidly increasing interests *who want to melt the pot.*

So far as Fifth Avenue was concerned, it was the pot that melted. At least, not the most intrepid Jewish leader will shout much about the American characteristics of the most conspicuous Jewish colony in the world, that of New York.

The lofty buildings in this district are filled with clothing workshops, of which the Jew has a monopoly in the United States. Coatmakers, pantmakers, button-hole workers, ladies' garment workers, these men are engaged in the "needle trades" in which adult men of no other race participate.

Why the tendency of the Jew to the "needle trades"? It is explained by his aversion to manual labor, his abhorrence of agricultural life, and his desire to arrange his own affairs. Arriving in the city of his destination, the Jew would rather not leave it except for other cities. There is one Hebrew society whose charter would indicate that its work is the placing of Jews in the rural districts, but it does next to nothing in this respect. On the other hand, there is testimony that city colonization goes on apace. Widespread Jewish associations are on the lookout of likely towns in which to settle a few Jews, who in time become a larger colony, and in a little longer time run the place. There is nothing haphazard about it. The Jew is not an adventurer, he does not cut himself off from his base, but all his movements are made under consultation and direction. New York is the great training school in which the newly arrived immigrant receives his instructions as to the method of handling the American goyim.

Thus, preferring any kind of a life in the city, and not taking to the trades which involve much bodily effort, the Jew gravitates to the needle, not in the capacity of a creative artist, as is the commercial tailor, but in the production of quantities of ready-to-wear goods.

Aside from the "white collar quality of the job," the "needle trades" appeal to the Jew because at such work he can practically arrange his own hours. For this reason the Jew generally prefers piece work to day work, domestic industries to factories—he can arrange his own time. Many people wonder how the Jews of New York have so much time for revolutionary consultation, parades, meetings, demonstrations, restaurant debates and radical authorship. No other class of working people can get the time; other people work pretty steadily. The explanation is at hand: extreme Socialism and Bolshevism have a great deal of "time off."

Trotsky, the present head of Russia, lived that way in New York. His main arrangement was for leisure to work up his scheme. All the East Side leaders knew that Trotsky was to "take the Czar's job," even though he never had an extra dollar to spend. There was nothing haphazard about it. It was prearranged, and the appointed men went directly to their preappointed places. The East Side has other rulers ready now, and they live in the midst of the revolutionary "needle trades."

One main point that should not be overlooked in all this, of course, is that the "needle trades" being exclusively Jewish, all their abuses are Jewish too. This is said for the benefit of those apologists for Russian Bolshevism who explain that the reason for it all is the way the poor "Russian" was treated in America. If Americans will ever learn to remember that the Russian is not a Jew, and that Bolshevism is not Russian but

Jewish, and if in addition to that the American will ever learn to remember that every Russian-Jewish laborer in New York comes into contact with a Russian-Jewish employer, and every Russian Jew tenant pays his exorbitant rent to a Russian Jew landlord, it will then be clear that once more has the United States been made to bear a slander that does not belong to it.

It may be well to remember also that it was on account of these Russian and Polish Jews, while they yet resided in Russia, that the United States broke off her trade treaty with that country—broke off with the Russia that was a country and a government before America was discovered; and, having by that act contributed to the Jewish throttle on Russia through Germany, it is now proposed that the United States, on account of these same Jews, enter into trade agreements with the present Russian tyranny. Verily, the diplomacy of Judah has come very near determining our foreign policy. If they were strong enough, in spite of President Taft's refusal, to make us break with Russia, they may also be strong enough to make us shake hands with Bolshevism.

The Jewish trade union is exclusively Jewish for the reason that the trades affected are exclusively Jewish. That is, the Jewish trade union is not an American trade union, it is not a mixed trade union, it is Jewish. Like all other Jewish activities the purpose of the trade union is to advance Jewish interests alone. These unions are one aspect of United Israel.

This should be borne in mind with reference to the widespread strikes in the clothing trade and the rapid increase in the price of clothing to the 99,000,000 non-Jews in the United States. In spite of all the strikes, the profits advanced enormously; it may be said that the strikes were essential to the advance of profits; and the country as a whole paid.

Look at some of the figures of the "needle trades" before the war. In the entire United States, the men's and women's clothing manufactured in 1914 had a value of $932,099,000.

In New York alone, $542,685,000 was produced. The rest was produced by the Jewish clothing centers in Chicago, Cleveland, New Jersey and Philadelphia.

The figures for the period of the war and since will be staggering. Clothing in the regular trade began to mount in price, until at the end of the war in 1918, it had attained an increase of 200 per cent and 300 per cent. Until well into 1920 the monopoly held up the price. This was done in face of the declaration by the manufacturers of *cloth* that the whole profiteering persistence was due to the manufacturers of *clothing*. Russian-Polish Jews, in this country only a few months, drew $50 to $80 a week. Threats of strike were used to get a five per cent increase in wages, which was met by a 20 per cent increase in the cost of clothing. The American public paid.

If, however, these statements were merely an attempt to arouse indignation that for once the workers got more than they earned, the attempt would be a failure. It is pretty hard to find anyone to regret the workers getting hold of a bonanza. The high wages weren't of much use, as it proved, but people at least had the satisfaction of handling them.

These statements are made to show that during the war the Jewish unions waxed fat, a fact which has a bearing on their Bolshevik attitude today. Not all the wage was the gain of the man who earned it—there was the union to pay. Girls in the fur trade in New York earned $55 a week, of which they paid in $27.50 a week to the unions. Other workers paid in like proportion. There was great talk of what would be done. In Russia, of course, they had the government's gold vaults immediately upon the success of the revolution, but in the United States the preliminary funds would have to be supplied by themselves. A great revolutionary stroke was planned of which the written evidence still remains.

There are two divisions of Jewish wealth and power centering in New York. The first is German-Jewish, represented by the Schiffs, the Speyers, the Warburgs, the Kahns, the

Lewisohns and the Guggenheims. These play the game with the aid of the financial resources of the non-Jews. The other division is composed of the Russian and the Polish Jews who monopolize the hat, cap, fur, garment and toy trades. (By the way—it is the Russian and Polish Jew who controls the American stage and movies also.) Between them their grip and influence is far from negligible. They may sometimes have internecine quarrels regarding the division of the profits and eager publicists may zealously call attention to these quarrels as evidence of the lack of unity among the Jews, but in the Kehillah and elsewhere they understand each other pretty well, and on the question of Jew vs. "goy" they are indivisibly one.

Between these two forces the attempt to hold up prices was continued until late in 1920. The heads of the Jewish clothing would not be lowered. Solidly behind them were the associated Hebrew labor unions, so-called, which threatened dire things if the prices came down. The first great store to reduce prices in New York was Wanamaker's a non-Jewish house. In fact there was not reduction of prices among Jewish manufacturers and merchants generally, until in the month of November less than a dozen Jews were called into the presence of a non-Jewish financier, after which a belated effort was made to save the buying market by sensational reductions. The Jewish controllers of the clothing business had just previously stated that not only would prices not go down, but the 1921 prices would go still higher.

There is a distinction between what the Jewish coalition *would* do and what it *could* do, but its will and its power never so closely correspond as when the non-Jewish mind is asleep, and never are Jewish will and power so widely divorced as when the non-Jewish mind is alert. When the non-Jewish financial mind made itself felt in November, 1920, the bottom dropped out of Jewish trade prophecies and policies. The only thing to fear is not the alert Jew, but the consequences of sleepiness among the Christians. *The Jewish Program is checked the moment it is perceived and identified.*

Ordinary people who for five years have been paying high tribute to the clothing trust are entitled to know who comprise that trust. But that is a trifling affair compared with the political uses to which the clothing trust has been put in this country. The clothing trust, being composed exclusively of Jews, most of whom have formed the ax-head of Jewry in the fight against certain Old-World governments, is today the heart and center of a movement which, if successful, would leave not a shred of the Republic, its institutions, nor even the liberty, which is every American's by inheritance.

What is the strength of these people? How are they banded together? What are the facts concerning them?

In New York City alone there are 2,760 Jewish cloak and suit manufacturing concerns; 1,200 Jewish clothing manufacturers; 2,880 Jewish fur manufacturers; 600 Jewish skirt manufacturers; 600 manufacturing tailoring establishments; 800 Jewish merchant tailoring concerns.

These employers have organized themselves into associations such as the following:

Associated Boys' Clothing Manufacturers of Greater New York.
Associated Fur Manufacturers.
Associated Shirt Manufacturers.
Association of Embroidery and Lace Manufacturers.
Children's Dress Manufacturers' Association.
Cloak, Suit and Skirt Manufacturers' Protective Association.
Cotton Garment Manufacturers of New York.
Dress and Waist Manufacturers' Association.
East Side Retail Clothing Manufacturers' Association.
Ladies' Hat Manufacturers' Protective Association.
Mineral Water Dealers' Protective Association.

National Association of Separate Skirt Manufacturers.
National Society of Men's Neckwear Manufacturers.
New York Association of House Dress & Kimono
    Manufacturers.
New York Tailors' Verein.
Shirt Manufacturers' Protective Association.

Among the employed Jews, the unions are numerous but all gathered up into one central organization. For example, the International Fur Workers' Union of the United States and Canada, is made up of the following:

Feather Boa Makers' Union.
Fur Cap Makers' Union.
Fur Cutters' Union.
Fur Dressers' Union.
Fur Dyers' Union.
Fur Floor Walkers' Union.
Fur Hatters' Union.
Fur Head and Tail Makers' Union.
Fur lined Coat Finishers' Union.
Fur Nailers' Union.
Fur Operators' Union.
Fur Pluckers' Union.
Muff Bed Workers' Union.

In the garment industry, the organizations include every operation in the process of making clothes. There are separate unions for buttonhole makers, vest makers, pants makers, coat cutters, coat operators, coat pressers, coat tailors, coat basters, lapel makers, knee pants makers, clothing turners, overall workers, palm beach workers, shirt makers, vest pressers, and even a washable sailor suit union. These together comprise the Amalgamated Clothing Workers of America.

In children's clothing we have another complete organization:

'Children's Jacket Makers (three unions).
Children's Jacket Pressers.
Children's Sailor Jacket Makers' Union.
Children's Cloak and Reefer Workers' Union.
Children's Dressmakers' Union.

In women's wear, there are unions organized around every garment known to the wardrobe, some of which are:

Amalgamated Ladies' Garment Cutters' Union.
Bonnaz, Singer and Hand Embroiderers' Union.
Buttonhole Makers and Button Sewers' Union.
Children's Cloak and Reefer Workers' Union.
Cloak and Suit Tailors' Union.
Cloak and Suit Piece Tailors and Sample Makers' Union.
Cloak Examiners, Squarers and Bushelers' Union.
Cloak Makers' Union.
Cloak Operators' Union.
Cloak, Skirt and Dress Pressers' Union.
Ladies' and Misses' Cloak Operators' Union.
Ladies' Tailors Alteration & Special Order Union.
Ladies' Waist and Dressmakers' Union.
Skirt and Cloth Dressmakers' Union.
Waterproof Garment Workers' Union
White Goods Workers' Union.
Wrapper, Kimono, House Dress and Bath Robe Makers' Union.

These unions comprise the International Ladies' Garment Workers' Union.

The reader will have an idea, after reading these lists, that the employes represented in these unions are women. The majority are men. It may require something of an effort to remember that, but it is essential. These organizations control an essential business which *before the war* produced over One Billion Dollars' worth of goods a year, and since the war has probably received for its products each year the amount of a big fat Liberty Loan; and these unions have received 30 to 40 per cent of that for wages and propaganda funds.

Now, let it be said at once that these Jewish unions are not to be confused with the regular Labor Union Movement, as we know it in the United States.

They are not Jews who have gone into the American trades unions. They have started unions of their own which are Jewish in membership, control and purpose. It is true, of course, that the regular trades union movement which heads up in the American Federation of Labor is under the presidency of a Jew, Samuel Gompers, but the membership is mixed, the large majority being non-Jews, and the purpose is not racial.

These Jewish unions comprise a body by themselves and are to be reckoned with, not only as labor union groups, but as racial and political groups whose purposes can be determined by the character and utterances of their leaders, as well as by the actions authorized and approved by the unions themselves.

Now, *this Hebrew union movement is a part of the New York Kehillah.* Jewish leaders have sought to counts ᵃct THE DEARBORN INDEPENDENT'S account of Kehillah activities by saying that the Kehillah is such a little weak thing. Admittedly, however, the Jewish clothing trust and the Jewish garment workers' unions are among the biggest and most powerful aggregations in the country. Not even a Jewish leader would have the temerity to deny that. Well, the Amalgamated Clothing Workers of America and the International Ladies' Garment Workers' Union are affiliated with the Kehillah.

More than that: this Kehillah, which Jewish spokesmen with cool contempt for truth would have the public believe was weak and unimportant—*this same Kehillah, in its Executive Committee, constitutes The American Jewish Committee.*

Is the American Jewish Committee a nonentity? Ask any President of the United States, any Senator or Governor.

The American Jewish Committee heads up in District No. 12 *is also the Executive Committee of the Kehillah.*

The men who represent before the world the combined organizations mentioned in this article *are* the Kehillah, and they *are* the American Jewish Committee, and besides, they are the men whose failure in candor has left such an impression of dissatisfaction throughout the masses of the Jewish people.

Who are they? Who are these men with whom the Kehillah is said to be such a puling thing?

Louis Marshall, of the law firm of Guggenheimer, Untermeyer and Marshall. Mr. Marshall is not only head of District No 12, but he is also head of the American Jewish Committee. His headship of the A. J. C. makes him Jewish leader of the United States. His headship of District No. 12 makes him head of the New York Kehillah. Quite an important man? Yes; and an important place, in spite of lying Jewish spokesmen.

Who are the others? Eugene Meyer, Jr., formerly of the Capital Issues Committee of the United States war government.

Who else? Judah L. Magnes. Judah L. Magnes is the organizer and active leader of the New York Kehillah. The two bodies are linked up again. They are linked up by the Kehillah's constitution which is able to decree that its executive committee shall be the American Jewish Committee as far as District No. 12 (New York City) is concerned.

There are other names on the American Jewish Committee which also constitutes the executive committee as the Kehillah—Adolph Lewisohn, Cyril L Sulzberger, Felix Warburg, and so on, 36 in all.

In the current annual report of the American Jewish Committee this relation with the Kehillah is acknowledged in a note at the foot of page 123, just as in the constitution of the

Kehillah its relation with the A. J. C. is acknowledged and explained.

Now to recapitulate.

The Hebrew labor unions, both of employes and employers which are in complete control of the garment industry of the United States, represent one wing of Jewish aggression in the realm of political revolutionism. It is not a small wing in itself. Certainly it does not become smaller by its connection with the Kehillah nor the Kehillah by its gain of these workers. The two unions mentioned above number over 337,000 members. That figure is conservative. Besides these there are associated with the Kehillah the members of 1,000 other Jewish organizations, such as synagogues, charitable societies and educational bodies, and 1000,000 individual members who belong on their own account.

Link this organization with the powerful American Jewish Committee, and at once the protest of the editors and the spokesmen that the Kehillah is a weak, unimportant body becomes a deliberate falsehood.

And as for those "Gentile fronts" who are ready victims of Jewish propaganda, and who, without personal knowledge, are describing the Kehillah as a large and flourishing charitable society (bad teamwork there!) let them read in the next article what some of the Kehillah leaders are trying to do to the United States.

Issue of April 16, 1921

L.

Jew Trades Link With World Revolutionaries

THERE are more Bolsheviks in the United States than there are in the Soviet Russia. Their aim is the same and their racial character is the same. If they are not able to do here what they have done there, it is because of the greater dissemination of information, the higher degree of intelligence and the wider diffusion of the agencies of governmental authority, than obtains in unhappy Russia.

The power house of Bolshevik influence and propaganda in the United States is in the Jewish trade unions which, almost without exception, adhere to a Bolshevik program for their respective industries and for the country as a whole.

This fact is proving most embarrassing to the Jewish leaders at the present moment. It is bad enough that Russian Bolshevism should be so predominantly Jewish, but to confront the same situation in the United States, is a double burden of which Jewish leaders do not know how to dispose.

Yet it is difficult to see how the International Jew can be absolved either from the necessity of being confronted with it, or from the necessity of bearing sole responsibility for it. Russian Bolshevism came out of the East Side of New York where it was fostered by the encouragement—the religious, moral and financial encouragement—of Jewish leaders. Leon Trotsky (Braunstein) was an East Sider. Whether he was a member of the New York Kehillah is not known. But the forces which fostered what he stood for centered in the Kehillah, and both the Kehillah and its associated American

Jewish Committee were interested in the work he set out to do, namely, the overthrow of an established government, one of the allies of the United States in the recent war. Russian Bolshevism was helped to its objective by Jewish gold from the United States. And now that it is found to be numerically much stronger in the United States than it is in Russia, the fact causes no little embarrassment.

Denial is useless, for the thing is too blatant and has advertised itself too long. What amazes the student of the Jewish Question in the United States is the stupidity which permitted Jewish Bolshevism to flaunt itself so openly during the past few years. The only explanation that seems at all adequate is that the Jews never dreamed that the American people would become sufficiently awake to challenge them. The present widespread exposure of Jewish tactics in the United States has doubtless come as a surprise to the Jewish leaders, and this cannot be accounted for otherwise than that they thought they had gained too strong a grip on the American mind to make a challenge possible.

It remains to be seen whether the Jewish leaders shall be able to control the Frankenstein that their false policies have created.

Following exactly the program which the Jewish leaders approved for Russia, the organized Jews of New York are exhibiting a zeal and a directness which Jewish leaders would like to curb for the present, if we are to judge from some of the complaints that the Bolshevik Jews are making.

Benjamin Schlessinger, president of the International Garment Workers' Union, whose membership numbers 150,000, and which is a part of the New York Kehillah, is one of the complainants. His union, of course, is not the regular American labor union formed for the betterment of working conditions and wages; it is a revolutionary union for the complete change of the social system, involving also a change of government. In an interview printed in the *Jewish Forward* of

April 8, Schlesinger complains against the manner in which Jewish judges have recently come to interfere with Jewish strikes:

" ' And Jewish judges come to their assistance. They issue injunctions; and it is said that they do it to save the Jewish name, so that it shall not be said that "all Jews are Bolshevists." So the injunctions become a Jewish affair. . . .

" 'We have a gigantic wide-branched Kehillah in New York. In all corners, Jews! All over, what you see and what you hear—Jews. And, of course, also dress; politicians and greater ones.'

"But only *we* may say this. And I understand Schlessinger . . . Schlessinger explains it this way: Several reasons are given why judges like (here a Jewish judge is named) twist the law . . . . The real purpose is to break our strike . . . . But then, after all, there is a reason, a Jewish reason. He wants to demonstrate to the American community, he claims, that not all Jews are Bolshevists."

This excerpt shows several things: that only "we" may say certain things; that Jewish authority is trying to cover the blemish of Bolshevism; and that this is done in order to demonstrate to "the American community" a certain desirable thing. The Jewish community, it is presumed, is not so easily impressed. The Kehillah is apparently flown too high in the rarefied atmosphere of revolutionism.

Another big union which makes part of the New York Kehillah is the Amalgamated Clothing Workers of America, whose membership is about 200,000. It is officered by Russian Jews whose pronounced Bolshevik utterances have been widely reported in the Jewish press of New York, until plain and unprivileged Americans have wondered how far treason to the United States Government could go on our own soil.

Sidney Hillman, the president, is one of the most radical Socialists in the United States—so radical that he would probably spurn the name of Socialist as ordinarily used. He is a Sovietist. He is so far "advanced" that to him the regular type of American labor union is "a scab union." The purpose of the American labor union is stated to be the improvement of the workers' condition in industry and the establishment of their industrial rights, whereas the object of Hillman's union is the overthrow of industry and its communization in the hands of the radical element. That is to say, Russia over again. Hillman was born in Russia. He personally knows most of the Bolshevik Jews now ruining that great land.

The secretary of the Amalgamated is Joseph Schlossberg, also born in Russia. Schlossberg has a very free gift of words. One of his promises to his Jewish followers, publicly made at Madison Square Garden, is this:

"The clothing industry is ours. We are not going to permit the employer to determine where his factory shall be, or how many hours we shall work."

Abraham Shiplacoff, a Socialist member of the New York board of aldermen, and next to Sidney Hillman in command of the Amalgamated, is also a free speaker, as the following excerpt will show:

"We are going to move heaven and earth to educate our people that they and they alone are the owners of industry. The workers of Russia have found it out, God bless them!

"If I knew old Sammy Gompers knew as much as that, I would tell you to go and do what the workers did in Turine. Ten thousand of them marched to the factory with music and a flag, and they opened the doors and went to work and said, 'To hell with the owners of the factory.'

"Everybody knows it is war. We are going to control the industry."

Always the omission, of course, that the factories so spectacularly captured, cease to run soon after. The Hillmans and the Schlossbergs and the Shiplacoffs are heroic figures on the platform, but in manufacturing the common commodities of life and making both ends meet so that the consumer may be served and the producer rewarded, they have been the most tragic failures. "The workers of Russia have found it out, God help them!"

As a matter of fact, besides the I. W. W., the Amalgamated is the only organization which not only preaches Bolshevism but actually practices it—all in the United States, and all apparently in perfect consistency with its membership in the Kehillah and under the officership of the high gentlemen of the American Jewish Committee. The Amalgamated actually does run the industry which has mulcted such a heavy tax from the American public since 1914.

They tell the factory manager where the factory is to be located.

They have a minimum wage of $12 a day, independent of skill or production. They enforce that rule, that an employe who has worked for two weeks has thereafter a job for life.

No improved machinery can be introduced without the union's permission.

The employer cannot hire even a cartage firm that the union has not first approved.

The employer cannot withdraw from business unless he goes into bankruptcy, else the whole force of the union and its allies will be marshaled against him and his. He must inform the union of all his plans in advance.

This, of course, is part of the endowment of Trotsky to the East Side. He did great missionary work there while waiting to go across and take the Czar's place. Even to this day in the Jew-controlled theaters that crowd Broadway, the picture of Trotsky brings wild delirious cheering, while the portrait of the President of the United States is hissed. A favorite stage scene is the Star of David high over all flags. The recent debate between Senators King and France, said to have been organized with the assistance of two rabbis, developed into such an outrageously anti-American pro-Soviet demonstration, that prudence intervened to prevent a vote. Recently when pro-Jewish Germans endeavored to stir up trouble by holding a great mass meeting to protest the alleged "Black horror on the Rhine," the audience was packed with Jews. Not that they love Germany more, but they love any regular government less. While a few days later, at a great American meeting, the Jews of New York, according to the testimony of incredulous observers, were most conspicuous by their absence.

Now, the Jewish leaders must admit that the Jewish Question does not consist in American citizens uncovering these facts and helping other American citizens to become aware of them; the Jewish Question inheres in the facts themselves and in Jewish responsibility for the facts. If it is "anti-Semitism" to say that Bolshevism in the United States is Jewish, so be it; but to unprejudiced minds it will look very like Americanism.

There is not a single, solitary American-born citizen serving as officer or directory of those great unions which form part of the New York Kehillah. These men have not the faintest idea of what America stands for. They are not here to become Americanized, but to change America to their own model. In this they have the articulated support of most of the Jewish rabbis who have been very keen to explain that *Americanization does not at all mean what the American means by it.*

America will have become what these people want it to be when America is sovietized with Jewish radicals in control, and that is the objective toward which they are working now.

The other officers of the Amalgamated are Jacob Petowsky, secretary, who is a Russian Jew, and J. B. Salutsky, who is also a Russian Jew and "National Director of the Educational Department," which means that he is the propagandist of the union in the United States.

Regarding the assertion that the great radical unions are not officered by native-born citizens (the statement has been made that Russian Jews do not usually complete their citizenship but stop short at the "declaration of intention"), there is some interesting material in a study of 2,000 presidents of Jewish organizations in New York City.

Of this number, 1,054 were born in Russia, 536 in Austro-Hungary, 90 in Rumania, 64 in Germany and four in Palestine. These countries produced 89.1 per cent of Jewish leaders in New York.

Of this number, 531 entered the country between the ages of 14 and 21, and 977 entered over the age of 21.

Of this number, 1,270 are still under 50 years of age.

These figures include all organizations from synagogues to trade unions.

How far they have been Americanized, or wish to be, can only be judged by the policies and activities of the organizations which they direct.

The big Jewish labor organizations are the direct offspring of the Jewish Socialist Bund of Russia. It is due to the propaganda of the Bund in the United States that the united Hebrew trades have gone over to the ranks of radicalism. Bundists swarmed to the United States after the abortive revolution of 1905 at which time they failed to put Bolshevism over in Russia, and these Bundists gave their time to the Bolshevizing of the Hebrew Trade Unions in this country. An Agitation Bureau was formed which propagated radical Socialism through the medium of the Yiddish language, which is one of the official languages of the New York Kehillah, made so by the demands of the Kehillah's overwhelming radical constituency.

The Bundists incorporated in 1905 in New York an organization known as "The Workmen's Circle" and "swelled the ranks of the Jewish trade unions," to quote the Kehillah's Register. After a brief attempt to propagate Socialism without reference to the Jewish Question, it was given up, and in 1913 a resolution was adopted declaring that the whole purpose of the work was Jewish. This is attributed, in the Kehillah record, to the spread of "the idea of Jewish nationalism."

Now, care would have to be exercised to avoid confusion between the Hebrew labor unions, radical as they are, and the avowed communistic bodies, radical, if it were not the fact that the unions and the communists are so inextricably interlocked as to make distinctions unnecessary.

That this is not a judgment dictated by mere adverse attitude may be seen from the following facts:

The Workmen's Circle has 800 branches throughout the United States and is officered by Jews throughout. The membership is 98 per cent foreign-born and is Jewish in like proportion.

Among the higher officers of this organization are Joseph Schlessinger, Sydney Hillman, Benjamin Schlossberg, Sam Feinstein and J. B. Salutsky. The names will probably have become familiar to the reader by this time. They form part of the interlocking directorate so commonly found among Jewish organizations, a system which finally heads up in the executive committee of the Kehillah which also composes the leaders of the American Jewish Committee, of which the great public lights of Jewry are members.

Schlessinger is president of the Union of Ladies' Garment Workers, and made a trip to Russia in behalf of communism in the United States, to finance which the members of the Communist party were assessed $1.50 each.

Hillman is president of the Amalgamated Clothing Workers of America.

Schlossberg is secretary of the Amalgamated Clothing Workers of America.

Feinstein is secretary of the United Hebrew Trades.

Salutsky is food commissar to the striking Amalgamated, and is national director of Bolshevik propaganda carried on by his crowd.

They are, of course, all Jews.

The line-up is this: Hebrew trade union leaders are also members of the Workmen's Circle and of the Communist party, and the majority of their trade union followers go with them into the other associations. The reverse process is this: Communism and radical Bolshevism then find their way to the consciousness of the American public by the Bolshevik demands of the so-called trade unions of Jewry.

An extreme defense of all this activity might be that these Jewish leaders and workers are only enamored of the *idea* of Bolshevism, are playing with it academically, and are not to be considered as actively the proponents of a form of government contrary to the Constitution of the United States and to be established by "direct action."

This defense, however, appears insufficient when confronted by another set of facts in which these same union leaders and Communists are shown to be in communication with the Soviet government in the United States—and the Soviet government in the United States is not a mere *idea*, it is a *program*. Moscow has repeatedly stated that the purpose of the Lenin-Trotsky government has been World Revolution. And one reason for the colossal economic failure of the Soviet governmental experiment has been the Jewish Soviet leaders' neglect of their proper work to follow this fetish of World Revolution. If one-tenth the effort had been made to govern and feed Russia that has been made to sow Bolshevik ideas in other countries, Russia might today have been in a less unhappy plight. Propaganda is the sole art which the Bolsheviks have mastered.

This Soviet government in the United States, therefore, must be regarded by those who know anything about it. It is so regarded by those who ordered the deportation of L. C. A. K. Martens, the "Soviet Ambassador." Martens was announced to be here for the purpose of opening up trade relations with the United States. He had a vast fund of gold—indeed, it was to explain his gold hoard that he used the story about trade relations. The Government of the United States judged, however, that his purpose here was World Revolution—and the government was right.

Martens has departed but the Soviet Embassy remains. As stated in a former article, Martens' successor is Charles Recht, who is a Russian Jew about 36 years of age. In the same building with Recht is Isaac A. Hourwich, another Russian Jew and attorney, whose office is supposed to be the headquarters whence proceeds much of the Russian Bolshevik propaganda.

Now, the people who go to the offices of Recht and Hourwich are the same people whose names we have been tracing all through this interlocker, with some notable additions. Into the sanctum of ambassadorial Bolshevism in the United States, come, of course, Recht the representative and Hourwich the attorney for Lenin and Trotsky in this country.

Another caller is Judah L. Magnes, head of the New York Kehillah. He is a rabbi without a synagogue, an extreme extremist, a master of the language of agitation, and pro-Bolshevist in his influence and associations. He is credited with being the mediator between rich Jews and radicals when the latter are in need of funds. This is the Judah L. Magnes, head of the Kehillah, who tried to tell New York newspaper reporters what a weak and innocent foundling the New York Kehillah is; the same Judah L. Magnes whom the *American Hebrew* tried to picture as a diaphanous idealist broken-hearted because the ghetto doesn't fall in with his educational schemes. The Kehillah is *not* a welfare institution in the charitable sense; it is a nerve-center of Jewish power; in Rabbi Magnes' own words, "a clearing house"; and if it amounted to nothing politically and nationally, the men who are now prominent in it would soon desert it. Kehillah is just what the word signifies—the whole Jewish community.

Then, of course, there are Benjamin Schlessinger again, president of the Ladies' Garment Workers, and Sydney Hillman, president of the Amalgamated Clothing Workers, and Joseph Schlossberg, another Amalgamated official whose Bolshevik utterances were quoted earlier in this article, and others of the Hebrew trades crowd whose radical relationships have been shown.

In addition, there are certain immigration inspectors from Ellis Island—all Jews, of course; occasionally a courier from Russia who has slipped into the country for a secret purpose; occasionally also a courier to Russia bearing messages from Recht and Hourwich.

Then I. W. W. leaders—Jews. Among them Baletin, secretary of the I. W. W. Metal Machinery Workers' Branch, and Peltner, joint secretary of the I. W. W. branches in New York.

In close touch with these Jewish radicals are a number of revolutionists of other countries, representing various violent programs against the established order.

It is through the office of Charles Recht that passports, issued by the State Department of the government of the United Stages, are being viséed. This statement refers to a regular practice known to have been followed until a few days preceding this writing, and there is no reason to believe it has since been altered. Ambassador Recht, or Acting Ambassador Recht, or whatever he may be called, is in close touch with Soviet authorities and has full notice of all their intentions regarding American affairs.

A frequent subject of conferences in Recht's office is the Soviet propaganda in America. Men like Hillman and Schlossberg and Schlessinger are merely liaison officers between the Soviets and the Hebrew trades unions. The orders received from Moscow are thus transmitted to the Jews in America, and are obeyed along perfectly defined lines.

Of course, Rabbi A. Magnes, head of the New York Kehillah, could hardly be expected to remain in ignorance of what the whole Kehillah knows. And that Magnes is temperamentally a radical, any two-minute perusal of his speeches will show. He is head of what Schlessinger calls the "gigantic, widebranched Kehillah," the foremost political racial organization in this country, a close community of a single racial type which has its own code and its own customs and its own method of gaining its ends. This is not the whole story by any means. Schlessinger and Schlossberg and Hillman and the rest are leaders, but they are not the higher-ups. The connections run straight up to the lofty heights of those who dwell in palaces and sway the finances of the nation, and to those who play large parts in the government of the United States. The Jews who finance radical publications—good conservative Jews who form the standing illustration in the argumentative question, "What possible gain can they hope from Bolshevism?" Jews who pull official wires to gain immunity and privilege for known traitors and revolutionists. Jews who replenish the coffers of dangerous elements. It is a long story, and all of it does not require telling, for the point to be gained is not that everyone should be told, but that the involved persons should be aware that it is known, proved, safely put away, in hope that the occasion to use it may never come. However, it is due the public to tell at least a part of it.

The Jewish leaders never played so stupid a card as when they endeavored to minimize the Kehillah and the place it fills. Nor did their Gentile echoes ever fall for so miserable an imposition.

Issue of April 23, 1921

LI.

Will Jewish Zionism Bring Armegeddon?

W HEN the British Army passed into Jerusalem in the memorable capture of the city in 1917, the Protocols went in with it. A symbolic circle was thus closed, though not in the way the Protocolists had hoped. The man who carried the Protocols knew what they signified, and they were carried not in triumph but as the plans of the enemies of world liberty.

Zionism is the best advertised of all present Jewish activities and has exerted a greater influence upon world events than the average man realizes. In its more romantic aspects it makes an appeal to Christian as well as to Jew, because there are certain prophecies which are held to concern the return of the Jews to Jerusalem. When this return takes place, certain great events are scheduled to ensue.

Because of this admixture of the religious sentiment, it will be rather difficult for a certain class of people to scrutinize modern Political Zionism; they have been too well propagandized into believing that political Zionism and the "return" promised by the prophets are the same thing. Having succumbed to the initial confusion of mistaking Judah for Israel they have entirely mistaken the ancient writings that relate to these two, and have made the single tribe of Judah (whence comes the name of Jew) the hub around which all history and humanity swing. Judah was the tribe with which Israel could not live in peace over two thousand years ago, and which has the fateful gift of stirring up the same kind of dissension today. And yet no one ever thought of charging the Ten Tribes of Israel with "anti-Semitism."

Zionism is challenging the attention of the world today because it is creating a situation out of which many believe the next war will come. To adopt a phraseology familiar to students of prophecy, it is believed by many students of world affairs that Armageddon will be the direct result of what is now beginning to be manifested in Palestine.

For these, if for no other reasons, the subject becomes important.

With Zionism as a dream of pious Jews this article has nothing to do. With Zionism as a political fact, every first class government is now compelled to have something to do. It is a bigger question than the German indemnities or American immigration, because it lies back of both, and is rapidly proceeding under cover of both.

It is worthy of note, if only in passing, that Zionism in the active modern political sense took its rise racially and geographically where Bolshevism arose, namely, in Russia, and that its center, the seat of its Inner Actions Committee, was at Berlin. There was always a close relationship between the Zionists of Russia and the New York Kehillah, as is evidenced by public utterances made in Russia after the Revolution in which the Kehillah is extolled.

At the time the war was declared in 1914, the Inner Actions Committee was spread about in various countries. For example: Dr. Schmarya Levin, of Berlin, was in the United States and remained here. He was Russian rabbi, German scholar, and cosmopolitan. Although his headquarters were Berlin, he remained in the United States and became recognized as the leader of the leaders of Zionism, until the great Jewish shift to Versailles. Another member of the Inner Actions Committee was one Jacobson, who was in Constantinople. "When he saw that Constantinople could no longer be the center of Zionist politics, he left and went to Copenhagen, Denmark, where in a neutral country he could be of practical usefulness to the Zionists *by transmitting information and funds.* (Guide to Zionism, page 80.)   In fact, the entire Inner Actions Committee, with headquarters at Berlin, moved freely through a war-locked world, the only two exceptions being Warburg and Hantke—and there was no need for the Berlin Warburg to move about, for there were others who represented him.

Dr. Levin gave his sanction for the shifting of the center of Jewish gravity from Berlin to America, and "as early as August 30, 1914, a month after the outbreak of war, an extraordinary conference of American Zionists was called in New York."

What this change of seat meant, has formed the subject of much discussion.   In 1914 the Jews apparently knew more about the probable duration of the war than did the principals. It was not to be a mere excursion through Belgium, as some fancied.   There was time to dicker, time to show the value of certain Jewish support to the governments.   Germany gladly pledged the land of Palestine to the Jews, but the Jews had already seen what Wilhelm had done in that ancient state when he enthroned himself on the Mount of Olives.   Evidently the Allies won in the contest of making promises, for on November 2, 1917, when General Allenby was pushing up through Palestine with his British Army, Arthur James Balfour, the British secretary of state for foreign affairs, issued the famous declaration approving Palestine as a national home for the Jewish people.

"The wording of it came from the British foreign office, but the text had been revised in the Zionist offices in America as well as in England.   The British declaration was made in the form in which the Zionists desired it, and *the last clauses were added* in order to appease a certain section of timid anti-Zionist opinion." (Guide to Zionism, pages 85-86.)

Now please read the declaration and note the italicized clauses just referred to:

"His Majesty's Government view with favor the establishment in Palestine of a national home for the

Jewish people and will use their best endeavors to facilitate the achievement of this object, *it being clearly understood that nothing shall be done which may prejudice the civil and religious rights of non-Jewish communities in Palestine, or the rights and political status enjoyed by Jews in any other country.*"
Zionism is of particular interest, not merely because of the quarrels which have arisen among the leaders over money—it is the war of "interest" against "capital"—but also because of the light it throws on the two great armies of Jews in the world, the way in which they use their power where they can, and the trouble that always embroils the nations which become Jewish tools.

People sometimes ask why Jewry, which is capitalistic, should favor Bolshevism, which is the announced enemy of capital. It is an interesting question. Why should a New York Jewish financier, an officer of the government of the United States, help finance a "Red" publication which even our tolerant government cannot stomach? In addition to the fact that it is only "Gentile capital" that is attacked, the answer is that the Jew who has fallen for the worship of the Golden Calf is anxious to keep in the good graces of the Jew of the East— the Mongolian Jews—who are rampaging against orderly systems of society. It is quite useful when there is a revolution in Paris to have the 600 houses which you may own spared by the incendiary mobs—as were Rothschild's houses. Zionism has been one of the subjects upon which Western and Eastern Jew can unite. Indeed, it was the Eastern Jew that compelled the Western Jew to take a favorable stand on this matter. The Jewish gentlemen who are receiving the freedom of our cities today in their various aspects as "German" and "British" scientists are Eastern Jews. They have come to a contest with the Jews of America on the question of Money. The Jews of America have smothered some very ugly charges. The Jews of the East, more recently of Germany or England, are not likely to be browbeaten by the moneybags of Jewish New York, for *the Eastern type of Jew knows of a situation in which money is the most useless thing in the world*—and that is why he is feared and favored by Western Jewry of the Golden Calf.

The Jewish defenders are just now capitalizing the "split" in Jewry. The real split in Jewry will come when Jews of vision begin to support the attempts which have been made to liberate the Jews from their leaders. This internal squabble means nothing but a squabble of leaders; but when the Jews themselves divide, one side for twentieth century light and the destruction of the class power of selfish leaders, then may we look up hopefully. When the Jew recognizes the honesty of his critics and the righteousness of what they charge, then will there be a "split," but not before. The division in Jewry as evidenced by the contempt of the revolutionary party for the financial party, and as even more strongly evidenced by the fear of the revolutionary party by the financial party, is being brought about by the insincerity of the Western Jew's Zionism. The Western Jew says that the United States is the Promised Land, profits and interest are the "milk and honey" and New York is Jerusalem; the Jew of Russia has another view.

A knowledge of Political Zionism is worth while also as an authoritative illustration of what the Jew does when he is in power. Heretofore there has been Russia to illustrate this, but now there is Palestine. With every fact against them, with every traveler and observer giving them the lie direct, there are still Jewish spokesmen and poor befuddled "Gentile fronts" who insist that Bolshevism is not Jewish and that Russia is not now governed by Jews. It is just this constant denial of facts, this failure to use their opportunity to be honest, that is going to be the judgment of Jewish leaders. Bolshevism all over the world, not in Russia only, but in New York, in Chicago, in New Orleans, in San Francisco, is Jewish.

However, there is no need further to insist upon that, except occasionally to add confirmatory illustrations of it. More to the present point is Palestine. It will be very difficult for the most irresponsible Jewish spokesman to deny that Palestine is Jewish. The government is Jewish, the plan of procedure is Jewish, the methods used are Jewish. Does anyone rise to deny that? Scarcely.

Very well, Palestine will do to illustrate the genius of the Jew when he comes to power.

Professor Albert T. Clay, in the *Atlantic Monthly* (will anyone declare that this long-established and thoroughly respectable Boston publication is "anti-Semitic"?) warns us that the information about Palestine which we receive in America comes to us through the Jewish Telegraph Service (which is the Associated Press of world-wide Jewry) and the Zionist propaganda. "The latter," he says, "with its harrowing stories of pogroms in Europe, and its misrepresentations of the situation in the Near East, has been able to awaken not a little sympathy for the Zionist propaganda."

This propaganda of pogroms—"thousands upon thousands of Jews killed"—amounts to nothing except as it illustrates the gullibility of the press. No one believes this propaganda, and governments regularly disprove it. But the fact that it continues indicates that something besides facts is necessary to keep the scheme going.

In Jerusalem, as this is being written, martial law is proclaimed. There has been a struggle between the native inhabitants, whom the Balfour declaration sought to protect, and the new-come Jews. As in the famous Easter disorders of last year, the wounded in the hospitals show that the Jews were armed and the natives fought with whatever weapons they could find on the spot; the conclusion of all impartial observers under the circumstances being that the Jews prepared for and sought the fight with unprepared natives.

The mark of disorder perpetrated by the Jews is all over the place, the "persecuted" turned persecutor, and lest this should be charged to the general wildness of the people in Palestine let it be said that the rioters were only expressing in deeds what cultivated American and English Jews have expressed in words —namely, that the lawful inhabitants of the land ought to be driven out, in spite of governmental promises to the contrary. One of the first Easter rioters, Jabotinsky, whom the British authorities sentenced to 15 years in prison, was released immediately upon the arrival of Sir Herbert Samuel, and is now travelling in state, and is talked of as a possible successor to Sir Herbert, although he is originally one of the Russian Bolsheviki come down to practice the gentle arts of that tribe in Palestine.

The government is Jewish. Sir Herbert Samuel is High Commissioner, representing the power of the British Government, which holds the mandate over Palestine. The head of the judicial department, who appoints the judges of Palestine, is a Jew. Christian or Moslem judges who do not give the Jews a shade the better of the proceedings are ousted—a condition not unknown in New York. Chaim Weizmann is head of the department of works—he is a Jew, now traveling in this country and having the polite lie passed to him occasionally by Judge Julian W. Mack. In fact, at the heads of all departments are Jews, a former New York Jew being head of the department of immigration, who has made splendid rules for the protection of Palestine from an undesirable class of Jews, rules so well adapted for the purpose that if the Congress of the United States should adopt them the cry of "persecution: would girdle the world.

It is to be noted that the Jewish government of Palestine is very much like that of Russia—mostly foreign. Trotsky came from the East Side of New York. A gentleman recently released from Bolshevik custody told the writer that the governor of his prison was an ordinary Jew who formerly lived on Fourteenth street, Detroit. Practically every big

American city is represented in the Bolshevik government of Russia. There is another full-fledged government waiting in this country for service wherever necessary.

The methods being adopted to get the land are such as will fill the world with indignation once the world fully understands what is being done. And that it is done with the knowledge and approval of the Zionist Commissioner is indicated by the fact that he suspended the activities of the British officer who endeavored to stop the abuse. It was the old game of lending money at an exorbitant rate of interest to people hard pressed by war and crop failure, and then seizing their land when they could not pay. The bank that did this was the Anglo-Palestine Bank, a Zionist concern. This British officer, to save the people and the land, made arrangements with a British bank to lend them money at 6 1/2 per cent, with five years to pay. If payment failed, the land was to go to the government for redistribution, not to the Zionist bank. This was the humane plan which the Zionist Commissioner forbade, whereupon the British officer resigned. Some effort was afterward made to redress the terrible act, but there it stands as the well-considered action of Jewry in power.

Then follows what is described by every impartial observer as an "arrogant" attempt to expropriate everything in sight. In Russia it could have been done very easily under the plea of "nationalization," but there was Great Britain whose laws do not condone theft. The only schools that have been established in Jerusalem have been built and manned by the so-called "Gentiles," although the Jews of Jerusalem have been the pensioners of world-wide Jewry for centuries. As long ago as 1842 Dr. Murray M'Cheyne noted that the Jerusalem Jews cared nothing for schools because their children were only growing up into pensioners too. But Christians, with a warm regard for the Holy City, set about to improve the miserable condition of the Jewish inhabitants, and thus it came that at the time of the Zionist invasion a considerable number of Jewish children were in attendance at the schools. The new-come Zionist leaders demanded that the best of the schools be given up to them. Of course, this was refused.

"The Council of Jerusalem Jews" then caused it to be published in the Hebrew daily that parents who did not withdraw their children from the schools would be punished. And now look at the typical punishments threatened:

If any parent refused whose name was on the list of the American Relief Fund, the relief would be withdrawn. An interesting bit of news to subscribers to that fund.

Doctors would be forbidden to visit the families that had children attending the enlightened schools.

Their names would be sent to the blacklist at the places where circumcision was performed, so that new-born descendants of the recalcitrants might be refused the rite of Moses.

They would be denied all share in Zionist benefits or funds.

If they were in business, they would be boycotted.

If they were workmen, they could get no work.

"Anyone who refused, let him know that it was forbidden for him to be called by the name of Jew. They will be fought by all lawful means. Their names will be put upon a monument of shame and their deeds made to reproach them to the last generation. If they are supported, their support will cease. If they are rabbis, they will be moved far from their office. They shall be put under the ban and persecuted, and all the world will know that in this justice there has been no mercy."

It is the Jewish Bolshevist spirit all over again, that spirit which so many people have been vainly endeavoring to reconcile with the Russian temperament—because it is so un-Russian.

It is tyranny, and not the tyranny of strength, but of meanness and darkness. It is now perfectly clear what was meant by Dr. McInnis, who is Anglican Bishop of Jerusalem, when he said: "The emigrants so far brought in (to Palestine, under the Commission) did not include many respectable English Jews; but they did include a great number of Russians,

Poles and Rumanians, many of them thoroughly Bolshevik in their attitude to the government."

If this spirit obtains at the beginning of a movement which the Christian world has been taught by propaganda to regard as a profoundly religious and respectable exodus, it burdens the imagination to forecast what will be done in a period of full and unquestioned rule.

Observing and weighing the events and tendencies of Jewish rule thus far in Palestine, it is not difficult to see the purpose in it all. The Jews still distrust their ability to make a State. They do not distrust the world's willingness to let them have a State; indeed, it is amazing how naturally the Jews place confidence in that portion of the world they have always affected to despise. But deep-seated in the Jew is a distrust of himself. He doesn't know how his people will contrive to live together. He doesn't know how they will contrive to drop the principles and practices which are so destructive of social comity elsewhere. And he feels that, patient as the mandatory power may be now, it is doubtful how long that patience will hold out under the blunders and brutalities that will be inseparable from Zionist rule, if any deductions can be drawn from the facts at hand. Therefore, feeling that the time may be short, he is endeavoring by such actions as interference with the cultural question, with the racial rights of the natives, and by such schemes as the land-grabbing device described above, to get so strong a hold on the situation as will seriously complicate it whenever Great Britain shall feel it to be her duty to the world to step in and attempt to bring some kind of order out of the chaos.

It begins to be very clear that Jewish nationalism will develop along the line of enmity to the rest of the world. Already the dangerous proposal has been made to organize a Jewish army for the protection of the Suez Canal. Instead of thinking of roads and farmsteads, of vineyards and oil presses, of schools and sanitary villages, the Jews are thinking of elevating themselves into the military power that shall stand between East and West on that most strategic strip of ground in the world. The whole situation is fraught with danger, and men who wish well to the Jews are alarmed and saddened by the prospect.

There are three elements of danger in the situation as it exists today: the overwhelmingly predominant Bolshevik element that is being poured into Palestine; the intense, egotistic and challenging nationalism that Zionists exhibit even before they get a potato patch—the taste for world politics and world power; and the racial confusion which now exists in Palestine.

These combined are dynamite. The first is more vital than many realize. Already the Jews who have gone to Palestine at great sacrifice and for pious reasons are complaining that instead of the Psalms of David the people are singing songs of the Red Revolution, and instead of meeting for instruction and prayer there are riotous gatherings extolling Trotsky as Messiah and the Soviet as the kingdom of heaven. On the third anniversary of the Jewish Revolution in Russia, the streets of Jerusalem were placarded with sentiments of blasphemy and treason, and May Day this year was devoted to the exaltation of anarchy.

This fact will be of interest to students of prophecy. It is as certain as any human forecast can be that this sort of thing will not be permitted to go forward in the face of the world. It is unimaginable that the nations responsible to humanity for the conduct of that important strip of territory will remain supine while Bolshevism spreads under the false pretense of a religious movement favored by Christendom. An attempt will be made to stop it. The Jews of Palestine will turn on their sponsor nation. The Jews of Russia will come down to help. Great Britain and perhaps the United States will defend the old pure vision of a Jerusalem redeemed. Then will come to pass the prophecy of Zachariah:
"And Judah also shall fight against Jerusalem."

Judah also! It is a thought to make a Jew bethink himself where the lawlessness of the East and the materialism of the West will lead him. Against Jerusalem! What a terrible ending of Judah's present mad delusion.

Palestine has been called the center of the earth. It is. The power that controls Palestine controls the world. Although exercising no sovereignty over the land itself, Great Britain's control of adjacent waters and of Egypt and Persia and India, forms the key of her power. The white race has thus far been the Chosen People to whom the dominion of the earth has been given. Palestine is the key to world military strategy and trade. In question 12 of the Questions and Answers published by the department of education, Zionist Organization of America, this occurs:

12. What are the commercial possibilities of Palestine?

The location of Palestine *between the three continents* favors foreign trade.

All this lends itself to dreams of future glory, and many Christian friends of the Jew have pleased themselves by conceiving a universal Hague at Jerusalem and a new social order going out to bless the nations from Zion. It is the idea conveyed by men like A. A. Berle in books like "The World Significance of a Jewish State." All this might be expected if the Jews of today were Old Testament people, anxious to re-establish the social laws of Moses, which are conceded to be the best safeguards ever devised against pauperism on the one hand and plutocracy on the other. But Palestine has not fallen into the hands of that sort of Jews. Before the dream can be fulfilled Judah must come to himself, as he has not yet, for from of old the Word is—

"And Judah also shall fight against Jerusalem."

The racial situation in Palestine just now is very delicate. Americans do not understand it. The Zionist propaganda has always been accepted on the assumption that Palestine is the Jews' land and that they only need help to go back. It is an historical and political fact that Palestine has not been the Jews' land for more than 2,000 years. There are in Palestine 500,000 Moslems, 105,000 Christians and 65,000 Jews. The industry of the land is agriculture. Engaged in this are 69 per cent of the Moslems, 46 per cent of the Christians and 19 per cent of the Jews. Neither numerically nor industrially have they held the land. Yet, as the result of a war bargain, it is handed over to them as regardless of the native inhabitants as if Belgium had been handed over to Mexico. Many of the natives are Semites, like the Jews, but they do not want the Jews among them.

That is a strange fact for those who use the term "anti-Semitism"; why do real Semites also dislike the Jews? Surely Semites are not victims of "anti-Semitism."

The Balfour Declaration, as well as the terms of the Mandate adopted at San Remo, recognized the rights of the native races. Indeed, everyone who knows about the people who have been native to Palestine for 2,000 years recognizes their rights, everybody except the Jews. Bethlehem was a Christian town, as befits the birthplace of Christ. Yet the Jews have contrived that 2,000 Bethlehemites leave Palestine rather than submit to what they see coming. The other races are not so placid about it, hence the trouble. It is now that the last clauses, added as the Zionist historian declares, "in order to appease a certain section of anti-Zionist opinion," begin to get a meaning for the reader. Was the purpose only to quiet disturbing questions until all the arrangements were made? Evidently. It was then a dishonest appeasement! Such may have been the Zionists' intention, but no one need expect perjury on the part of the responsible nations. The end of the matter will see those last clauses redeemed by honest application of their terms to the people involved.

General Allenby promised those native races of Palestine that their rights would be respected. So did the Balfour Declaration. So did the San Remo Conference. So also did President Wilson in the twelfth of his Fourteen Points.

But Judah says, "Let them get out!" "The last clauses were added in order to appease a certain section of timid anti-Zionist opinion."

"Let them get out!" says Israel Zangwill. "We must gently persuade them to 'trek.' After all, they have all Arabia with its million square miles, and Israel has not a square inch. There is no particular reason for the Arabs to cling to those few kilometers. To fold their tents and silently to steal away is their proverbial habit; let them exemplify it now." Aside from the falsity of using the term "Arab," there is the delightful Jewishness of it—let them give it up to us, we want it! Americans have been in their land less than 150 years as a nation, and there is China and Arabia or Siberia for us to go to if we should want to, but we prefer out own country, and so do the native races of Palestine, who have dwelt there for 2,000 years.

The watchmen on the towers of the world are alarmed at what seems brewing in Judah's geographical caldron.

Issue of May 28, 1921

LII.

How the Jews Use Power—
By an Eyewitness

T HE Jewish Question continues to mount the scale of public attention, attracting ever a higher type of mind to the discussion of its significance. When THE DEARBORN INDEPENDENT first began to print some of the results of its research into the Question, the initial response was largely from those who disliked the Jew because he was a Jew. This class expected to find in THE DEARBORN INDEPENDENT a spokesman for all their coarse humor and abuse.

The method that was followed by this paper, however, was not abusive enough, nor bitter enough to satisfy Jew-baiters and Jew-haters, and gradually a new response from a better class began to be heard, which by this time has attained massive proportions. The better class of people, seeing that racial and religious prejudice had no part in the work, began to consider the Question with relation to our American life and the future of this nation as a Christian people.

Upon this ascent of the discussion to its proper plane, the better periodicals began to give thoughtful attention to the matter. These publications have been referred to in previous articles. There is to be added to the list the Century Magazine for September, which contains an article by Herbert Adams Gibbons which clearly intends to be fair and is certainly able, in spite of a difference of opinion that might exist with regard to some of the author's conclusions. Mr. Gibbons states some matters more plainly than they have been stated outside the pages of THE DEARBORN INDEPENDENT, and some matters he states just as plainly: and he will be justified by the unprejudiced reader.

One of the most notable studies of the Jewish Question has come out of the University of the South, at Sewanee, Tennessee. It is entitled "Zionism and the Jewish Problem," the author being the Rev. Dr. John P. Peters, formerly canon residentiary of the Cathedral of St. John the Divine, Morningside Heights, New York, also rector emeritus of St. Michael's Church, New York, and professor of New Testament Languages and Literature in the University of the South. The article has been reprinted from the Sewanee *Review* and makes a brochure of 29 pages.

Dr. Peters begins with an historical sketch of the development of the two lines of thought among the Jews, the nationalistic which made for exclusiveness, and the religious which made for inclusiveness, and he describes the domination of the latter by the former with the coming of modern Zionism which he finds to be racial and not religious. He says "the dominant control of the Zionist party is at present in the hands of those who are not religious but merely racial Jews." He believes that the development of race-consciousness along these lines "must be inevitably in the end to make the Jews bad citizens of the United States or of any other country and to keep alive and increase the hostility to the Jews . . . ."

This monograph by Dr. Peters will repay study. By permission, THE DEARBORN INDEPENDENT reprints the article from page 20 to the end, this portion being selected because it deals with Dr. Peters' testimony as an eyewitness of certain conditions in Palestine: (The italics are ours, there being none in the university reprint.)

"The experiment of the Zionist homeland is now being tried. It is too early to determine fully how it will work, but it is at least of interest to consider its manifestations so far. My earliest contact with Zionism and Zionistic influences in

Palestine dates from 1902. When I first visited Palestine, in 1890, the Jews in Jerusalem were almost exclusively of old oriental Sephardic families. Jerusalem was then still the old Jerusalem within the walls. There were no houses without. Jewish colonization, economic and philanthropic in character, had just then begun on the Sharon plain, but what little there was in the way of colonization was a feeble, unsuccessful exotic—an attempt to replace the persecuted Jews of Russia on the land, where, however, the Jew, unused to manual and especially farm labor, sat under an umbrella to protect himself from the sun and engaged native Syrians to do the work.

"On my next visit, in 1902, more colonies had been planted, and a serious effort was being made to turn the Jewish colonists into farmers. The majority of the Jews who had come to Palestine, however, were settled about Jerusalem, and the new Jerusalem without the walls was larger, in space at least, than the old Jerusalem within. The Alliance Israelite had developed there splendid schools to teach agriculture, and manual and industrial arts. I was urgently solicited by the management to visit and inspect these schools. Here I found Jew, Moslem and Christian working side by side without prejudice. This was, in my judgment, the best work of any sort being done in Palestine, for two reasons: first, these schools were teaching the dignity and the worth of manual labor, which the oriental of all sorts had theretofore despised, regarding it as unworthy of any man of intelligence or capacity; secondly, because they brought Moslem, Christian and Jew together on a plane of common work and common worth, the most valuable agent for the breaking down of those ancient prejudices, religious, racial and social, which have been the curse and bane of the land.

"I was asked to put this down in writing because, I was told, *great pressure was being exerted—I regret to say, especially from America—to prevent the management from continuing this particular work of* teaching Jew, Christian and Moslem on the same plane, the demand being that the Jew should not be brought into such contact with the Moslem and the Christian, and that he alone should be trained, that he might not be infected, as it were, by the others, *and that they might not be prepared to compete with him for possession of the land. This spirit I met in a more thoroughly organized and offensive form on my latest visit in 1919 and 1920.*

"I found immense progress in the development of agricultural colonies. There was still difficulty in persuading the Jew, except only the African or Arabian Jew, to do the actual work of the colony, but colonies were prospering, and fruit-culture, vine-culture and especially the manufacture of wine and liquors on a grand and most scientific scale, had progressed wonderfully. In general, the land occupied by those colonies was not in a proper sense ancient Jewish land. They were on the Sharon and Esdraelon plains and in the extreme upper end of the Jordan Valley; but those regions were being enriched, and the country at large benefited by the colonists. The great bulk of the Jews were still gathered in Jerusalem as heretofore, and there were on one hand the intellectuals and on the other the parasitic or pauperized Jew, what would ordinarily be regarded as the very best and the very worst. Life in the colonies was often very sweet and very lovely, a wholesome, normal family life, and an exhibition in peace and prosperity of what religious Judaism at its best may be.

"In Jerusalem one found the extremes of intensely narrow and bitter orthodoxy, and unbelief with extreme Bolshevik radicalism. Here, too, aggressive Zionism manifested itself in an attitude of bumptiousness and aggressiveness. The country was for the Jew. It belonged to him and he would shortly take possession. One was made to feel that one's presence in the land was objected to. The Hebrew press contained angry diatribes against the existence of Christian schools and missions. The attitude taken by these Zionists at first alarmed, then aroused and irritated enormously, the native population, both Christian and Moslem, making the Jew an object of dread and hatred as he had never been before. I had opportunities to talk on intimate and friendly terms with leaders in all camps, albeit I was unable through language difficulties, to communicate with the rank and file as freely as I should like to have done. I myself felt the annoyance and in some places the danger of the animosity aroused. Under government order I was not permitted to visit certain sections of the country on account of the raids or uprisings of the Arabs, partly due to the animosity roused by their apprehension of the Jewish invasion, and partly due to banditry, which took advantage of that as an occasion. In other parts it was difficult to travel, because any stranger, unless he could prove the contrary, was suspected of being an agent of the Zionists, spying out the land for possession by the Jews. It was difficult to obtain lodgings or food, and there were sometimes unpleasantly hostile demonstrations on account of these suspicions. Everywhere it was believed that the Jew by unfair means was seeking to oust the true owners and to take possession of their land.

"In Jerusalem it was asserted that the Zionist funds, or the Jewish funds which the Zionists could influence or control, were used to subsidize Jewish artisans or merchants to underbid Christians and Moslems and thus oust them by unfair competition, and that similar means were being used to acquire lands or titles to lands. It was even believed by many that the English authorities were unduly favoring and helping the Jews in these endeavors, as is shown by a letter from a Christian in Jaffa published in the *Atlantic Monthly*:--

" 'We are already feeling that we have a government within a government. British officers cannot stand on the right side because they are afraid of being removed from their posts or ticked off.'

"From time immemorial the Jews the world over have contributed for the help of pious Jews in Jerusalem and the other sacred cities, Hebron, Tiberias and Safed, the so-called halukha or dole, in return for which the Jews in those cities were to win merit for themselves and those who contributed to their support by study of the law, prayer and pious observances. St. Paul carried over the same practice into the Christian Church, causing alms to be collected in the different congregations to be transferred to Jerusalem for the benefit and support of the Christians living there. To this day annual collections are taken the Roman Catholic churches throughout the world which go to the Franciscans for the same use in Jerusalem. The Greeks and Armenians have like customs. In the past there had been no prejudice with regard to these doles, but now, it was claimed, the Zionist committees were using the moneys thus collected or contributed to organize and help their people in a systematized attempt to gain the upper hand in the land.

"Perhaps the attitude of the extremists who possessed the dominating power in the community can best be shown by the utterances of one of their own organs, written in Hebrew. (It should be stated that *the English edition of this journal was, as a rule, quite different in its contents from the Hebrew edition.* One article, entitled 'Malignant Leprosy,' is a denunciation of parents who allow their children to go to any school except those under the control of Jews and conforming to the demands of the local Zionist Committee. Parents are notified that a list has been made by the Zionist Committee of all children who are attending foreign schools, even though they are not subjected to any religious teaching, and it is demanded that they shall be withdrawn from those schools and placed in schools where they shall be taught the Hebrew language, customs and traditions, and kept separate from contamination by the Gentile, with his different ways and customs. Those teaching in foreign schools, or schools not complying with the conditions laid down by this committee, are ordered to withdraw from their positions. The 'malignant leprosy' is the contamination with the Gentiles. It is admitted in this article, in answer to protests, that the opportunities in some of the non-Jewish schools are better than in the Jewish schools—for example, in the teaching of foreign languages, so important for conducting business or securing employment; that there is greater diligence in instructing; and better hours and better care of pupils. Nevertheless, parents are informed that they must sacrifice for the sake of their race those chances for their children, doing their best meanwhile to raise their own schools to the higher level. Those who are failing to live up to these ideals are designated as 'traitors' and by other opprobrious names, and the article ends with this threat of persecution to any who do not obey the orders of the Zionist Committee thus conveyed:

" 'Let him know at least that it is forbidden him to be called by the name of Jew and there is to him no portion of inheritance with his brethren, and if after a time they will not try to reform, let them know that we will fight against them by all lawful means at our disposal. Upon a monument of shame we will put their names for a reproach and blaming forever, and unto the last generation shall their deeds be written. If they are supported, their support will cease, and if they are merchants, with a finger men will shoot at them, and if they are Rabbis, they will be moved far from their office, and with the ban shall they be persecuted, and all the people of the world shall know that there is no mercy in judgment.'

"This was followed about a month later by a second article, also in Hebrew, entitled 'Fight and Win,' which announced that the threatened persecution would now be carried out:

" 'The names of the traitorous parents and of the boys and girls who have not taken notice of the warnings ought to be published at once and without delay, in the papers and on public notices, placarded at the entrance of every street. The list of these names should be sent to the heads of every institution and to the rulers of the synagogues, to hospitals, to those who arrange and solemnize marriages, and to the directors of the American Jewish Relief Fund, and so on. It should be the title of "Black List" and "Traitors to Their People." An order should go forth to all, and if one of these men has a son, he shall not be circumcised; in case of death the body is not to be buried among Israelites; religious marriages will not be sanctioned; Jewish doctors will not visit their sick; relief will not be given to them when they are in need, if they are on the list of the American relief fund—in short, we must hunt them down until they are annihilated. Men will cry to them: "Out of the way, unclean, unclean!" Because these people will be considered as malicious renegades, there can be no connecting link between them and us. Again, the society of young men and girls of Jerusalem must accept it as a principle to expel from their societies all those who visit these schools; to point the finger of scorn at them; and to make them see that they are put out of the camp. These traitor scholars, boys and girls, must understand themselves that they are sinners and transgressors, who are isolated, driven from all society, separated from the Jewish community, after they have once despised Israel and its holiness, and it will be interdicted to all sons of Israel to come near them . . . .War against the traitors among our people. War by all means legal. War without pity or mercy; that the traitors may know that they must not trifle with the sentiment of a people. Fight and win.'

"The Zionist Committee, *of whom one was an American,* followed this by a printed announcement that the time of grace had passed and that forthwith the names of those who were still refractory would be posted publicly on street-corners, and the boycott begin. Miss Landau, a devout Jewess, the head of the best and highest Jewish school for girls in the city, the Eva Rothschild School, one of those, however, whose pupils and teachers were threatened under these rulings because they would not follow the dictates of the Zionist Committee, appealed to the civil authorities. The committee was haled into court and the threatened boycott enjoined

"With such an attitude on the part of Zionist leaders in Jerusalem it might be expected that violence would ensue. Easter is a time of great excitement and unrest in Jerusalem for Christians, Jews and Moslems alike, for with Easter coincide the Jewish Passover and the Moslem pilgrim feast of Nebi Musa, when Moslems gather from all over Palestine to hear sermons in the Haram Esh-Sherif, and then march to the so-called tomb of Moses near the Dead Sea. The religious excitement of that season which vents itself in curses of each against the others, is always likely to produce physical outbursts if the cursers come into contact with one another. The Turks wisely segregated at that time each religion in its own quarter. This, in spite of warnings and requests from the Moslem religious leaders, the English failed to do, either through ultra-confidence in the *pax anglicana,* or because of objections from Jewish representatives against such segregation as applied to them. For days beforehand hot-heads among the Jews and Moslems were inciting to riot, and in their quarter Jewish trained bands were preparing for the conflict, a preparation of which Moslems from long want probably had no need. On Easter morning, 1920, the fanatical Moslems of Hebron arrived at the Jaffa gate with their sacred banner, singing their songs of religious intolerance. There numerous Jews were waiting to greet them. The English Tommies with their officers were all in church. Whose insults were the worst and who struck the first blow is not clear. Battle was speedily joined. *The Jews were better armed,* with guns against the Moslem knives; but the Moslems were the better fighters. The city within the walls was speedily in their hands. The Jews living there were the old-time Sephardic families, dwelling close-packed in miserable slums, with no sympathy with Zionism, peaceful and quite unprepared. Moslem fury vented itself on these poor wretches. Without the walls the Jews were in the vast majority. All told, by official count there were at that time 28,000 Jews, 16,000 Christians and 14,500 Moslems in Jerusalem. What the Moslem did within the walls the Jew endeavored to do without the walls. Before my eyes an Arab camp just below the great Jewish quarters was set upon, burned and plundered, the poor inhabitants fleeing for their lives while guns popped from the Jewish quarter. Two men were killed there. When the troops reached the scene the great bulk of rioters whom they rounded up were Jews. The subsequent court proceedings also seemed to place the chief responsibility for the outbreak on them. The major sentences were equally divided between Jews and Moslems, but of *the criminals who received lighter sentences the majority were Jews.* For a week we lived in a state of siege, not allowed to pass in or out of the city gates, or to show ourselves on roof or balcony after sundown, and for months there were guards at every turn, assemblies were prohibited and there was continual danger of a new outbreak.

"The appointment of Sir Herbert Samuel, a Jew, as governor of the new protectorate under the Zionist Mandate, greatly increased the excitement. In Moslem towns like Nablus it was openly said in my presence that no Jew might enter the place and live. The Christians, who had taken no part in the riots, were nevertheless to a man in sympathy with the Moslems, and one saw the curious spectacle of Cross and Crescent making common cause. It was prophesied that should Sir Herbert come as governor, he would never enter Jerusalem alive. In point of fact, he landed at Jaffa and came up to Jerusalem under strong guard, *with machine-guns before and behind,* and the following week made a visit to Nablus and

Haifa in the same manner. That was the situation when I left Palestine. Sir Herbert had at that time just issued his declaration and his interpretation of the mandate. *English officers and officials almost to a man were against the Zionist Mandate,* and their utterances in many cases were extraordinarily frank. Some of the most prominent and best trained sought transfers to other posts because of their feelings on the matter, and some resigned.

"It has since that time been extremely difficult to obtain reliable information of prevailing conditions. It would seem, however, from all the information I have been able to gather , that Sir Herbert, who is, I believe, not himself a Zionist, has acted with singular tact and discretion. He has shown great fairness and indicated his intention to govern with impartiality, granting no special favors to any, nor allowing outside committees or local organizations to dictate or assume to dictate unfair policies. When I left Palestine, Jews were leaving in considerable numbers, especially those claiming American citizenship, so that the outgo was larger than the income. Since then, if I may judge by reports, Jews have been coming in, chiefly from eastern European countries, some parasitic and objectionable, others of a higher type. Some of the latter, graduates of universities, both men and women, may be seen engaged in hard manual labor, I am told, building roads and the like, not despising to do such work in order to secure their Palestinian home and fulfill their aspirations.

"It is too soon to judge the future of the Zionist experiment in Palestine. If the English authorities will give fair play to all, and if the Jews will pursue the old policy of the Alliance Israelite and its schools of seeking to benefit all dwellers of the land alike, to break down, not to build up, religious, racial and social prejudices, then the Jew may perhaps overcome the present prejudice against him, and his invasion of Palestine may prove to be a blessing both to himself and to the land. The methods of those in control of the Zionist movement in Palestine while I was there were, however, aimed in the opposite direction and tended to make the Jew an object of hatred and violence wherever the opportunity for violence offered. This has been illustrated again by the recent bloody riot in Jaffa which compelled the expedition of a British warship to that port; and the order issued holding up all immigration shows that not Jaffa only but the whole country is unsafe. *The Jews in Palestine are now protected only by force of British arms. Were the British troops withdrawn, the Jews would be exterminated by the angry natives, of whom the Moslems alone outnumber them in the ratio of more than ten to one; and with such action the neighboring countries would sympathize, yielding ready assistance if any were required. Mesopotamia and Egypt are seething with disaffection against British rule, and racial-religious ferment, and Palestine is to them and to the Arabs of Arabia a holy land included in the heritage of Islam. Moslem India also feels this keenly, and the British have been obliged to withdraw Moslem Indian troops from Palestine, because they will not fight fellow-Moslems.*

"In this country the Jewish problem which ., ` have hitherto had to face is not a result of religious antipathy. Religiously, politically and economically, the Jew has the same opportunity as everyone else. The Jewish problem here has been merely a matter of social prejudice, resulting from the extremely difficult task of amalgamating with great rapidity an enormous population, alien in race, culture, custom and habit. In 1880 there were, according to Jewish statistics, 250,000 Jews in this country. The Jews now claim 3,500,000, for the most part an undistributed mass huddled together in a few of the great cities—one-third of them in New York. Coming in such great numbers in so short a time and herding together thus, intentionally or unintentionally they help one another to resist the process of Americanization. This enormously increases the incidence of social prejudice. Those who have no conscious prejudice either of religion or of race are in danger of imbibing or developing such prejudice as a method of protection of their institutions, their traditions and their habits. The Zionist movement, with its intentional development of race consciousness and race peculiarity on the part of the Jew, is an additional obstacle against the efforts of those Jews and those Christians who are seeking to break down prejudice and to bring Jew and Christian together within a common recognition of the Golden Rule: that each should treat the other as he, in like instance, would wish to be treated by him. One of the greatest of English Jews, honored and respected by Jew and Christian alike for his learning, his philanthropy and his godly piety, says of this racial-political Zionism that it has broken his heart, and set the clock backward for his people a hundred years. The Christian lover of his country and his fellow-men may well express a similar feeling on his side."

_____

Issue of September 17, 1921

LIII.

How Jews Ruled and Ruined
Tammany Hall

W ITHIN the memory even of young men, Tammany Hall has been the synonym of all political trickery, in the vocabulary of popular criticism. Tammany Hall was held up as the worst example of boss rule and political corruption that it was possible to find in either of the parties. Its very name became a stigma.

But even the most unobservant newspaper reader must have observed the gradual facing out of Tammany Hall from public comment, the cessation of the hosts of good citizenship to do battle against the grim bossism that maintained its headquarters at the Wigwam.

Why this change? Is it due to the dying out of Tammany Hall as a political force? No, Tammany is still there, as any New York politician will tell you. Is it due, then, to a reform of that organization? No, the Tammany tiger has not changed its stripes. Then, perhaps, this change is due to public sentiment? Not at all. The explanation is to be found along other lines.

There was a time when fearless publications told the truth about Tammany, but *Harper's Weekly* and others which waged fierce war against the Tiger, have either gone out of existence or have fallen under control of the Jews. The silence which has shrouded certain matters must not be noted and set aside without reference to the changed control of the press. There was a time when public bodies like the Citizens' Union organized to oppose Tammany and to keep a volunteer vigil on

141

its activities; these groups have succumbed to Jewish contributions and officership and no longer stand guard.

The outcry against Tammany seemed to be hushed the moment that Tammany patronage fell into the hands of New York Jews, where it now reposes, the Kehillah being the real political center, and Tammany but a distributing station--a sort of organizational "Gentile front" for the more powerful Kehillah. A few Tammany leaders are permitted to strut out in front, but everyone knows that from the Wigwam chiefs the power has departed, it is now to be found in Jewish conferences. Murphy is still the titular head of Tammany, but like a Samson shorn, he is not feared and obeyed as of yore. In fact, the Judaization of Tammany Hall is now complete. Once in a while the Irish—always a match for the Jews—rear their heads and show battle, but for the most part Jewish money rules and the Tiger lies down.

Tammany Hall was one of the strongest political organizations ever seen in the United States, potent not only in municipal and state politics, but often exercising a decisive influence on national affairs. It was, without exaggeration, *powerful.*

If there is one quality that attracts Jews, it is power. Wherever the seat of power may be, thither they swarm obsequiously. As Tammany was power and the gate of power, it was natural that the Jews of the biggest Jewish city in the world should court it. Doubtless, they were also affected by the incongruity of the fact that in the biggest Jewish city, the most solid political power was non-Jewish. That was a condition which called for correction.

When the German Jewish banker, Schoenberg, came to this country under the name of August Belmont to represent the interests of the Rothschilds, his keen eye at once took in the situation and at once he began to court the favor of Tammany. He became a member and a supporter. It was good business for this Jewish banker, because the funds of the Rothschilds were heavily invested in New York tractions. The properties of city tractions were and to a great extent still are, as in all American cities, at the mercy of the local Tammany power, by whatever name it may be known. Belmont was insinuating himself under the wing of power to protect the investments for which he was responsible.

August Belmont eventually attained the coveted eminence of Grand Sachem of the Tammany Society. The Belmont family for a time represented the sole Jewish banking support of Tammany Hall, but that honor is now divided among many.

In Richard Croker's day, when corruption went hand in hand with power, and power apparently was none the weaker for it, we find that this notorious leader's intimate friend, business partner and political associate was a Jew—Andrew Freedman. Freedman and Croker lived together at the Democratic Club in Fifth Avenue, Tammany politicians even then having become rich enough to despise Fourteenth Avenue. Freedman held the purse strings of the organization, as head of the Committee on Finance, and he was Croker's representative and mouthpiece when the chief went into exile on an over-sea estate.

The most recent Jewish power in Tammany Hall, and one of the most liberal contributors to Tammany campaign funds, is the lawyer, Samuel Untermeyer, whose specialty of recent years seems to be to serve as the battering ram of the Jewish power against interests which it wants destroyed, and whose efforts are usually camouflaged under exaggerated journalistic advertisements as being wholly in the public interest. Mr. Untermeyer is not in particularly good humor with Tammany these days, because of the recent defeat of his son, Irving Untermeyer, for a judgeship. There was somewhere a slip. The Jews deserted the Wilson ship anyway, apparently seeing what was coming in the way of retribution for the colossal and amazing mismanagement of war business which was prin-

143

cipally in their hands; and in the ensuing mix-up, a scion of the house of Untermeyer tasted defeat.

Tammany numbers other Jews among its supporters. Nathan Straus, one of the owners of R. H. Macy & Company, has been for years an active member of the organization and one of the rulers of its inner councils.

A Jewish ghetto politician, Henry M. Goldfogle, has represented the Jewish interests in Congress for a number of years, and expected to continue, but he slipped in the election and has recently been "taken care of " by a city appointment.

There is also Judge Rasalsky who has been implicated in a number of interesting matters which illustrates the completeness of the Jewish network of control in New York City.

One might mention also M. L. Erlanger and Warley Platzek, justices of the supreme court of the state of New York, but if one began a list of the Jewish judiciary of that city, where would one end?

Another Tammanyite is Randolph Guggenheimer, founder of the corporation law firm of Guggenheimer, Untermeyer and Marshall—Untermeyer being the aforesaid grand inquisitor of Gentile activities generally and Marshall being head of the American Jewish Committee and the Kehillah.

It was doubtless necessary for a Jewry that contemplated control of the judiciary as well as special protection for certain powerful Jewish enterprises that are near enough the borderline of the law to merit question—it was necessary to obtain control of the supreme political engine through which favors were disbursed in local politics. And control of such organizations can always be had by money.

Not that the Jews threw themselves entirely into Tammany. The Jew's natural political home seems to be in the Republican party, for thither he returns after the venture elsewhere. But his predilection for the Republican party does not move the Jew to make the mistake of being exclusively the partisan of one group. It is better, as he knows, to control both groups.

As a matter of political fact, strong as is the Jewish element in Tammany, it is still stronger in the ranks of the Republican party, while New York Socialism is completely headed and manned by Jews. This renders it extremely easy for the Jews to swing support in whichever direction they choose, and for Kehillah to fulfill any threat it may make. It also insures that any Jewish candidate on any ticket will be elected. The fluke in the case of Young Untermeyer is perhaps not to be entirely explained politically: other causes were doubtless working in that matter.

It is a long time since Ferdinand Levy bore the distinction of being the first Jew in New York to hold a political job. He was only a coroner, and the man who appointed him was only a fire commissioner, but that fire commissioner was Richard Croker. And Levy was solidly backed by the Independent Order of B'nai B'rith, whose success in this matter laid the foundation for more ambitious demands later.

But at the beginning, the Kehillah Jews adopted the ancient policy, not of putting forward their own people, but non-Jews who could be useful to Judah. The difference between pro-Jewish politicians who are not themselves Jews, and politicians of the Jewish race, is that the former in office can sometimes go further than the Jew in office can, without detection. This has been true at least up to this time, but it will probably not be true very long, now that the people's eyes are being opened. The Jewish officeholder is only standing up for his race, but the "Gentile front" has betrayed the people for the pottage of Jewish favor.

Thus, in the early days of Tammany, indeed until comparatively recent years, we see the "Gentile front" in Tammany offices and basking in the glory of Tammany publicity, but in the background there is always his "Jewish control." This also is a formula for citizens who wish to know the meaning of things otherwise unexplainable—"look for the 'Jewish control.' "

To this end, therefore, the Jews have been strong in all parties, so that whichever way the election went, the Jews would win. In New York it is always the Jewish party that wins. The campaign is staged as an entertainment, a diversion for the people; they are permitted to think and act as if they were really making their own government, but it is always the Jews that win.

And if after having elected their man or a group, obedience is not rendered to the Jewish control, then you speedily hear of "scandals" and "investigations: and "impeachments," for the removal of the disobedient official. Usually a man with a "past" proves the most obedient instrument, but even a good man can often be tangled up in campaign practices that compromise him.

It has been commonly known that Jewish manipulation of campaign matters has been so skillfully handled, that no matter which candidate was elected, there was ready made a sufficient amount of evidence to discredit him in case his Jewish masters needed to discredit him. To arrange this is part of the thoroughness of Jewish control. And, of course, the American people have been sufficiently trained to roar against the public official immediately the first Jewish political hound emits its warning bay.

Amazing as is the technique of the Jewish political process, the readiness with which the American people can be counted on to do their part in 'forwarding the game is still more amazing.

What Mr. Hylan, the present mayor of New York has done to merit chastisement, is scarcely clear to a non-partisan investigator. But the fact that the Jews have set out to "get" him for something is evident on every side.

In the Untermeyer so-called "housing investigation," the people hauled up were non-Jews, and the result of the whole business has been a stronger Jewish hold than ever on the housing affairs of New York. Jews are exempt from such inquisitions. The choice prey are non-Jewish business houses whose secrets may be forced and whose good name may be stained under cover of a legal procedure. There is such a thing as blackmail so entirely respectable as to be unsuspected.

Governor Sulzer, of New York, was the choice of the Jews. They subscribed money for his campaign, forced it on him, and kept careful account of it. Finally, under pressure of a compelling sense of justice, Sulzer pardoned a non-Jewish valet of an important Jewish New York family, a young man whom a coterie of Jews very prominent in the political, financial and social worlds had contrived to "put away" for a period of 30 years. Sulzer had no option but to pardon young Brandt. But he paid the penalty. He was impeached. The Jews who supported him testified against him and their checks were used to assist his dismissal.

The story of young Brandt hangs heavily over the heads of some of the proudest Jewish names in New York.

Playing on both sides of the political fence, and always retaining a string on the men they elect to office, are two Jewish characteristics which should not fail to be reckoned with. THE DEARBORN INDEPENDENT, in its recent articles showing the hand of Paul Warburg in the Federal Reserve System, was able to prove by Mr. Warburg's own words that his firm, Kuhn, Loeb & Company, during the three-cornered fight between Roosevelt, Taft and Wilson, supported all three. The Jewish owners of R. H. Macy & Company, New York, illustrate the same principle; while Nathan Straus looked after affairs at Tammany Hall, his brother and partner, Isador Straus, was one of the most active opponents of Tammany. Were the interests of the two men therefore different? Not at all.

Take the firm of Guggenheimer, Untermeyer and Marshall. This is a notable firm for the part it plays in the people's business. Every community in America has been affected by Louis Marshall's decisions as head of the American Jewish Committee. Untermeyer is the arch-inquisitor for Jewry. Randolph Guggenheimer, the founder of the firm, achieved the foremost influence of any except the Chief in the old Wigwam, and was a power to be reckoned with in all matters. But Louis Marshall is a "staunch" Republican and a member of the Republican Club. Here again is the favorite method of including all parties under the capacious wing of the Jewish program.

Hence the popularity of "Fusion" in New York City elections. It has become the fad, but its most notable purpose is to insure the election of a Jew whatever his politics may be. In some Assembly Districts it is impossible to find anyone but a Jew to vote for. When Otto A. Rosalsky, a jurist who was implicated in the Brandt scandal, was re-elected Judge of General Sessions in 1920, he was the "Fusion" candidate on both the Democratic and Republican tickets. It was perhaps fortunate for his candidacy that he was. The point just now is that whenever a candidate may be vulnerable, it is very desirable to forestall a fight upon him by eliminating all opposition before the election. "Fusion" is another matter that should be carefully scrutinized in behalf of American rule of American cities.

By the way things are going in New York, these inter-party and "fusion" expedients may soon be unnecessary, because in any event it will be most difficult to avoid electing a Jew. Of the candidates of all parties for the offices of justice of the supreme court of New York, numbering 26, 14 were Jews. Of the Democratic presidential electors, 13 were Jews. Of the Republican presidential electors, 14 were Jews. Of the Socialist presidential electors, 22 were Jews.

The strength of Tammany had exactly the same source as the strength of the Kehillah, namely, in the foreign population; the difference being that the Kehillah had a more compact foreign mass to draw upon. But both the Jewish leaders and the Tammany leaders have always been alertly aware of the fact that their power depended upon an uninterrupted flow of immigration, to supply the losses sustained by the Americanization of the people. It is always the un-Americanized foreigner that makes the best material for the Kehillah's and Tammany's purposes. The Kehillah is based upon the principle of recognizing racial minorities, and Tammany has made a specialty of giving representation of racial minorities in its councils. This was a liberal policy, and was thoroughly American in its original intent (as Tammany was a thoroughly American assemblage at its inception) but it was soon seized upon by the Jews and used to their own ends, and to the eventual ruin of all except Jewish representation. Thus all through the history of immigration activity, Tammany has been on the side of the wide open gate without any restrictions. The lower the type of immigrant, the more easily amenable it is to the ward boss's orders.

Tammany of recent years has been the able seconder of the Kehillah in all efforts to frustrate control of immigration.

The third great influx of immigration into the United States occurred in 1884 and was really the cause of the beginning of the degeneration of Tammany Hall. The great wave was composed of Russian, Austrian and Hungarian Jews, whose arrival was followed by a memorable period of crime, the marks of which remain to this day. Indeed, the downfall of Richard Croker was a direct result.

At the time the police department and the police courts before which all criminal cases in the city were first brought, were in the hands of Tammany Hall. The result was a partnership between local government and crime which has not been duplicated outside of Semitic countries.

Immigrant Jews of the shadier type organized an association called The Max Hochstim Association, which was known during the Lexow Investigation as "The Essex Market Court Gang." One of its chief rulers was Martin Engel, Tammany leader of the Eighth Assembly District. The "king" of this Jewish district was a man named Solomon who had changed his name to the less revealing one of "Smith," and who became known as "Silver Dollar Smith" because of the fact that he ruled his little empire from the Silver Dollar Saloon, which gained its name from the silver dollars that

149

were cemented into the floor of his place of business. This saloon was just opposite the Essex Market Court, which was thronged daily by hordes of Yiddish criminals, the bondsmen, false witnesses and lawyers.

Let not the fastidious reader deem it unnecessary to linger longer round the old police court at Essex Market, for out therefrom came a word which has fixed itself in common English speech—the term "shyster," by which a certain type of lawyer is described. A Clinton street lawyer named Scheuster, whose practices were quite characteristic, made himself very obnoxious to Justice Osborne. "Whenever another Yiddish lawyer attempted a shady trick, the judge would openly denounce it as "Scheuster practice," and so it came that the first men in the profession to bear the name "shyster" were the Yiddish lawyers of Essex Market Court.

To make a nasty story brief, the Max Hochstim Association became the first organized White Slaver group in America, and the revelations made by the Lexow Committee are shuddering glimpses into that lowest form of depravity- a coolly conducted, commercialized, consolidated traffic on women. The traffic was made to yield dividends to politicians, to Tammany Jews in particular. The Ghetto became the Red Light District of New York. The first man to undertake the export trade in women with foreign countries, especially South America, was a man who later became a Tammany notable.

The surprising fact is that, although these matters are written in official documents, and although the same matters have been written into the record of every similar investigation which has been made, Jewish leaders persist in denying that the leaders in this particular form of depravity are Jews. When the United States Government made a nation-wide investigation, it found and recorded the same facts. The New York Kehillah came into existence as a defense organization at a time when the exposure of the

Jewish White Slave traffic threatened to overwhelm the New York ghetto.

The Max Hochstim Association was not the only organization of its kind. The other was the New York Independent Benevolent Association, which was organized in 1896 by a party of Jewish white slave dealers as they were returning from the funeral of Sam Engel, brother of Martin Engel, Tammany leader of the red light district.

The gangs that formed the backbone of Tammany power in the slum districts were made up of "cadets." Their principal field of operation was the cheap dance halls. Paul Kelly's gang originated in the halls about lower Broadway. Monk Eastman's gang grew strong in the Russian Jewish District below Delancy street. And Kid Twist's gang developed close to a dance hall for Galician Jews on the far East Side. All of these three were Jewish gang leaders. They were slavers as their forbears were in the days of Rome's decline; they were bootleggers before the days of prohibition; and they constituted a strong support of the international narcotic ring which to this day has defied the law by corrupting the officers of the law.

It was to associations like these that the lights of Tammany lent their names. Tim Sullivan was a vice president of the Max Hochstim Association. The name of the Honorable Henry M. Goldfogle also appeared on the picnic announcements.

The exposure which resulted when the white people of New York finally succeeded in getting the forces of the law to function impartially for a little while, caused many of the implicated Jews to change their names. These names are now representative of some of the best Jewish families, whose concealed bar sinister is the fact that the foundation of the family fortune was laid in the red light district. Society, sliced down to its seeds, is a queer growth.

It is due in justice to say that men like Tim Sullivan were not the originators of the Jewish abuses referred to, nor willing participants in the gains therefrom. Tammany would do favors for its friends, at the police court or elsewhere; Tammany had its occasional political upheavals; Tammany believed that they who profited by political spoils should divide with the Wigwam's treasury; but with such traffic as seduction and barter in women, Tammany had never been compromised until the Yiddish invasion of New York and the Judaization of the Wigwam. This much must be said for the Irish and American leaders.

The situation is the same in Boston. An Irish city, its chief political control is in the hands of Jews. The old-time Irish leaders are still permitted to be out in front, but the inner power has departed from them. One Boston ward, where once none but Irish lived, now contains only Jews, but the old-time Irish boss retains his seat. This is by favor of the Jews and nothing else.

The same state of facts accounts in large degree for the connection between a man like Tim Sullivan and the Jews. "Tim," as everyone knew him, was leader of a district inhabited by Irish and Germans. Then the Jews came in. And then began the Jews' practice of profiting by the people's dislike of them.

Foreign Jews well know that they are disliked. It is one of their assets which never fails to produce dividends. They choose the part of the city where they desire to live, and a few move in. Their immediate neighbors move out. More Jews move in—more of the others move out. The property nearest the Jews always goes down in value. People will sell at a loss rather than live engulfed in a ghetto.

It was so in Tim Sullivan's district. As the Jews swarmed in, the Irish and Germans fled north. Sullivan stood his ground. It was his old territory. He would not leave it, nor remove his family. He cultivated the new arrivals and made a partnership with the ex-kosher chicken butcher, Martin Engel.

The Jews lived under Sullivan's rule for a time, awaiting the moment when they should know what to do for themselves. The Yiddish flood increased until the district was crowded, and then the Jews demanded representation for themselves. With a premonition that a new force had arisen, Tim Sullivan played safe and helped the Jews to get recognition—Martin Engel was made leader of the old Eighth. But Sullivan had previously gone to Tammany—or to what remained of the old non-Jewish Tammany—and exacted an understanding that his rule should be left unchanged below Fourteenth street.

From that time forward, in spite of the understanding, Sullivan's power began to wane, principally because he continued to get in deeper and deeper with the Jews. He went into Jewish lines of business. He formed a theatrical partnership with George Kraus, among his enterprises being the Imperial Music Hall, the Dewey Theater, and the traveling Eagle Burlesque Company. Still the old district continued to become crowded and overcrowded and saturated with Yiddish newcomers, for whom neither the name Sullivan nor the traditions of the district had any meaning.

In his closing years, scarcely more than a hanger-on around the former scene of his power, Tim Sullivan bitterly lamented the ease with which he was led into associations that undermined his power.

Crocker was destroyed in public confidence by the terrific shock of the exposure attending the Jewish "cadet" activities. Sullivan, equally picturesque, was the slowly shoved-out victim of Jewish infiltration. There were other occurrences and other downfalls, all of which are a part of the real story of Tammany.

Issue of September 24, 1921

"I need hardly explain that I do not think Jews ought to insist overmuch on their rights or nationality in a negative sense. They ought to be as much Jews as they can, but ought to be as little as possible of what is merely anti-Christian. For the Jews to try to get a song out of the public schools because it praises Jesus is natural but perhaps hardly wise. I admit that question, however, is an extremely complex and baffling one. Again, the Jews have naturally taken a great interest in this war, but in the case also they ought to choose as far as possible the more tolerant view. Too much hostility to Russia was shown, it seems to me, when some of their spokesmen were fighting over the wording of the Immigration Act. They seemed to be fighting not for a real gain, but simply to rub their political power in America into the Russian mind."
—Norman Hapgood

LIV.

Jew Wires Direct Tammany's Gentile Puppets

T HE proposal that non-Jews emigrate from New York City, 500,000 in the first exodus, and 500,000 in the second, to hasten the event which is held to be certain of occurrence, namely, that New York shall become an all-Jewish city, may be a joke; but it is no joke that the Jews themselves discuss and have proposed that the City of New York be separated from the state of New York, and made both a state and city in itself. This would entail three governments—state, county and municipal—whose offices the Jews could parcel out as they pleased. Besides, it would rid them of Albany. It is a most amazing fact that the state capital, bad as it is, has always been able to defeat the New York Jew in his most ardently pursued quests, as notably, his insistent appeal to abrogate the Sunday law.

Of course, if the non-Jews emigrated from New York, the Jews would soon follow. They are not self-sufficient. If New York could be isolated, Jewish initiative would not suffice to provide enough potatoes for the inhabitants.

It is too trite to say that New York is already in the hands of the Jews. But it would be most startling to give a schedule illustrating how completely this is so. The New Yorker himself can scarcely comprehend the extent of his vassalage to the Jew. The average intelligent New Yorker does not know what the Kehillah is, nor yet how it works. Like the child born within sound of Niagara Falls, the New Yorker takes Jewish supremacy as a matter of course, as the way things should be, and as the way they probably are elsewhere. The New Yorker is thus like a native of the Balkans.

The Hylan administration, ostensibly non-Jewish, is really Jewish, as any New York administration must necessarily be, except there should arise a man whose ambition would be to prove that New York could be better governed if the Jews should be excluded from the government. Well-informed New Yorkers say that the power of Hylan is Hirschfield.

This is a rather peculiar situation to those who do not understand how the Jewish leaders work. Directly you say the Hylan administration is Jewish, it is objected: "But it is the arch-Jewish inquisitor, Untermeyer, who is trying to break down the Hylan administration!" Exactly. That is the game. It's inside and outside that does it. There is power gained in making them and there is power gained in breaking them, and often it is profitable to try both ways with the same man. That is the way Russia went: there were Jews plentifully sprinkled throughout the government of Russia (in spite of the "Persecution") and there were Jews outside. Between the two, they got Russia. It is the same in a Texas city today. Four non-Jewish candidates for postmaster were made the center of a political deadlock--up through the deadlock pops a Jew as a compromise candidate for all sections. A sufficient number of Jews were available in that city to keep all the non-Jewish candidates in a deadlock until their own man was trotted out. The "Gentile mind," of course, does not easily realize these turnings and twistings of group conspiracy. And that is why the Jews feel safe, as a rule; they rely on what they call "Gentile stupidity." The Gentile says, "incredible!" And the traditional Jewish game is incredible, until by mountainous proofs and centuries of illustration the actuality of it is forced home to the mind.

But to return to the New York City government: The police department has its Jewish streak in the higher offices—a Jewish police commissioner who has fortunately escaped thus far the full story of his career. The department of health, where it actually touches the people, is Jewish, although occasionally a distinguished non-Jewish name meets the eye in the roster of the higher officials. The public health is becoming more and more a Jewish monopoly in all our cities. The department of accounts, the board of child welfare, the board of inebriety, the municipal service commission, the board of taxes and assessments, are all under the leadership and domination of Jews.

The judiciary becomes increasingly Jewish, litigation is almost overwhelmingly Jewish, and the consequences to the reputation of the courts for justice and the profession of the law are well understood. Real estate exploitation and speculation is strictly Jewish, the profiteers treating even their own co-nationalists with the utmost cruelty.

In short, New York's most influential press (within New York) is the Yiddish press; New York's real government is the Yiddish Kehillah; New York's real administration of the law is the Yiddish administration; New York's real politics is Jewish. A little more, and New York's official language would be the Yiddish dialect.

In all this Tammany Hall is little more than a na...e; it is one of the rallying centers which the Jews have left the non-Jew who still interests himself in New York politics. There must be rallying places for the non-Jews, and one or two do not hurt. The Jew has the double advantage in such a matter, for while he claims equality with all, he denies equality with any. That is, any Jew proclaims his right to join any fraternity, or any club, or any society, or any party whose members are chiefly non-Jewish, but where is the Jewish fraternity, or club, or society that admits non-Jewish members? The newspapers carried the report, after a certain occurrence, that hundreds of Jews had offered to join the Knights of Columbus! It was very typical of Jewish character. But let any non-Jew attempt to join the B'nai B'rith or the Hebrew Young Men's Association, or the Menorah Society, or any of the others: he will see how far the principle of equality operates. "We want to be part of yours, but we want our own for ourselves," is the Jewish attitude.

So, politically, the New York Jew has the advantage. He belongs, together with the non-Jew, to organizations like Tammany or the Republican Club—but the non-Jew cannot with him belong to the Kehillah.

It is all so very familiar: the Jew insists on double everywhere. In the Balkans he insists on double citizenship. He insists on a double protection. He insists on a double standard of education. He insists on all his own religious rights as strenuously as he insists that all Christian majority rights shall be stamped out in this country. He insists that he shall have his Sabbath and that you shall not have yours. He wants his own social rights and yours too—but he wants you to have only your own and not his with it. It casts serious doubts on Jewish intelligence that this course should be so seriously pursued, as if on the one hand the humor of the "nerve," and on the other hand the disgusting impudence of it, had never appeared to his consciousness.

In New York, therefore, the Jew politically belongs twice, while all non-Jews belong but once, and it can easily be perceived that this is an advantage.

In the previous article it was rehearsed how Tammany besmirched its name by association with Jews who used the organization as a protection for their traffic in vice. This was in 1894. The revelations were so terrible that in any other community they would have led to a complete abolition of any possible chance of recovery, but as it was never made plain to the people that the traffic in vice was not a sudden appearance of rottenness among Americans, but was the normal activity of an alien racial strain, the moral power of exposure was dissipated. The people were left staggered by what they were allowed to believe about the origin of the horror. People said it was Tammany because the press said it was Tammany, and yet people could not understand how it could be Tammany, and so in the midst of hesitancy the fire of reform burned out. It was exactly like these days when we are told that "American business men" abroad are doing terrible things; yet even while the press declares them to be "American" we cannot understand how Americans could do such things—and we never get the key to the matter, nor see the solution, until we stumble on to the fact that these so-called "Americans" are not Americans at all, but alien Jews. Over in Canada the name "American" is becoming a stigma because it is borne by men who are not Americans. What Canadians point out in the United States as definitely "American" is mostly Jewish, but how are the Canadians to know? The national name suffers. The whole course of evil is camouflaged and a nation pays the price of a racial group's misdeeds. There should be some method of protecting this forging of national names.

Thus Tammany became a synonym for what was not characteristically Tammany at all, but what was characteristically Jewish.

The exposure of 1894 disclosed that vice was really a thing of cold blood. Evil that springs from passion and impulse really amounts to far less than is commonly supposed. It is when passion is deliberately cultivated and impulse stimulated, that the great bulk of the world's social evil occurs. And this stimulation is undertaken in cold blood by those who make profit out of providing the means of gratification —like the old-fashioned bar keepers who served very salty free lunches to stimulate the sale of beer.

This kind of vice is not a thing to be shamed by exposure as can be done with involuntary vice, as it might be called. This cold-blooded merchandising of human weakness was merely a matter of profits, and if business had been interfered with by a Lexow Committee it was rather unfortunate, but good business required that operations be resumed at the earliest possible moment. And so, though the investigations of 1894 were successful and the exposure duly made, it was not to be expected that mere oratory and printers ink would suffice to keep the serpent down.

It was only seven years before scandal flamed again throughout the length and breadth of New York, and strangely enough—strange enough in all conscience for "Gentile fronts" of this day and generation to heed!—it was found again that the traffic in evil and its ramifications all over the land, and even to foreign countries, was in the hands of Jews. There was no doubt about it. There was even no accident about it. The fact was as continuous as it was colossal.

William Travers Jerome, then Justice of the Court of Special Sessions, made in 1901 a ringing indictment of conditions in the city and used the full power of his court to punish wrongdoers; he even went so far as to specify individuals and political connections—but he did not mention the keyword of it all, which was "Jew." It was doubtless wise for him that he did not, else he could not have enjoyed the subsequent political career which came to him.

Tammany was defeated in the election of 1901. The defeat was due to the same cause—the stigma of Jew-controlled vice traffic under political protection.

It was at this time that Richard Croker "abdicated." He was a rich man. He sailed for Ireland, where he became a country squire on his Wantage estate.

Public curiosity was fed the statement that Croker had selected Lewis Nixon to be his successor, but this turn in Tammany's career is too important to be thus misstated. The truth is that *when Croker left he surrendered Tammany to the Jews.*

Croker could confirm this if he would talk, if he should be permitted to talk. It is, however, not well to have garrulous old men spilling the secrets of other days. Croker in his age took a bride who is said to be of "Indian descent," and he has not been much in touch with his family nor the public since.

Lewis Nixon was the convenient and perhaps unconscious "Gentile front." The real ruler of Tammany in Croker's stead was Andrew Freedman, mentioned in the former article as Croker's friend and house mate.

(Judging from the habit of individual Jews to room with baseball players before the baseball scandal, and the result of another Jew's living with Croker, it might be just as well to keep an eye on those other men who are in positions to do favors or influence legislation, whose close cronies happen to be Jews. Some of these friendships may indeed be perfectly conceived; but there are numerous instances where the plans of the "Jewish friend" are very completely matured through the agency of the "Gentile chum.")

So, upon the departure of Croker from these shores, we find Tammany under the dictatorship of a Jew who was Croker's chief influence, if not his absolute master.

But by the time this occurred, it was useless for Tammany to rebel. Tammany men who had noticed the infiltration of Jews and were alarmed by it had consoled themselves with the thought that, at least, the higher offices were immune from Jewish occupation. This consolation served only to permit the filling of the lower offices by Jews, with less protest from the membership. By the time the Jews were ready to permit Croker to "abdicate," they had permeated every part of the Wigwam and the assumption of supreme control was thus made a simple matter. Croker stepped aside; instantly into his place stepped the Jew, Freedman, operating through Nixon.

It was too late for Tammany to remonstrate. Tammany could not protest against the Wigwam *becoming* Jewish, because the Wigwam already *was* Jewish. To remonstrate then was to ruin Tammany. Becoming reconciled to what seemed to be inevitable, Tammany leaders saw that their only hope of survival came through preserving Jewish support.

Presently even Nixon was relegated to the background and Freedman issued his orders directly. The Jews, however, with great astuteness continued to make much of Nixon, because he was the last thin veil which concealed the change which had come over Tammany, and he was valuable to that extent. He was, unwillingly, perhaps, their puppet, but even puppets must be accorded their proper dignity. Nixon was tendered a great reception in 1902, but the influential men on the reception committee were mostly Jews: Andrew Freedman was chairman; then followed the names of Oliver H. P. Belmont, Max F. Ihmson, Samuel Untermeyer, Nathan Straus, Randolph Guggenheimer, Henry M. Goldfogle, Herman Joseph, and others.

On the executive committee of Tammany Hall at this time were Randolph Guggenheimer, Isaac Fromme, Nathan Straus, Henry M. Goldfogle, O. H. P. Belmont, and other Jews.

On the committee on law were Samuel Untermeyer, M. Warlet Platzek, Abraham Levy, Henry W. Unger, Morris Cukor and Fred B. House.

Andrew Freedman had complete control of the committee on finance that was nominally headed by Lewis Nixon.

Randolph Guggenheimer was president of the municipal council.

Ferdinand Levy was on the committee on resolutions and correspondence.

Jews had so spread themselves as to constitute a controlling group in all the assembly districts that were under tribute to Tammany. In the "Fighting Eighth" district, Martin Engel was leader. His chief aid was "Manny" Eichner, chairman of the Isidor Cohn Association and of the Young Men's Democratic Association. His other assistants, Max J. Porges, Max Levein, and Moe Levy were floor managers of the dances and balls of the Florence Sullivan Association.

In the Tenth district, Simon Steingutt, "Mayor of Second Avenue," was one of the hardest workers in Tammany affairs.

Edward Mandell was the active Jewish Tammany man in the Twelfth district.

In the Eighteenth district, Maurice Blumenthal was one of the principal workers. He devoted his career chiefly to the training of Jewish speakers for the Wigwam.

The Eighteenth district was known as "the Gashouse district," notorious for the Gashouse scandals over padded pay rolls, and here Charley Murphy ruled, his aides being Julius Simon, Edward E. Slumasky, Joseph Schlesinger, Leopold Worms, Hugo Siegel, Alfred B. Marx, Nathan Fernbacher, and other Jews.

And so on through the list. Among the Sachems of the Tammany Society there were to be found the wealthier and more socially exalted Jews.

However, the Jews made their cyclically recurring mistakes: they carried things with too high a hand, and rebellion broke out. It is this Jewish tendency to boast and overdo that has always given the game away. Superficial observers and writers like John Spargo and Norman Hapgood have observed the recurrent periods of protest against Jewish presumption and bumptiousness and have explained them as being recurrent spasms of a vile poison which is supposed to reside in the blood of the Gentiles—the vile poison of anti-Semitism. That, of course, is the conventional Jewish propagandist explanation, and Spargo and Hapgood are merely retailing it. They say it always breaks out after wars. Why after wars? Because in wars the world sees more clearly than at other times the real purpose and personality of the Jew. Thus, it is not anti-Semitism that breaks out—it is Semitism, gross and exaggerated Semitism; and the serum that forms in the social body to encist and control the germ of Semitism, comes in the form of public exposure and protest. That serum is working now—the serum of publicity, and the Jewish program cannot endure it. Study the history of all things whatsoever into which Jews inject themselves, from summer resorts to empires, and you see the same cycle appearing.

Thus it happened in Tammany Hall—"Too much Jew" engendered revolt. Lewis Nixon became aware of his position. As a gentleman of standing and responsibility he could not continue in a position whose falsity had become clear to him. When he accepted the leadership of Tammany Hall, it was not with a purpose to continue the old order. His understanding was that he was to be left free to restore Tammany to the plane of its former serious purpose and respectable character. He discovered that he was being used as the "respectable Gentile front" behind whose name the Jews expected to carry on the old game. Therefore, in May 1902, three months after the great reception above mentioned, Nixon resigned as leader of Tammany Hall. Doubtless the reception that was tendered him was for the purpose of inducing him to love the exaltation of his position so much that he would sacrifice its moral obligations.

Nixon accompanied his resignation with a speech in which he protested that ever since he had accepted the leadership of Tammany he had been hampered in his every action by a group headed by Andrew Freedman; they dictated the names that were to be placed on the list of Sachems: "When I rebelled, I found that at every turn I would be opposed by this coterie of interferers; I found that all my important acts had to be viséed before they could become effective." He said he could no longer retain his position and his self-respect; he had to give up one or the other.

With this Mr. Nixon vanished from the scene of Tammany politics.

The resignation of Mr. Nixon had a bad effect on the reputation of Tammany with the public. The plan had been to allow him to serve a long as ordinarily and then replace him with a Jew by means of the usual process of selection. But the resignation and the explanation that accompanied it, showing as it did the Jewish influence in Tammany, made it seem inadvisable to follow with a Jewish leader. So the district leaders were obliged to find another "Gentile front," only this time one who would prove sufficiently docile. There was enough rankling disfavor against the Jews in the old organization to warrant this observance of appearances, at least.

The dictatorship of Freedman was seen to be a failure, much as the dictatorship of Trotzky is seen to be a failure. A rearrangement of committees automatically eliminated him from control, at the same time the name of Croker was dropped. A triumvirate of leaders was chosen, of whom Charles F. Murphy became and remains the chief. "Boss Murphy" he is called. Mr. Murphy has been an ideal "front," not attempting to do anything, not attempting to interfere with the Jews doing anything, keeping wisely silent and thereby gaining a reputation for silent wisdom. Mr. Murphy is a millionaire. Those who do the higher Jewish leaders' bidding get their reward that way; there is no other reward they can hope for; certainly they never have the reward of public confidence and the people's gratitude.

That is the status of Tammany Hall at the present time. A few of the Old Guard are left at their posts, but they are officers in name only. Tammany is no longer denounced by the public press, but the Jewish leaders of Tammany live daily to a chorus of praise in the Jewish-controlled newspapers of New York. Samuel Untermeyer, for example, receives more publicity in New York than does the President of the United States, but it is not discriminating publicity; it does not penetrate to the inner purposes and consequences of his actions.

Those who were the lesser Jewish lieutenants of Tammany a few years ago have now arrived at posts of influence and affluence. Morris Cukor was made president of the municipal service commission, to be succeeded by former State Senator Abraham Kaplan. Fred B. House rose to be a city magistrate. The city marshals are mostly Jewish. Jews predominate in the College of the City of New York. Jews control the municipal courts, the city magistrates' courts, the city court, the New York state supreme court. They rule in the departments enumerated in the fore part of this article. The New York judiciary has a distinctly Semitic complexion.

The leadership of the Tammany-controlled districts tells the same story. In the second, the leader is M. S. Levine; in the Sixth, David Lazarus; in the Eighth, S. Goldenkranz, F. Bauman and S. Salinger; in the Ninth, Mrs. P. Lau, in the Seventeenth, Nathan Burkan—and so on.

The Jewish conquest of Tammany, however, is only one phase of the conquest of New York. The Jewish objective is more than political. Merely to strive that the lucrative and powerful officers of the city shall fall to their people, is not the end in view. New York has been turned into the Red Center of America. There most of the alien treason carried on against the government of the United States has its source. The United States Government has been compelled at times to regard New York as almost alien soil, but even that watchfulness on the part of the national government is relaxed as Jewish influence becomes more potent at Washington. Tammany is a convenient cover for ostensible political activity as the Kehillah is for the more radical racial and anti-American racial activity. The United States Government could not do better than to investigate—through a committee of invulnerable Americans— the Jewish activities of that center. And that there is much to investigate is indicated by the rush of Jews to Washington when it was recently proposed in the United States that such a thing be done.

Issue of October 1, 1921

LV.

B'nai B'rith Leader Discusses the Jews

T O THE pro-Jewish spokesmen who have filled the air with cries of "lies" and "slander," to those self-appointed guardians of "American ideals" who rule out with rare finality all those who would dare suggest that possibly there is a hidden side of the Jewish Question, it must come as something of a jolt to be reminded that in this series there is scarcely a line that is without high Jewish authority.

The Protocols themselves are written for centuries in Jewish authoritative teachings and records. All the plans that have been described from time to time in these articles are written in the fundamental laws of the Jews. And all that the ancients have taught the modern Jews have reaffirmed.

The writer of these articles has had to take constant counsel of prudence in his selection of material, for the Jews have always counted confidently on the fact that if the whole truth were told in one comprehensive utterance, no one would believe it. Thus, bigots and minds bursting with the discoveries they have made, have never been feared by the Jews. They counted on the incapacity of the non-Jews to believe or receive certain knowledge. They know that facts are not accepted on proof, but only on understanding. Non-Jews cannot understand why human beings should lend themselves to certain courses. They are, however, beginning to understand, and the proof is therefore becoming more significant.

There are yet more important revelations to be made, always following closely the best Jewish sources, and when

167

these revelations are made, it will be impossible for the
Jewish leaders to keep silent or to deny. The time is coming
for American Jewry to slough off the leadership which has led
it and left it in the bog. Leadership knows that. Indeed, it is
amazing to discover the number of indications that the
attempts made to suppress THE DEARBORN INDEPENDENT have
been made principally *to prevent the Jews reading it.* The
leaders do not care how many non-Jews read these articles;
but they do not desire their own people to read them. The
Jewish leaders do not desire their people's eyes to be opened.

Why? Because, just now, only Jews can truly know
whether the statements made in these articles are true or
not. Non-Jews may know here and there, as their observations may confirm the printed statements. But informed
Jews really *know.* And large numbers of the masses of the
Jews really know. When they see the truth in all its
relationships in these articles, the hitherto "led" Jew may not
be so tractable. Hence the effort to keep the non-Jewish point
of view away from him.

In support of the statements that these articles have been
based on Jewish authority, we quote today a series of
declarations by one of the most able of the presidents of the
B'nai B'rith, Leo N. Levi. Mr. Levi was American-born and
died in 1904. He was a lawyer of distinction and attained the
presidency of the international Jewish order, B'nai B'rith, in
1900. He took part in the international politics of his people
and is credited with collaborating with Secretary of State
John Hay on several important matters. The utterances here
quoted were for the most made while he was president of
B'nai B'rith, but all of them were published under B'nai B'rith
auspices. There is no question therefore of their Jewishness.

Non-Jewish defenders of the Jewish program have
pretended to much indignation because of references that
have been made to the Oriental character of certain Jewish
manifestations. The references in these articles have been

two in number, once regarding Oriental sensuality as it has been introduced to the American stage by Jewish theatrical panderers, and again in quoting Disraeli, the Jew who became premier of Britain, to the effect that the Jews—his people—were "Mosaic Arabs."

But it never seemed to have occurred to Leo N. Levi to deny the Oriental character of his race. Instead, he asserted it. On page 104 of the B'nai B'rith memorial, he excuses certain social crudities of the Jew on the ground "that hailing originally from the Orient and having been compelled for twenty centuries to live in a society of his own, he has preserved in his tastes much that is characteristically Oriental." Again on page 116, he excused the multiplicity of religious rites as being due to the fact that the Jew "drew upon his Oriental imagination for a symbolism that appealed to his ideal emotions." On page 312, he speaks of the Jews' "Oriental devotion to their parents." This easy recognition of the fact is commended to those bootlicking editors who, out of the vastness of their ignorance of the Jewish Question, have seen in the reference to Orientalism an "insult" to the Jews and an unfailing indication of anti-Semitism.

The Jewish Question! Ah, that is another point which pro-Jewish spokesmen hasten to deny, but they will be somewhat disturbed by the candor with which true Jewish spokesmen admit the Question.

In a strong passage on page 101, Mr. Levi says:

"If I have dwelt so long upon this subject, it is because I recognize that if the Jew has been denied so much that is rightfully his, he often claims more than is his due. One of these claims, most persistently urged, is that there is no Jewish Question; that a Jew is a citizen like any other citizen and that as long as he abides by the law and does not subject himself to criminal prosecution or civil action, his doings are beyond legitimate inquiry by the public at large.

"This contention on his part would certainly be well based if he claimed nothing further than the right to live in peace, but when he demands social recognition the whole range of his conduct is a legitimate subject of inquiry against which no technical demurrers can be interposed . . . . nor must the Jew be over-sensitive about the inquiry.

"The inconsistencies and the unwisdom exhibited in the consideration of the Jewish Question are not to be found altogether on the side of those who are hostile to the Jews."

"Since then the refugees from Russia, Galicia and Rumania have raised the Jewish Question to commanding importance. Since then it has dawned on the world that *we are witnessing another exodus which promises soon to change the habitat of the Jews to the Western Hemisphere.*" (Page 59)

"The Jewish Question cannot be solved by tolerance. There are thousands of well-meaning people who take to themselves great credit for exhibiting a spirit of tolerance toward the Jews." (Page 98)

Mr. Levi also lays down rules for "the study of the Jewish Question," and he says that if they were followed the result "would be startling at once to the Jews and the general public." (Page 93) How far present Jewish leadership has departed from that frank and broad view taken by Mr. Levi, is everywhere evident.

Not that Mr. Levi was a critic of his people, but he was a lawyer who was accustomed to weighing facts, and he saw facts that weighed against his people. But he was pro-Jewish even in his most severe observations. He could make an attack on the rabbis, taunting them with the saying that "many of you are 'rabbis for revenue only,' " but he could also insist on Jewish solidarity and exclusiveness.

In this connection it may be interesting to see how strongly Mr. Levi supports the contention of Jewish leaders (as outlined in THE DEARBORN INDEPENDENT of October 9 and 16, 1920) that the Jews are a *race* and not merely a *religion,* a nation and not merely a church, and that the term "Jew" is biological rather than theological. This is specially commended to the attention of those dim-minded shouters of "religious prejudice," who come into action whenever the Jewish Question is mentioned. (Of "religious prejudice" there are may examples to give in future articles.)

"Certain it is that thus far the race and the religion have been so fused, as it were, that none can say just where the one begins and the other leaves off." (Page 116)

Attacking the contention of the "liberals" or "reformed Jews" to the effect that "Jew" is the name of a member of religious denomination, and not of a member of a certain race, Mr. Levi says:

"Nothing to my mind is more pregnant with error than this postulate of unreason. (Page 185) It is not true that the Jews are only Jews because of their religion." (Page 189)

"The Jews are not simply an indiscriminate lot of people who hold to a common belief." (Page 190)

"A native Eskimo, an American Indian might conscientiously adopt every tenet of the Jewish church, might practice every form and ceremony imposed by the Jewish laws and the Jewish ritual, and as far as the religion is concerned, be a Jew, but yet, no one who will reflect for a moment would class them with the Jews as a people. If the truth were known, a very large percentage of so-called Christians would be found to be believers in the essentials of the Jewish religion, and yet, they are not Jews.

"It requires not only that men should believe in Judaism, but that they should be the descendants in a direct line of that people who enjoyed a temporal government and who owned a country up to the time of the destruction of the second commonwealth.

That great event took away from the Jews their country and their temporal government; it scattered them over the face of the earth, *but it did not destroy the national and race idea* which was a part of their nature and of their religion."

"Who shall say, then, that the Jews are no longer a race? . . . . Blood is the basis and sub-stratum of the race idea, and no people on the face of the globe can lay claim with so much right to purity of blood, and unity of blood, as the Jews."

"If I have reasoned to any purpose, the inquiry of rights in the premises is not to be limited to Jews as exponents of a particular creed, but *to the Jews as a race.*" (Pages 190-191)

"The religion alone does not constitute the people. As I have already maintained, a believer in the Jewish faith does not by reason of that fact become a Jew. On the other hand, however, *a Jew by birth remains a Jew, even though he abjures his religion.*"(Page 200)

This is the view of such men as Justice Brandeis, the Jew who sits on the Supreme Court of the United States. Justice Brandeis says, "Let us all recognize that we Jews are a distinct nationality *of which every Jew, whatever his country, his station, his shade of belief, is necessarily a member.*"

Believing all this, Mr. Levi subscribes to the Jewish law and practice of exclusiveness.

Describing the state of the Jews, Mr. Levi says (page 92): "The Jews have not materially increased or diminished in numbers for 2,000 years. They have made no proselytes to their religion . . . . They have imbibed the arts, the literature and the civilization of successive generations, but have abstained very generally from intermixture of blood . . . . They have infused their blood into that of other peoples but have taken little of other peoples into their own."

As to intermarriage between the Jew and non-Jew, Mr. Levi calls it miscegenation. "In remote countries, sparsely populated, the choice may lie between such marriages and a worse relation." Those are his words on page 249. He does not advise the worse relation, but he has said quite enough to indicate the Jewish view of the case. He continues:

"It seems clear to me that Jews should avoid marriages with Gentiles and Gentiles with Jews, *upon the same principle that we avoid marrying the insane, the consumptive, the scrofulitic or the Negro."* (Page 249)

This exclusiveness goes down through all human relations. The Jew has one counsel for non-Jews and another for himself in these matters. Of the non-Jew he demands as a right what he looks down upon as shady privilege. He uses the Ghetto as a club with which to bludgeon the non-Jew for his "bigotry," when as a fact he chooses the Ghetto for well-defined reasons. He condemns the non-Jew for the exclusion of the Jew from certain sections of society, when as a Jew his whole care is to keep himself unspotted from that very society to which he seeks entrance. The Jew insists on breaking down non-Jewish exclusiveness while keeping his own. The non-Jewish world is to be public and common, the Jewish world is to be kept sacrosanct. Read the teachings of this enlightened leader of Jewry as published by the B'nai B'rith.

He favors the public school for non-Jewish children, not for Jewish children; they are to be kept separate; they are the choice stock of the earth:

"Because the government tenders free education, it does not follow that it must be accepted; if education be made compulsory, it does not follow that government schools must be attended . . . . As a citizen I favor free schools, because the education they afford, imperfect as it is, is better than none, and society is benefited thereby; but as an individual I prefer to pay to support free schools and send my children to more select places." (Page 253) He speaks of the fact that "all classes of children frequent the public schools" as an argument against Jewish children going there.

"In my judgment, Jewish children should be educated in Jewish schools." (page 254) "Not only is it a positive and direct advantage to educate our children as Jews, but it is absolutely necessary to our preservation. Experience has shown that our young people will be weaned from our people

if allowed indiscriminately to associate with the Gentiles."
(Page 255)

Discussing the possibility of Jews losing their crudeness,
Mr. Levi asks, "How shall we best accomplish that end?"
Then he quotes the frequent answer: "Since the exemplars of
gentility most abound among the Gentiles, we should
associate with them as much as possible, in order to wear our
own rudeness away." He meets the suggestion this way:

"If gentlemen were willing to meet all Jews on a parity
because they are Jews, we should doubtless derive much
benefit from such association. But, while it is true that no
gentleman refuses association with another because that
other is a Jew, he will not, as a rule, associate with a Jew
unless he be a gentleman. As we are far from being all
gentlemen, we cannot reasonably expect to be admitted as a
class into good society. So, better keep by ourselves,"
concludes Mr. Levi. (Page 260)

That is, Mr. Levi admits the willingness of society to meet
Jews on equal terms, as with all others, but not on unequal
terms. And this being so, Mr. Levi holds they had better meet
as little as possible, they had better keep apart; in the
formative years, certainly, Jewish young people should be
kept rigidly apart from non-Jews. The exclusiveness of which
the Jews complain is their own. The Ghetto is not a corner
into which the non-Jews have herded the Semites; the Ghetto
is a spot carved out of the community and consecrated to the
Chosen People and is therefore the best section of the city in
Jewish eyes, the rest being "the Christian quarter," the area
of the heathen. Mr. Levi himself admits on page 220 that
there is no prejudice against the Jew in this country.

Certain wild-eyed objectors to the series of studies on the
Jewish Question have made the assertion that THE DEARBORN
INDEPENDENT has declared cowardice to be a Jewish trait.
That the statement is false as regards this paper does not
change the fact that the subject has been generally discussed
in and out of army circles. If it ever becomes necessary to

discuss it in these studies, the facts will be set forth as far as they are obtainable. But the point just now is that Mr. Levi has had somewhat to say which may repay reading:

"Physical courage has always been an incident, not an element, of Jewish character. It has no independent existence in their make-up, and always depended on something else. With some exceptions this may be said of all Oriental people. The sense and fear of danger is highly developed in them, and there is no cultivation of that indifference to it which has distinguished the great nations of Western Europe." (Page 205)

Were a non-Jew to call attention to this difference between the Jews and others, he would be met with the cry of "anti-Semitism" and he would be twitted with the fact that all his relatives may not have served in the war. Loudest to twit him would be those who served in what our soldiers called "the Jewish infantry," the quartermaster's corps in the late National Army.

It is to this aversion to danger, however, that Mr. Levi attributes the Jews' greatness among the nations. Other nations can fight, the Jews can *endure*, and that, he says, is greater. Note his words (the italics are his own):

"Other nations may boast conquests and triumphs born of aggression, but though the fruits of victory have been manifold, they have not been enduring; *and it may be truly said that the nation whose greatness grows out of valor* passes through the stages of discord and degeneracy to decay . . . . In the virtue of endurance I believe the Jews have a safeguard against the decay that has marked the history of all other peoples."

It appears, therefore, that the draft-dodger, if he can *endure* long enough, may yet come to own the country.

Jewish leaders have lately tried to minimize as "wild words" the disclosures made by Disraeli with reference to the Jews' participation in European revolutions. What Disraeli

said can be found in his "Coningsby," or in the quotations
made there from in THE DEARBORN INDEPENDENT of December
18, 1920. With reference to the German Revolution of 1848,
Disraeli wrote—before it had taken place:

"You never observe a great intellectual movement
in Europe in which the Jews do not greatly participate
. . . That mysterious Russian Diplomacy which so
alarms Western Europe is organized and principally
carried on by Jews. That mighty revolution which is at
this moment preparing in Germany, and which will
be, in fact, a second and greater Reformation, and of
which so little is yet known in England, is entirely
developing under the auspices of Jews."

It is interesting, therefore, to hear Mr. Levi confirming
from the American side those significant statements made by
Disraeli.

"The revolution of 1848 in Germany, however, influenced
a great many highly educated Jews to come to America."
(Page 181) "It is unnecessary to review the events of 1848;
suffice it to say, that not a few among the revolutionists were
Jews, and that a considerable number of those who were
proscribed by the government at home, fled to the United
States for safety." (Page 182) These German Jews are now
the arch-financiers of the United States. They found here
complete liberty of their powers. They still maintain their
connections with Frankfort-on-the-Main, the world capital of
International financial Jewry.

With these quotations from the speeches and writings of
Leo N. Levi, a famous president of the B'nai B'rith, it would
seem to be a fair question as to the reason for the denial and
denunciation which have followed the making of these
statements in the course of this series of studies. Leo N. Levi
studied the Jewish Question because he knew a Jewish
Question to exist. He knew that the Jewish Question was not
a non-Jewish creation but appeared wherever Jews began to
appear in numbers. They brought it with them. He knew the

justice of many of the charges laid against the Jews. He knew the impossibility of disproving them, the futility of shrieking "anti-Semitism" at them. He knew, moreover, that for the Jews to solve the Jewish Question by departing from the peculiar racial traditions of superiority, would be to cease to be Jews. Therefore, he threw his whole influence on the side of the Jews remaining separate, maintaining their traditions of The Chosen Race, looking upon themselves as the coming rulers of the Nations, and there he left the Question just about where he found it.

But in the course of his studies he gave other investigators the benefit of his frank statements. He did not put lies into the mouths of his people. He was not endeavoring to maintain himself in positions by prejudiced racial appeals. He looked certain facts in the face, made' his report, and chose his side. Several times in the course of his argument, his very logic led him up to the point where, logically, he would have to cast aside his Jewish idea of separateness. But with great calmness he discarded the logic and clung to the Jewish tradition. For example:

"The better to facilitate such happiness in every country and in every age, various kinds of organizations have existed as they exist today. The Jews have theirs.

"For many reasons they are exclusive. In theory they should not be so. In our social organizations we should, in deference to the argument which I have already named, admit any congenial and worthy Gentile who honor us with his application. But what may be theoretically correct may be found practically wrong. It certainly is a wrong to exclude a worthy person because he does not happen to be a Jew; but on the other hand, where are you to draw the line?"

This is frankness to a fault. Of course, it is wrong, but the right is impractical! Logic goes by the boards in the face of something stronger. Mr. Levi is not to be blamed for having gone to his tribe. Every man's place is with his tribe. The criticism belongs to the lick-spittle Gentile fronts who have no tribe and become hangers-on around the outskirts of Judah, racial mongrels who would be better off if they had one-thousandth of the racial sense which the Jew possesses.

This brief survey of the philosophy which Mr. Levi both lived and taught, and which is shared by the leaders of American Jewry, is in strict agreement with Jewish principles all down the centuries. In his published addresses Mr. Levi does not touch upon all the implications of the separateness which he enjoins upon his nation. Why do they keep by themselves? What is it that keeps them distinct? Is it their religion? Very well; let us regard them as a sect of religious recluses and wish them well in their endeavors to keep themselves unspotted of the world. Is it their race? So their leaders teach. Race and nationality are strictly claimed. If this is so, there must be a political outlook. What is it? Palestine? Not that any one can notice. A great deal may be read about it in the newspapers, the newspapers in turn being supplied through the Associated Press with the Jewish Telegraph Agency's propaganda dispatches; but no one in Palestine notices the Land becoming more Jewish. Jewry's political outlook is world rule in the material sense. Jewry is an international nation. It is this, and nothing else, which gives significance to its financial, educational, propagandist, revolutionary and immigration programs.

Issue of May 14, 1921.

LVI

Dr. Levy, a Jew, Admits His People's Error

A JEW of standing, Dr. Oscar Levy, well known in English literary circles and a lover of his people, has had the honesty and the wisdom to meet the Jewish Question with truth and candor. His remarks are printed in this article as an example of the methods by which Jewry can be saved in the estimation of Twentieth Century Civilization.

The circumstances were these: George Pitt-Rivers, of Worcester College, Oxford, wrote a most illuminating brochure entitled, "The World Significance of the Russian Revolution," which is published and sold for two shillings by Basil Blackwell, Oxford. The book is the result of unpɪ ᵔudiced observation and study and agrees with the statements made in THE DEARBORN INDEPENDENT about the personnel of Bolshivism. The manuscript was sent to Dr. Oscar Levy, as a representative Jew, and Dr. Levy's letter was subsequently published as a preface to the book.

That the reader may understand the tenor of Mr. Pitt-Rivers's book, section XVI, pp 39-41, is herewith given in full, and is followed by Dr. Levy's comments. The italics throughout are intended to remind the reader of remarks on similar lines made in this series:

It is not unnaturally claimed by Western Jews that Russian Jewry, as a whole, is most bitterly opposed to Bolshevism. Now although there is a great measure of truth in this claim, since the prominent Bolsheviks, who are preponderantly Jewish, do not belong to the orthodox Jewish

179

Church, it is yet possible, without laying oneself open to the charge of anti-Semitism, to point to the obvious fact that Jewry, *as a whole*, has, consciously or *unconsciously*, worked for and promoted an international economic, material despotism, which, with Puritanism as an ally, has tended in an ever-increasing degree to crush national and spiritual values out of existence and substitute the ugly and deadening machinery of finance and factory. It is also a fact that Jewry, as a whole, strove every nerve to secure and heartily approved of the overthrow of the Russian monarchy, which they regarded as their most formidable obstacle in the path of their ambitions and business pursuits. All this may be admitted, as well as the plea that, individually or collectively, most Jews may heartily detest the Bolshevik regime, yet it is still true that the whole weight of Jewry was in the revolutionary scales against the czar's government. It is true their apostate brethren, who are now riding in the seat of power, may have exceeded their orders; that is disconcerting, but it does not alter the fact. It may be that the Jews, often the victims of their own idealism, have always been instrumental in bringing about the events they most heartily disapprove of; that perhaps is the curse of the Wandering Jew.

Certainly it is from the Jews themselves that we learn most about the Jews. It is possible that only a Jew can understand a Jew. Nay, more, it may be that only a Jew can save us from the Jews, a Jew who is great enough, strong enough—for greater racial purity is a source of strength in the rare and the great—and inspired enough to overcome in himself the life-destructive vices of his own race. It was a Jew who said, "Wars are the Jews' harvest"; but no harvest so rich as civil wars. A Jew reminds us that the French Revolution brought civil emancipation for the Jews in Western Europe. Was it a *Jew* who inspired Rousseau with the eighteenth century idea of the sameness of man according to nature? Dr. Kallen, a Zionist author, writes: "Suffering for

1,000 years from the assertion of their difference from the rest of mankind, they accepted eagerly the escape from suffering which the eighteenth century assertion of the sameness of all men opened to them . . . . They threw themselves with passion into the republican emancipating movements of their fellow subjects of other stocks." It was a Jew, Ricardo, who gave us the nineteenth century ideal of the sameness of man according to machinery. And without the Ricardian gospel of international capitalism, we could not have had the international gospel of Karl Marx. Moses Hess and Disraeli remind us of the particularly conspicuous part played by Jews in the Polish and Hungarian rebellions, and in the republican uprising in Germany of '48. Even more conspicuous were they in the new internationalism logically deducible from the philosophy of Socialism. This we were taught by the Jew Marx, and the Jew Ferdinand Lasalle, and they but developed the doctrine of the Jew David Ricardo.

It was Weininger, a Jew—and also a Jew hater—who explained why so many Jews are naturally Communists. Communism is not only an international creed, but it implies the abnegation of real property, especially property in land, and Jews, being international, have never acquired a taste for real property; they prefer money. Money is an instrument of power, though eventually, of course, Communist claim that they will do away with money—when their power is sufficiently established to enable them to command goods, and exercise despotic sway without it. Thus the same motives prompt the Jew Communist and his apparent enemy, the financial Jew. When owners of real property in times of economic depression feel the pinch of straightened circumstances, it is the Jewish usurers who become most affluent and who, out of goodness of their hearts, come to their assistance—at a price.

To these and other statements, Dr. Levy, as a Jew, made this reply:

Dear Mr. Pitt-Rivers:

When you first handed me your MS. on *The World Significance of the Russian Revolution,* you expressed a doubt about the propriety of its title. After a perusal of your work, I can assure you, with the best of consciences, that your misgivings were entirely without foundation.

No better title than *The World Significance of the Russian Revolution* could have been chosen, for no event in any age will finally have more significance for our world than this one. We are still too near to see clearly this Revolution, this portentous event, *which was certainly one of the most intimate and therefore least obvious, aims of the world-conflagration, hidden as it was at first by the fire and smoke of national enthusiasms and patriotic antagonisms.*

It was certainly very plucky of you to try and throw some light upon an event which necessarily must still be enveloped in mist and mystery, and I was even somewhat anxious, lest your audacity in treating such a dangerous subject would end in failure, or what is nearly the same, in ephemeral success. No age is so voracious of its printed offspring as ours. There was thus some reason to fear lest you had offered to this modern Kronos only another mouthful of his accustomed nourishment for his immediate consumption.

I was, I am glad to report, agreeably surprised—surprised, though not by the many new facts which you give, and which must surprise all those who take an interest in current events—facts, I believe, which you have carefully and personally collected and selected, not only from books, but from the lips and letters of Russian eye-witnesses and sufferers, from foes as well as from friends of the great Revolution.

What I appreciate more than this new light thrown on a dark subject, more than the conclusion drawn by you from this wealth of facts, is the psychological insight which you display in *detecting the reasons why a movement so extraordinarily bestial and so violently crazy as the Revolution was able to succeed and finally to overcome its adversaries.* For we are confronted with two questions which need answering and which, in my opinion, you have answered in your pamphlet. These questions are: (1) How has the Soviet Government, *admittedly the government of an insignificant minority,* succeeded not only in maintaining but in strengthening its position in Russia after two and a half years of power? and (2) Why has the Soviet Government, in spite of its outward bestiality and brutal tyranny, succeeded in gaining the sympathies of an increasing number of people in this country? . . . .

You rightly recognize that there is an ideology behind it and you clearly diagnose it as an ancient ideology. There is nothing new under the Sun, *it is even nothing new that this Sun rises in the East* . . . .

For Bolshevism is a religion and a faith. How could these half-converted believers ever dream to vanquish the "Truthful" and the "Faithful" of their own creed, these holy crusaders, who had gathered round the Red Standard of the Prophet Karl Marx, and who fought under the daring guidance of *these experienced officers of all latter-day revolutions—the Jews?*

I am touching here on a subject which, to judge from your own pamphlet, is perhaps more interesting to you than any other. In this you are right. There *is no race in the world more enigmatic, more fatal, and therefore more interesting than the Jews.*

Every writer, who, like yourself, is oppressed by the aspect of the present and embarrassed by his anxiety for the future, MUST try to elucidate the Jewish Question and its bearing upon our Age.

For the question of the Jews and their influence on the world past and present, cuts to the root of all things, and should be discussed by every honest thinker, however bristling with difficulties it is, however complex the subject as well as the individuals of this Race may be.

183

For the Jews, as you are aware, are a sensitive Community, and thus very suspicious of any Gentile who tries to approach them with a critical mind. They are always inclined—and that on account of their terrible experiences—to denounce anyone who is not with them as against them, as tainted with "medieval" prejudice, as an intolerant Antagonist of their Faith and of their Race.

Nor could or would I deny that there is some evidence, some prima facie evidence of this antagonistic attitude in your pamphlet. You point out, and with fine indignation, *the great danger that springs from the prevalence of Jews in finance and industry, and from the preponderance of Jews in rebellion and revolution.* You reveal, and with great fervor, *the connection between the Collectivism of the immensely rich international Finance*—the Democracy of cash values, as you call it—*and the international Collectivism of Karl Marx and Trotsky*— the Democracy of and by decoy-cries . . . . And all this evil and misery, the economic as well as the political, you trace back to one source, to one *"fons et origo malorum"*—the Jews.

Now other Jews may vilify and crucify you for these outspoken views of yours; I myself shall abstain from joining the chorus of condemnation! I shall try to understand your opinions and your feelings, and having once understood them— as I think I have—I can defend you from the unjust attacks of my often too impetuous Race. But first of all, I have to say this: *There is scarcely an event in modern Europe that cannot be traced back to the Jews. Take the Great War that appears to have come to an end, ask yourself what were its causes and its reasons: you will find them in nationalism. You will at once answer that nationalism has nothing to do with the Jews, who, as you have just proved to us, are the inventors of the international idea.* But no less than Bolshevist Ecstasy and Financial Tyranny can National Bigotry (if I may call it so) *be finally followed back to a Jewish source*—are not they the inventors of the Chosen People Myth, and is not this obsession part and parcel of the political credo of every modern nation, *however small and insignificant it may be?* And then think of the history of nationalism. It started in our time and as a reaction against Napoleon; Napoleon was the antagonist of the French Revolution; the French Revolution was the consequence of the German Reformation; the German Reformation was based upon a crude Christianity; this kind of Christianity was invented, preached and propagated by the Jews; THEREFORE the Jews have made this war!. . . . Please do not think this a joke; it only seems a joke, and behind it there lurks a gigantic truth, and it is this, that *all latter-day ideas and movements have originally sprung from a Jewish source,* for the simple reason, that the Semitic idea has finally conquered and entirely subdued this *only apparently irreligious universe of ours.*

. . . ."There is no doubt that the Jews regularly go one better or worse than the Gentile in whatever they do, there is no further doubt that *their influence today justifies a very careful scrutiny, and cannot possibly be viewed without serious alarm.* The great question, however, is whether the Jews are conscious or unconscious malefactors. I myself am firmly convinced that they are unconscious ones, but please do not think that I wish to exonerate them on that account . . . . A conscious evildoer has my respect, for he knows at least what is good; an unconscious one—well, he needs the charity of Christ—a charity which is not mine—to be forgiven for not knowing what he is doing. But there is in my firm conviction not the slightest doubt that these revolutionary Jews do not know what they are doing; that they are more unconscious sinners than voluntary evildoers.

I am glad to see that this is not an original observation of mine, but that you yourself have a very strong foreboding about the Jews being the victims of their own theories and principles. On page 39 of your pamphlet you write: "It may be that the Jews have always been instrumental in bringing about the events that they most heartily disapprove of; that maybe is the curse of the Wandering Jew." If I had not the honor, as well as the pleasure, of knowing you personally, if I were not strongly aware of your passionate desire for light and your intense loathing of unfairness, this sentence, and this sentence alone, which tells the truth, will absolve you in my eyes from the odious charge of being a vulgar anti-Semite.

No, you are not a vulgar, you are a very enlightened, critic of our Race. *For there is an anti-Semitism, I hope and trust, which does the Jews more justice than any blind philo-Semitism,* than does that merely sentimental "Let-them-all-come Liberalism" which in itself is nothing but the Semitic Ideology over again. *And thus you can be just to the Jews, without being "romantic" about them.*

You have noticed with alarm that the *Jewish elements provide the driving forces for both Communism and capitalism,* for the material as well as the spiritual ruin of this world. But then you have at the same time the profound suspicion that the reason for all this extraordinary behavior may be the intense Idealism of the Jew. In this you are perfectly right. The Jew, if caught by an idea, never thinks any more in watertight compartments, as do the Teuton and Anglo-Saxon peoples, whose right cerebral hemisphere never seems to know what its left twin brother is doing; he, the Jew, like the Russian, at once begins to practice what he preaches, he draws the logical conclusion from his tenets, he invariably acts upon his accepted principles. It is from this quality, no doubt, that springs his mysterious force—that force which you no doubt condemn, but which you had to admire even in the Bolshevists. And we must admire it, whether we are Jews or whether we are Christians, for have not these modern Jews remained true to type, is there no parallel for them in history, do they not go to the bitter end even in our day? . . . .

Who stirred up the people during the late war in Germany? Who pretended to have again the truth, *that* truth about which Pontius Pilate once shrugged his shoulders? Who pleaded for honesty and cleanliness in Politics, *that* honesty which brings a smile to the lips of any experienced Pro-consul of today? Writers, who are mostly Jews: Fried, Fernau, Latzko, Richard Grelling—the author of "J'accuse." Who was killed and allowed himself to be killed for these very ideas and principles? Men and women of the Jewish race: Haase, Levine, Luxemburg, Landauer, Kurt Eisner, the Prime Minister of Bavaria. From Moses to Marx, from Isaiah to Eisner, in practice and in theory, in idealism and in materialism, in philosophy and in politics, they are today what they have always been: passionately devoted to their aims and to their purposes, and ready, nay, eager, to shed their last drop of blood for the realization of their visions.

"But these visions are all wrong," will you reply. . . . .Look where they have led the world to. Think, that they have now had a fair trial of 3,000 years' standing. How much longer are you going to recommend them to us and to inflict them upon us? And how do you propose to get us out of the morass into which you have launched us, if you do not change the path upon which you have led the world so disastrously astray?"

To this question I have only one answer to give, and it is this: "You are right." This reproach of yours, which—I feel it for certain—is at the bottom of your anti-Semitism, is only too well justified, and upon this common ground I am quite willing to shake hands with you and defend you against any accusation of promoting Race Hatred: *If you are anti-Semite, I, the Semite, am an anti-Semite too, and a much more fervent one than even you are . . . . We (Jews) have erred, my friend, we have most grievously erred. And if there was truth in our error 3,000, 2,000, nay 100 years ago, there is now nothing but falseness and madness, a madness that will produce an even greater misery and an even wider anarchy. I confess it to you, openly and sincerely, and with a sorrow, whose depth and pain an ancient Psalmist, and only he, could moan into this burning universe of ours . . . We who have posed as the saviours of the world, we who have even boasted of having given it "the" Saviour, we are today nothing else but the world's seducers, its destroyers, its incendiaries, its executioners* . . . . We who have promised to lead you to a new Heaven, we have finally succeeded in landing you into a new Hell . . . . There has been no progress, least of all moral progress . . . . And it is just our Morality, which has prohibited all real progress, and—what is worse—which even stands in the way of every future and natural reconstruction in this ruined world of ours . . . . I look at this world, and I shudder at its ghastliness; I shudder all the more as I know the spiritual authors of all this ghastliness . . . .

But its authors themselves, unconscious in this as in all they are doing, know nothing yet of this startling revelation. *While Europe is aflame, while its victims scream, while its dogs howl in the conflagration, and while its very smoke descends in darker and even darker shades upon our Continent, the Jews, or at least a part of them and by no means the most unworthy ones, endeavor to escape from the burning building, and wish to retire from Europe into Asia, from the somber scene of our disaster into the sunny corner of their Palestine. Their eyes are closed to the miseries, their ears are deaf to the moanings, their heart is hardened to the anarchy of Europe: they only feel their own sorrows, they only bewail their own fate, they only sigh under their own burdens* . . . . They know nothing of their duty to Europe, which looks around in vain for help and guidance, they know nothing even of their own great ancestor to whose heart the appeal of pity was never made in vain: they have become too poor in love, too sick at heart, too tired of battle, and lo! these sons of those who were once the bravest of soldiers are now trying to retire from the trenches to the rear, are now eager to exchange the grim music of the whistling shells with that of the cowbells and vintage songs in the happy plain of Sharon . . . .

And yet we are not all Financiers, we are not all Bolshevists, we have not all become Zionists. And yet there is hope, great hope, that this same race which has provided the Evil will likewise succeed in supplying its antidote, its remedy—the Good. It has always been so in the past—was not that fatal Liberalism, which has finally led to Bolshevism—in the very midst of that dark nineteenth century, most strenuously opposed by two enlightened Jews—Friedrich Stahl, the founder of the Conservative Party in Germany, and by Benjamin Disraeli, the leader of the Tory Party in England? *And if these two eminent men had no suspicion yet that their own race and its holy message were at the bottom of that unfortunate upheaval, with which their age was confronted:* how eager, how determined, how passionate will be the opposition of the Disraelis of the future, once they have clearly recognized that they are really fighting the tenets of their own people, and that it was their "Good," their "Love," their "Ideal," that had launched the world into this Hell of Evil and Hatred. A new "Good" as new Love, a true Love, an intelligent Love, a Love that calms and heals and sweetens, will then spring up among the Great in Israel and overcome that sickly Love, that insipid Love, that romantic Love, which has hitherto poisoned all the Strength and all the Nobility of this world. For Hatred is never overcome by Hatred: it is only overcome by Love, and it wants a new and a gigantic Love to subdue that old and devilish Hatred of today. That is our task for the future—a task which will, I am sure, not be shirked by Israel, by that same Israel which has never shirked a task, whether it was for good or whether it was for evil. . . .

Yes, there is hope, my friend, for we are still here, our last word is not yet spoken, our last deed is not yet done, our last revolution is not yet made. *This last Revolution, the Revolution that will crown our revolutionaries, will be the revolution against the revolutionaries.* It is bound to come, and it is perhaps upon us now. The great day of reckoning is near. It will pass a judgment upon our ancient faith, and it will lay the foundation to a new religion. And when that great day has broken, when the values of death and decay are put into the melting-pot to be changed into those of power and beauty, then you, my dear Pitt-Rivers, the descendant of an old and distinguished Gentile family, may be assured to find by your side, and as your faithful ally, at least one member of that Jewish Race, which has fought with such fatal success upon all the spiritual battlefields of Europe.

Yours against the Revolution and for Life ever flourishing,

OSCAR LEVY,

ROYAL SOCIETIES CLUB,
ST. JAMES STREET,
LONDON, S. W.,
JULY, 1920.

Issue of April 30, 1921

LVII.

Jewish Idea in American Monetary Affairs

M R. BRISBANE says that Jewish bankers exercise their large measure of control because they are abler than the other bankers. It was very good of Mr. Brisbane to say so, and it adds to the sum of his weekly, almost daily, worship at the Jewish shrine, but it is scarcely true. Jewish bankers do not as yet control the United States, and the principal reason they do not is that they are not abler than the other bankers. Doubtless they seek control; doubtless they have almost grasped it on several occasions; but not yet.

Nevertheless they form such a formidable force, and with their international connections constitute such a political problem, that the mere fact of their failing to top the column of control is not so reassuring as it sounds.

The great Jewish banking houses of the United States are foreign importations, as perhaps everyone knows. Most of them are sufficiently recent to be considered in their immigrant status, while the thought of them as aliens is stimulated by their retention of overseas connections. It is this international quality of the Jewish banking group which largely accounts for Jewish financial power: there is team-play, intimate understandings, and while there is a margin of competition among themselves (as at golf) there is also a wiping out of that margin when it comes to a contest between Jewish and "Gentile" capital.

Four conspicuous contemporary names in Jewish-American finance are Belmont, Schiff, Warburg and Kahn. All of them, even the most recent, are of foreign origin.

August Belmont was the earliest and arrived in America in 1837 as the American representative of the Rothschilds in whose offices he had been raised. His birthplace was that great center of Jewish international finance, Frankfort-on-the-Main. He became the founder of the Belmont family in America, which has largely forgotten its Jewish origin. Politics was a part of his concerns in this country, and during the critical time from 1860 to 1872 he was chairman of the National Democratic Committee. His management of the Rothschild interests was exceedingly profitable to that house, although the operations in which he engaged were quite simple compared with the operations of the present day.

Jacob Schiff is another Jewish financier who was given to the world by Frankfort-on-the-Main. He entered the United States in 1865, after having passed his apprenticeship in the office of his father, who was also an agent of the Rothschilds. The name Schiff runs a long way back without change, unlike the name of Rothschild. Originally named Bauer, this family of financiers took a new name from the red shield which adorned their house in the Jewish section of Frankfort and thus became "Rot-schild." Commonly the last syllable is pronounced as if it were "child"; it is "schild," shield. An epoch-making family in itself, it has trained hundreds of agents and apprentices, of whom Jacob H. Schiff was one. He became one of the principal channels through which German-Jewish capital flowed into American undertakings, and his agency in these matters gave him a place in many important departments of American business, especially railroads, banks, insurance companies and telegraph companies. He married Theresa Loeb, and in due time came to be head of the firm of Kuhn, Loeb & Company.

Mr. Schiff, too, was interested in politics with a Jewish angle, and was perhaps the moving force in the campaign which forced Congress and the President to break off treaty relations with Russia, then a friendly nation, on a strictly Jewish question which had been skillfully given an American aspect. Mr. Schiff was of inestimable assistance to Japan in the war against Russia, but is understood to have been disappointed by Japan's shrewdness in preventing too high a return being made for that assistance.

Associated with Mr. Schiff in Kuhn, Loeb & Company is Otto Herman Kahn, who is probably more international than were either of the two gentlemen mentioned above and is more constantly engaged in dabbling in mysterious matters of an international nature. This characteristic may be accounted for, however, by his experience of many countries. He was born in Germany and is also a product of the Frankfort-on-the-Main school of finance, having had connection with the Frankfort Jewish house of Speyer.

Of just how many countries Mr. Kahn has been a citizen is a question not easy to determine here because of the doubt that was recently cast upon his American citizenship by a protest against his being permitted to cast his vote last year and by his failure—the announced cause being physical indisposition—to cast his vote. If Mr. Kahn is a citizen of the United States (a status that will be readily proclaimed upon proof that he is), that probably increases the number of his citizenships to three. He was a German citizen by birth, and served in the German Army. And in 1914, in August, at the time of the outbreak of the European War, when efforts were being made, which afterward succeeded, to put Paul M. Warburg, a member of the firm of Kuhn, Loeb & Company, on the Federal Reserve Board, Mr. Warburg testified that at that time Mr. Kahn was not a citizen of the United States.

Senator Bristow—"How many of these partners are American citizens, or are they all American citizens. . . . "

Mr. Warburg—"They are all American citizens except Mr. Kahn."—(P. 7, Senate Hearings, August 1, 1914.)

Senator Bristow—"Now, the members of your firm, are they all American citizens except Mr. Kahn?"

Mr. Warburg—"Except Mr. Kahn, yes."

Senator Bristow—"Was Mr. Kahn ever an American citizen?"

Mr. Warburg—"No."

Senator Bristow—"He never was?"

Mr. Warburg—"No; he is a British subject."

Senator Bristow—"He is a British subject?"

The Chairman—"He lives in England, does he not?"

Mr. Warburg—"No. At one time he thought he would move to Europe, and that was when the question arose of his standing for Parliament; then he changed his mind and moved back to the United States."

Senator Bristow—"He was at one time a candidate, or a prospective candidate for Parliament, was he not?"

Mr. Warburg—"No; he was not; but there was talk about it; it had been suggested, and he had it in his mind. Something had been written about it in the papers."—(P.76, Senate Hearings, August 3, 1914.)

So, that if Mr. Kahn is a citizen of the United States now, which as a matter of fact has been disputed, then he has been a citizen of three countries, Germany and Great Britain being the other two.

Mr. Kahn, by the way, is one of those Jews whose adoption of another form of faith brings no denunciation whatever from the Jews themselves. A most peculiar circumstance! But doubtless not inexplicable. Mr. Kahn is not called a "renegade Jew" nor any of the other nasty names heaped upon Jewish converts to Christianity, because he does not deserve them. They would not fit him. He is not renegade. And he never was regarded for a moment by Jacob H. Schiff as anything but a Jew, else that "Prince of Israel" would not have chosen him to remain in America and run the business of Kuhn, Loeb & Company, at a time when it seemed undesirable to put the junior Schiff in full charge of it.

Doubtless it was Mr. Kahn's desire, just at the time Jacob Schiff made his wishes known, to go to England and stand for Parliament.

But from New York he fulfills probably as well as he could from London, those mysterious missions which frequently take him to the Continent, at which times he makes what are regarded as certain authoritative decisions, though just *whose* decisions it is not always possible to say. In Paris particularly, and at points east thereof, Mr. Kahn has been established in the position of spokesman of the American Financial Hierarchy, which, of course, he is not. But he undoubtedly is the spokesman of some group, possibly the group which so ably put through the Jewish program at the Peace Conference, the group that impressed Eastern Europe with the feeling that the United States of America was a very powerful Semitic empire. Mr. Kahn's trips abroad are usually unheralded, but their results richly repay observation.

A fourth member of the Jewish financial group in America (which is the form of statement which Mr. Chaim Weizmann would sanction, rather than to say "Jewish-American financiers") is Mr. Paul Warburg, to whose testimony we have just alluded.

Mr. Warburg is the most recent of all. He was born in Germany in 1868; he came to the United States in 1902; he became an American citizen in 1911. He came to the United States for the express purpose of reforming our financial system, and it is hardly possible to understand fully the system in operation today without reference to Paul Warburg. He is a man of very fine mind, a money-maker, but something more — a shrewd student of the systems by which money is made. There are two types engaged in the mere work of money-making which is better described as "money-getting," without reference to production; one type grubs away under whatever system obtains, regarding it as fixed as the solar system; another type is sufficiently detached to see the system as an artifice which may be mended, remodeled or supplanted altogether. Paul Warburg, scion of a long line of German Jewish bankers, is of the latter type. He is not content with the fact that the cash-register fills itself with money; he wants also to know how the cash-register works, and whether it can be worked. He is thus a student of money and of the number of ways in which it can be manipulated.

Perhaps it will be best to let him tell his own story as far as he goes. When he told it to the Committee on Banking and Currency of the United States Senate in executive session, there was some dispute as to whether the proceedings should be recorded by the stenographer. It was finally agreed that notes should be made but should not be divulged. The testimony was printed "in confidence" on August 5, 1914, and nominally "made public" on August 12.

The Warburgs are one of the international families whose importance was not realized until the war, and would not have been realized then if their internationalism had not been so apparent. It was an interesting spectacle to see brothers occupying important places of counsel on either side of the great struggle.

Paul Warburg learned the rudiments of banking in his father's bank at Hamburg, Germany, studying the over-sea trade which is the foundation of that city's business. The banking house of Warburg in Hamburg dates from 1796.

"After that I went to England, where I stayed for two years, first in the banking and discount firm of Samuel Montague & Company, and after that I took the opportunity of staying two months in the office of a stockbroker in order to learn that part of the business.

"After that I went to France, where I stayed in a French bank, so that—"

The Chairman—"What French bank was that?"

Mr. Warburg—"It is the Russian bank for foreign trade, which has an agency in Paris.

"And after that I went back to Hamburg and worked there again for a year, I think.

"Then I went round to India, China and Japan.

"And then I came to this country for the first time in 1893. I stayed here only a short time then, and went back to Hamburg, and then became a partner of the firm in Hamburg."

The Chairman—"How long were you in Hamburg then in the banking business?"

Mr. Warburg—"Until 1902 . . . . And then I moved over here to this country to become a partner of Kuhn, Loeb & Company."

"I explained in the curriculum which I gave you, Mr. Chairman, that by marriage I am related to members of the firm, the late Mr. Loeb having been my father-in-law, which brought about a desire on the part of the family to bring me over here . . . . I ought to say that I got married in this country in 1895 and that I have been in this country every year since, for several months . . . . That is the history of my banking education."

It will be recalled that Jacob H. Schiff also married a daughter of Mr. Loeb, so that Mr. Warburg married the sister of Mrs. Jacob H. Schiff. Felix Warburg, Paul's brother, who is also in the firm, married Mr. Schiff's daughter.

Mr. Warburg immediately cast a critical eye upon the state of financial affairs in the United States and it is significant of the grasp he already had on such matters that he found the country rather behind the times.

He conceived ambition—the very daring ambition —of taking hold of the United States' monetary system and making it what he thought it ought to be.

This alone would make him a remarkable man. It illustrates very well that detached point of view which the Jew is more fitted to take than any other man perhaps. He sees countries and systems with the same freedom from intimate bias with which another man would view assorted fish upon a market stall. Most of the world is engaged in doing its work and indulging its national, racial, domestic and social affections and inclinations; a small minority stands in the background and watches the entire mass at its unconscious maneuvers, and studies it as an observer studies a hive of bees. The man at work has no time except for his job. One man, standing back and studying 1,000 men at work, is able to see how he might utilize their labor or possess himself of a first toll on their production. Doubtless there must be men to stand at a sufficient distance from things to get a correct idea of their interrelationship, and doubtless such an attitude may be made of great service to the race, but doubtless it has also contributed to the selfish manipulation of natural and social processes.

Mr. Warburg testified: "When I came here I was at once impressed by the lack of system, by the old-fashioned nature of the system that prevailed here; and I got immediately into one of those periods of high interest rates, where call money went up to 25 and 100 percent; and I wrote an article on the subject then and there for my own benefit.

"I was not here three weeks before I was trying to explain to myself the roots of the evil. I showed the article to a few friends but I kept it in my desk, because I did not want to be one of those who try to inform and educate the country after they have been here for a month or so; and I kept that article until the end of 1906, shortly before the panic, when those conditions arose again, and when one newspaper wanted for an issue at the end of the year an article dealing with the conditions in our country.

"Then I took out that article and touched it up and brought it up to date; and that was the first article of mine that was published. It was called, 'Defects and Needs of Our Banking System.' . . .

"That was, however, the first time that I know of that the question of the discount system and the concentration of reserves was really brought out: and I got a great many encouraging letters asking me to go on and explain my ideas."

Mr. Warburg was perfectly willing to talk to the committee about himself, but not about Kuhn, Loeb & Company, his firm.

"I cannot discuss the affairs of my firm nor my partners," he said, "nor be asked to criticize acts of my partners, either to approve them or in any other way," but eventually he did tell a number of things which students of American financial affairs have considered interesting. Of which more later.

On page 77 of the testimony, more personal matters appear:

Senator Bristow—"When did you become a citizen of the United States, Mr. Warburg?"

Mr. Warburg—"1911. Did I not answer that?"

Senator Bristow—"Perhaps so. Did you intend to become a citizen when you came to the United States in 1902?"

Mr. Warburg—"I had no definite intentions then, because some of the reasons that brought me over here were family reasons; . . . .That had a good deal to do with my first coming here; and I was not sure at all that I would stay here when I came."

Senator Bristow—"When did you decide to become a citizen of the United States?"

Mr. Warburg—"In 1908, when I took out my papers."

Senator Bristow—"When you took out your first papers? You took out your second papers, then, in 1911?"

Mr. Warburg—"Yes."

Senator Bristow—"You made your declaration in 1908; that is when you decided to become an American citizen?"

Mr. Warburg—"Yes."

Senator Bristow—"Why did you wait as long as you did after you came to this country, before deciding to become a citizen of this country?"

Mr. Warburg—"I think that a man that does not come here as an immigrant; a man who has had, if you may call it such, a prominent position in his own country, will not give up his nationality so easily as a man who comes over here knowing that he does not care for his own country at all. I had been a very loyal citizen of my own country; and I think that a man who hesitates in giving up his own nationality and taking a new one, is apt to be more loyal to his new country when he does change his nationality than a man who gives up his old country more lightly."

Senator Bristow—"Yes."

Mr. Warburg—"I may add this: That a thing which had a great deal of influence on my making up my mind to remain in this country, was that monetary reform work, for I felt I had a distinct duty to perform here; and I thought I could do that; and in fact I have been working on it since 1906 or 1907.

"Then I felt that it was the right thing for me to become an American citizen and work here and throw in my lot definitely with this country."

Senator Bristow—"When you became an American citizen; and the motive which induced you to become an American citizen was, then, as I understand it, largely with a view of laboring to bring about a reform of the American monetary system?"

Mr. Warburg—"Well, you put it nearly exclusively on that. I think a man wants to feel that he is going to do some useful work in his country; that he has a mission to perform; and that is what happened to me . . . Moreover, I had been long enough in this country then to have thoroughly taken root and feel that I was a part and parcel of it."

Senator Bristow—"Yes. When did you first become active in promoting the monetary reforms in the United States?"

Mr. Warburg—"1906."

Senator Bristow—"What was your method of promoting your ideas with regard to monetary reforms?"

Mr. Warburg—"Mainly writing."

Senator Bristow—"Were you connected with the Monetary Commission?"

Mr. Warburg—"No, not directly . . . . "

Senator Bristow—"Were you consulted in regard to the report of the Monetary Commission in any way?"

Mr. Warburg—"Yes, Senator Aldrich consulted with me about details, and I gave him my advice freely."

Senator Bristow—"And in regard to the bill which was prepared by Senator Aldrich in connection with the commission, were you consulted in regard to that?"

Mr. Warburg—"Yes."

Senator Bristow—"What part did you have in the preparation of that bill, directly or indirectly?"

Mr. Warburg—"Well, only that I gave the best advice that I could give."

Most readers will recall that the name of "Aldrich" was, a few years ago, the synonym for the money power in government. Senator Aldrich was an able man and a tireless worker. His character for thoroughness and industry did more than anything else to disabuse the popular mind of the notion that such men were mere "tools of the money interest," or engaged in their work out of lust for gain, or out of sheer pleasure in legislating against the interests of the people. Senator Aldrich led on tariff and financial matters because he understood them; and he understood them by tireless study of them; and therefore, he was the master of other men who had not paid the price of knowledge. But, he understood these matters from the standpoint of the business interests only. He was sincerely desirous of the prosperity of the country, but that prosperity was written in banking balances. Fifteen years ago it might not have been possible to judge him thus calmly, because then he represented in the public mind, more than any individual does today, the concentrated power of the financial group. Their prosperity was his first care, possibly because he believed that their prosperity was also the country's.

It was such a man, then, that came to Mr. Warburg for advice. The labors of Senator Aldrich comprise many volumes of difficult material and Senator Aldrich's appeal to Mr. Warburg was a very high compliment to the quality of the latter's mind and financial experience—this, of course, assuming that Mr. Warburg's counsel was not forced upon the Aldrich committee by the New York money interests.

In his testimony, Mr. Warburg did not tell all. The omission, however, was supplied by an article in *Leslie's Weekly* in 1916, the author being B. C. Forbes.

It is a story of which *Current Opinion* said: "It reads like the opening in a shilling shocker."

It appears that the conferences between Mr. Warburg and Senator Aldrich took place on an isolated island off the coast of Georgia—Jekyl Island. Included in the party, besides Senator Aldrich and Mr. Warburg, were two New York bankers and the then Assistant Treasurer of the United States. The mysteriousness of it all was well brought out by Mr. Forbes:

"Picture a party of the nation's greatest bankers stealing out of New York on a private railroad car under cover of darkness, stealthily hieing hundreds of miles south, embarking on a mysterious launch, sneaking out to an island deserted by all but a few servants, living there a full week under such rigid secrecy that the name of not one of them was once mentioned lest the servitors learn their identity and disclose to the world this strangest, most secret episode in the history of American finance.

"The utmost secrecy was enjoined upon all. The public must not glean a hint of what was to be done. Senator Aldrich notified each one to go quietly into a private car which the railroad had received orders to draw up at an unfrequented platform. Drawn blinds balked any peering eyes that might be around. Off the party set. New York's ubiquitous reporters had been foiled. So far so good. After bowling along the railroad hour after hour into southern country, the order was given to prepare to disembark.

"Stepping from the car when the station had been well cleared of travelers, the members of the expedition embarked in a small boat. Silence reigned, for the boatmen must not find out how distinguished were their passengers.

"In due time they drew up at another deserted pier. They were at Jekyl Island, off Georgia. The island was entirely unpeopled save for half a dozen servants.

" 'The servants must under no circumstances learn who we are,' cautioned Senator Aldrich.

" 'What can we do to fool them?' asked another member of the group. The problem was discussed.

" 'I have it,' cried one. 'Let's all call each other by our first names. Don't ever let us mention our last names.'

"It was so agreed.

"The dignified veteran Senator Aldrich, king of Rhode Island and a power second to none in the United States Senate, became just 'Nelson'; . . . . and the quiet, scholarly member of the powerful international banking firm of Kuhn, Loeb & Company, became 'Paul.'

"Nelson had meanwhile confided to Harry, Frank, Paul and Piatt that he was to keep them locked up on Jekyl Island, cut off from the rest of the world, until they had evolved and compiled a scientific currency system for the United States, a system that would embody all that was best in Europe, yet so modeled that it could serve a country measuring thousands where European countries measured only hundreds of miles."

Mr. Forbes does not omit to write this further description of Mr. Warburg's condition at the time:

"...unable then to speak idiomatic English with perfect freedom and without an accent, an alien not naturalized."

Mr. Forbes also wrote—"Here is a "German-American, but the sort of one that makes the hyphen look like a badge of honor."

That was in 1916. Hyphens went out of fashion, though not entirely out of use, soon after.

Thus far the story of Paul Warburg.

Issue of June 18, 1921

LVIII.

Jewish Idea Molded Federal Reserve Plan

T he last view the reader had of Paul M. Warburg in the preceding article was as "an alien not naturalized" secretly closeted with Senator Nelson W. Aldrich and a party of bankers on an obscure island off the southeastern coast of the United States, all the members of the party concealing their identity even from the servants by calling each other by their first names.

That conference in its ultimate results was of the utmost importance to the United States, for then and there were formulated those fiscal devices, those financial methods, those "monetary reforms" which have exerted an influence on every citizen, rich and poor, of the Republic.

Much history was made in that little trip. It irresistibly calls to memory that other trip made in 1915—almost two years before America's entry into the war—by Bernard M. Baruch. As readers of THE DEARBORN INDEPENDENT of November 27, 1920, will recall, Mr. Baruch had been financial backer of the Plattsburg camp, and in his testimony he said he thought that General Wood would admit this. Then—"I went off on a long trip, and it was while on this trip that I felt there ought to be some mobilization of the industries, and I was thinking about the scheme that practically was put into effect and was working when I was chairman of the board. When I came back from that trip I asked for an interview with the President . . . The President listened very attentively and graciously as he always does." Mr. Baruch was an authority on the President's demeanor, for there was a long period in 1917 and 1918 during which he called at the White House every afternoon.

Two momentous trips in our recent history, both of them signalized and given their principal meaning by the presence of Jews. Not that there should not have been Jews in either case; to insist upon their total exclusion would be going too far. The Jew as a citizen, bearing his part, is one matter; the Jew as a master, directing the national show, is quite another thing. It is by no means agreed that Barney Baruch was the only man in the United States who could have run this nation's war business. That is the explanation made of the high place he took—that he was the *only* man who could do it. Nonsense! If that be so, let us close up the nation and hand the keys over to the New York Kehillah. Mr. Baruch could say—"I probably had more power than any other man did in the war; doubtless that is true," but he had that power because he was for the time the head and front of the Jewish group for war purposes.

If the explanation of Jewish mastery at critical moments were "brains," well and good, but if it were, it would be more evident to the people; brains do not need to be advertised, they advertise themselves. There is another reason.

The British public recently awoke to the fact that not Lloyd George but Mr. Montagu and Sir Alfred Mond were in charge of the recent negotiations over the German indemnities. These gentlemen are both Jews, one of them of German descent. Of all the British Empire are they the only two men to advise the premier in a great crisis? If they are, why is it? The Montagus, we know, control the silver of the world; Sir Alfred Mond, we know, turned the very neat trick of keeping the sign of the Cross off the war memorials raised to the soldiers of the empire; their Jewishness always so apparent. Both financiers; both the close advisers of the premier; as Baruch to Wilson, so they to Lloyd George.

Apparently there are no Anglo-Saxons on either side of the sea capable of managing these deep matters, if we are to judge them from the war administrations—those that have passed off the stage and those that still linger. Lloyd George, for once stung to the quick by the criticism of the British public of his tendency to closet himself with Jews when confronted with a crucial question, retorted bitterly—with what? With the old outworn Jewish propagandist boast, that it ill became people who sang Jewish psalms in church to rag the race that wrote them! A most illuminating defense! The world would give a good deal for a true psalm from Sir Alfred Mond, Mr. Montague, or even Sir Philip Sasoon, who is soon to become the premier's son-in-law.

In our own history, Barney Baruch boldly claims his place, he unhesitatingly asserts that he had more power than any man in the war. If Allenby in Palestine needed a locomotive, if the Americans in Russian needed clothing, if the munition mills needed copper—it was Baruch who gave or withheld the word.

Mr. Warburg, being of somewhat finer grain, probably due to his having less than Mr. Baruch of the rough experience of "the Street," does not make the claim that he is the chief factor in the present monetary system of the United States, nor does THE DEARBORN INDEPENDENT undertake to make it for him lest the cry of "anti-Semitism" wax wrathful again; but fortunately the fact is amply attested by a Jew whose knowledge of the matter is unquestionable.

Readers have doubtless become aware by this time that for a non-Jew to say that a certain Jew is a most important factor in any field is to be guilty of anti-Semitism, while for a Jew or a "Gentile front" to say it is perfectly proper. It is a rather odd etiquette in which simple minds sometimes become confused.

Professor E. R. A. Seligman, of Columbia University, is the sponsor of this great honor for Mr. Warburg. What Professor Seligman says is of such importance, both as to its source and its subject, that quotation is justified: (the italics in all cases are ours)

"It is in a general way known to the public that Mr. Warburg was in some way connected with the passage of the Federal Reserve Act, and his appointment to his present responsible position on the Federal Reserve Board was acclaimed on all sides with a rare degree of approval and congratulation; but I fancy *it is known only to a very few how great is the indebtedness of the United States to Mr. Warburg. For it may be stated without fear of contradiction that in its fundamental features the Federal Reserve Act is the work of Mr. Warburg more than of any other man in the country* . . . .

"When the Aldrich commission was appointed it was not long before Senator Aldrich—to his credit be it said—was won over by Mr. Warburg to the adoption of these two fundamental features.   The Aldrich Bill differed in some important particulars from the present law . . . .*The concession in the shape of the twelve regional banks that had to be made for political reasons is, in the opinion of Mr. Warburg as well as of the writer of this introduction, a mistake;* for it will probably, to some extent at least, weaken the good results which would otherwise have followed. On the other hand, the existence of a Federal Reserve Board creates, in everything but in name, a real central bank; and it depends largely upon the wisdom with which the board exercises its great powers as to whether we shall be able to secure most of the advantages of a central bank without any of its dangers . . . .

"In many minor respects also the Federal Reserve Act differs from the Aldrich Bill; but in the two fundamentals of combined reserves and of a discount policy, the Federal Reserve Act has frankly accepted the principles of the Aldrich Bill; *and these principles, as has been stated, were the creation of Mr. Warburg and of Mr. Warburg alone.*

" . . . .*It must not be forgotten that Mr. Warburg had a practical object in view.   In formulating his plans and in advancing slightly varying suggestions from time to time, it was incumbent on him to remember that the education of the country must be gradual and that a large part of the task was to break down prejudices and remove suspicions. His plans therefore contain all sorts of elaborate suggestions designed to guard the public against fancied dangers and to persuade the country that the general scheme was at all practicable. It was the hope of Mr. Warburg that with the lapse of time it might be possible to eliminate from the law not a few clauses which were inserted, largely at his suggestion, for educational purposes.*

"As it was my privilege to say to President Wilson when originally urging the appointment of Mr. Warburg on the Federal Reserve Board, at a time when the political prejudice against New York bankers ran very high, England also, three-quarters of a century ago, had a practical banker who was virtually responsible for the idea contained in Peel's Bank Act of 1840. Mr. Samuel Jones Lloyd was honored as a consequence by the British Government and was made Lord Overstone. The United States was equally fortunate in having with it a Lord Overstone . . . .

"The Federal Reserve Act will be associated in history with the name of Paul M. Warburg . . . ."—(pp. 387-390, Vol. 4, No. 4, Proceedings of the Academy of Political Science, Columbia University).

It surely cannot be considered invidious for THE DEARBORN INDEPENDENT thus to introduce to the people of the United States a gentleman whose influence upon the country is so vital. Just how vital can be understood only by those who have studied the puzzle of a country filled with the good things of life, and still unable to use them or to share them because of a kink in the pipe called "money."

But that Mr. Warburg himself is not entirely unaware of his position is indicated on page 56 of his testimony quoted last week. Mr. Warburg had just told the Senate Committee that he was making a heavy financial sacrifice to accept the position on the Federal Reserve Board offered him by President Wilson, and into the fitness of which appointment the Senate was carefully inquiring:

Senator Reed—"May I ask what your motive is, or your reason for making that sacrifice?"

Mr. Warburg—"My motive is that I have, as you know, taken a keen interest in this monetary reform since I have been in this country.

"I have had the success which comes to few people, of starting an idea and starting it so that the whole country has taken it up and it has taken some tangible form."

Professor Seligman advises us of the strategy that was used to get the whole country to take up Mr. Warburg's idea, and of the fact that some of the items inserted to appease the public might easily be removed when the public shall have become accustomed to Mr. Warburg and the Federal Reserve Board; but Mr. Warburg adds another hint, to the effect that you can do some things by administration which you cannot do by organization.

For example: Mr. Warburg wanted *only one central bank* which should be the sole arbiter of finance in the United States. The United States Government would have almost nothing to do save to make the money and stand back of it; the bankers of the United States, and the people thereof, would have nothing to do except what they were told; the one central bank would be the real financial governing authority.

When asked by Senator Bristow to state the fundamental difference between the Aldrich plan and the present Federal Reserve plan, Mr. Warburg replied:

"Well, the Aldrich Bill brings the whole system into one unit, while this deals with 12 units, and unites them again into the Federal Reserve Board. It is a little bit complicated, which objection, however, *can be overcome in an administrative way:* and in that respect I freely criticized the bill before it was passed."

There is evidently, then, a method of administration for which severe critics might even use the word "manipulation," by which the plain provisions of a banking law, whatever they may be, may be, if not evaded, then somewhat adapted.

This idea is brought to mind by a more colloquial expression of Mr. Warburg's to be found in his address on "bank acceptances" delivered in 1919.

"In this connection I am reminded of a story I once heard concerning a man belonging to a species now soon to be extinct and to be found by our children in Webster's dictionary only, the 'bartender.' A man of this profession, in pre-historic times, was abandoning his position and was turning over his cash-register to his successor. 'Please show me how it works,' said the newcomer. *'I will show you how it works,'* said the other, *'but I won't show you how to work it.'* "

The politics of Mr. Warburg and the firm of Kuhn, Loeb & company formed part of the inquiry, and Mr. Warburg made some interesting revelations, which illustrate the oft-repeated statement that it is part of Jewish policy—perhaps of large financial firms generally—to attach themselves to both parties so that certain interests may be the winners regardless of which party is defeated.

Senator Pomerene—"What are your politics?"

Senator Nelson—"No; we have not raised that before this committee."

Senator Reed—"It has not been raised here, but I should like to know."

Senator Pomerene—"It has been raised before the Senate."

Senator Reed—"I will say why I should like to know."

Senator Pomerene—"Well, I have no objection to saying what was in my own mind."

The Chairman—"I will say that I do not know what Mr. Warburg's politics are."

Senator Pomerene—"Well, I did not."

Senator Shafroth—"I do not know and I do not care to know."

Senator Pomerene—"I heard the statement made that the entire board was Democratic, and I had understood that Mr. Warburg was a Republican, or had been, in his affiliations."

Mr. Warburg—"Well, so I was; and my sympathies were entirely, in the early campaign, for Mr. Taft against Mr. Roosevelt in the first fight. When later on Mr. Roosevelt became President Wilson's opponent my sympathies went with Mr. Wilson. . . ."

Senator Reed—"Well, you would count yourself a Republican, generally speaking?"

Mr. Warburg—"I would."

Senator Bristow—"It has been variously reported in the newspapers that you and your partners directly and indirectly contributed very largely to Mr. Wilson's campaign funds."

Mr. Warburg—"Well, my partners—there is a very peculiar condition—no; I do not think any one of them contributed largely at all; there may have been moderate contributions. My brother, for instance, contributed to Mr. Taft's campaign."

Senator Bristow—"Just what would you consider a moderate contribution to a presidential campaign?"

Mr. Warburg—"Well, that depends who the man is who contributes; but I think anything below $10,000 or $5,000 would not be an extravagant contribution, so far as that should be—"

(Examination resumed another day.)

Senator Bristow—"Now, Mr. Warburg, when we closed Saturday some Senator asked you in regard to political contributions, and I understood you to say that you contributed to Mr. Wilson's campaign."

Mr. Warburg—"No; my letter says that I offered to contribute; but it was too late. I came back to this country only a few days before the campaign closed."

Senator Bristow—"So that you did not make any contribution?"

Mr. Warburg—"I did not make any contribution; no."

Senator Bristow—"Did any of your firm make contributions to Mr. Wilson's campaign?"

Mr. Warburg—"I think that is a matter of record. Mr. Schiff contributed. I would not otherwise discuss the contributions of my partners, if it was not a matter of record. I think Mr. Schiff was the only one who contributed in our firm."

Senator Bristow—"And you stated that your brother had contributed to Mr. Taft's campaign, as I understand it?"

Mr. Warburg—"I did. But again, I do not want to go into a discussion of my partners' affairs, and I shall stick to that pretty strictly, or we will never get through."

Senator Bristow—"I understood you also to say that no members of your firm contributed to Mr. Roosevelt's campaign."

Mr. Warburg—"I did not say that."

Senator Bristow—"Oh! Did any members of the firm do that?"

Mr. Warburg—"My answer would please you probably; but I shall not answer that, but will repeat that I will not discuss my partners' affairs."

Senator Bristow—"Yes. I understood you to say Saturday that you were a Republican, but when Mr. Roosevelt became a candidate, *you then became a sympathizer with Mr. Wilson and supported him?*"

Mr. Warburg—*"Yes."*

Senator Bristow—*"While your brother was supporting Mr. Taft?"*

Mr. Warburg—*"Yes."*

Senator Bristow—*"And I was interested to know whether any member of your firm supported Mr. Roosevelt."*

Mr. Warburg—*"It is a matter of record that there are.*

Senator Bristow—*"That there are some of them who did?"*

Mr. Warburg—*"Oh, yes."*

Senator Bristow—"Will you please indicate —or do you care to indicate—what members of your firm supported Mr. Roosevelt in that campaign?"

Mr. Warburg—"No, sir; I shall have to go on the principle that I cannot disclose the business of a member of my firm."

The result was this: that in a three-cornered fight between three candidates. Roosevelt, Taft and Wilson, the men who constituted the firm of Kuhn, Loeb & Company, chief Jewish financial institution of the United States, distributed their support among all three. Schiff for Wilson; Felix Warburg for Taft; and an unknown for Roosevelt—was that unknown Mr. Kahn? In any case, Wilson won, and the above examination relates to a member of the firm of Kuhn, Loeb & Company receiving an important appointment which gave him large power over the finances of the United States.

The point of not discussing the affairs of Kuhn, Loeb & Company was frequently made by Mr. Warburg.

"I cannot discuss the affairs of the firm nor my partners, nor be asked to criticize acts of my partners, either to approve them or in any other way. I would like to say that before we come to the point where I would feel that I should not answer any question," said Mr. Warburg.

The principle of this objection was conceded by the Senate Committee, but that it ought to serve as a blanket injunction against a number of pertinent inquiries was doubted.

Senator Bristow—"But you are a partner in this firm, and have not had something to do with its operations and its management?"

Mr. Warburg—"Yes."

Senator Bristow—"Does that not go to show your general views and practices as a financier and as a citizen and as a business man?"

Mr. Warburg—"Yes; but you have got to take them individually . . . . I cannot permit my firm to be drawn into this discussion."

Senator Bristow—"But how can you divest yourself from your firm when you have been one of the managers of the firm?"

Mr. Warburg—"I shall divest myself of the firm."

Senator Bristow—"If the firm has done something that I might think was improper—to illustrate, being called upon to say whether or not I approve your nomination to this responsible position—have I not a right to know what your attitude was in regard to that transaction which your firm performed?"

Mr. Warburg—"Well, inasmuch as my answer there might be a criticism of my firm, I would beg to be excused, and I would leave it to the committee to draw its own conclusions . . . ."

In examining Mr. Warburg about the handling of $100,000,000 Southern Pacific securities, the same difficulty was experienced; Mr. Warburg objected, "but we are getting here again into the transactions of my firm!"

To which Senator Bristow retorted—"Ah! but when you participated in the profits of the transaction, is it not a part of your business life?"

Mr. Warburg—"Certainly it is a part of my business life, and there is no reason why I should not be proud of it. But as a matter of principle I think we should not get into a discussion of the business of my firm."

Senator Bristow—"I am discussing your business."

215

Mr. Warburg—"No, you are discussing the firm's business."

Senator Bristow—"Did you get any of the profits that came from the handling of this $100,000,000?"

Mr. Warburg—"You may take it that whatever my firm did I got my profits—my share in the profits."

Senator Bristow—"Your share in the profits. Now, without being specific, I take it for granted that this was quite material; that that was quite a material interest in size; that is, that you are one of the important members of the firm."

Mr. Warburg—"I am one of the important members of the firm."

Senator Bristow—"Yes, I think the testimony and the report here show that you are the third important member—or the second, which is it?—of the firm."

Mr. Warburg—"We are not numbered."

Senator Bristow—"You are not; all right."

Mr. Warburg—"There is Mr. Jacob H. Schiff who is the senior."

Senator Bristow—"Yes."

Mr. Warburg—"And the others rank very much alike."

Senator Bristow—"Yes. We may take it for granted, then, that whatever profits accrued to your firm in the handling of this business here since you became a member of it, you participated in the profits as one of the partners?"

Mr. Warburg—"Yes, sir."

Senator Bristow—"Yes. So I will assume then, of course, that you participated in the marketing of $113,000,000 of Union Pacific, and so on."

The responsibilities of a member of the Federal Reserve Board, especially such a member as Paul M. Warburg would be (for it was recognized that because of his purpose and connections he would become a dominating factor), were very great, especially at the time when the appointment was being considered. They are as important now, of course, but in a different way; it is not now a question of military safety. This thought was evidently in the mind of the senators, as the following shows:

Senator Hitchcock—"Mr. Warburg, *one of the important functions of the board is to guard the gold supply of the country,* and it has been thought that *it was very important to have men on the board who had at heart only the interests of the United States,* and had no foreign interests or alliances. You have said that you proposed to; divest yourself altogether of your banking connections in Germany. Have you any other interests in Europe?"

"No, not to speak of," said Mr. Warburg. "I may have very unimportant things, like everybody has; but I could dispose of those; it would not amount to anything."

Senator Hitchcock—"Nothing in the line of banking?"

Mr. Warburg—"No."

A few moments later the chairman, Senator Owen, said— (the date was August 1, 1914)—"We are on the eve of a great European war, and the organization of this board is of great national importance."

At this time, Mr. Warburg was a member of the Hamburg firm. He testified (p. 7)—"I am going to leave my Hamburg firm, though the law does not require me to do so."

A part of the German firm of his father and brothers, a part of the American firm to which he and his brother were related by marital as well as financial ties, Mr. Warburg repeatedly said he would break off all business relationships so that he, like Caesar's wife (to quote himself), should be above suspicion.

Issue of June 25, 1921.

LIX.

Jewish Idea of Central Bank for America

ACCORDING to his own statements and the facts, Paul M. Warburg set out to reform the monetary system of the United States, and did so. He had the success which comes to few men, of coming an alien to the United States, connecting himself with the principal Jewish financial firm here, and immediately floating certain banking ideas which have been pushed and manipulated in what is known as the Federal Reserve System.

When Professor Seligman wrote in the Proceedings of the Academy of Political Science that "the Federal Reserve Act will be associated in history with the name of Paul M. Warburg," a Jewish banker from Germany, he wrote the truth. But whether that association will be such as to bring the measure of renown which Professor Selligman implies, the future will reveal.

What the people of the United States do not understand and never have understood is that while the Federal Reserve *Act* was governmental, the whole Federal Reserve *System* is private. It is an officially created private banking system.

Examine the first thousand persons you meet on the street, and 999 will tell you that the Federal Reserve System is a device whereby the United States Government went into the banking business for the benefit of the people. They have an idea that, like the Post Office and the Custom House, a Federal Reserve Bank is a part of the Government's official machinery.

It is natural to feel that this mistaken view has been encouraged by most of the men who are competent to write for the public on this question. Take up the standard encyclopedia, and while you will find no misstatements of fact in them, you will find no direct statement that the Federal Reserve System is a private banking system; the impression carried away by the lay reader is that it is a part of the Government.

The Federal Reserve System is a system of private banks, the creation of a banking aristocracy within an already existing autocracy, whereby a great proportion of banking independence was lost, and whereby it was made possible for speculative financiers to centralize great sums of money for their own purposes, beneficial or not.

That this System was useful in the artificial conditions created by war—useful, that is, for a Government that cannot manage its own business and finances and, like a prodigal son, is always wanting money, and wanting it when it wants it—it has proved, either by reason of its inherent faults or by mishandling, its inadequacy to the problems of peace. It has sadly failed of its promise, and is now under serious question.

Mr. Warburg's scheme succeeded just in time to take care of war conditions, he was placed on the Federal Reserve Board in order to manage his system in practice, and though he was full of ideas then as to how banking could be assisted, he is disappointingly silent now as to how the people can be relieved.

However, this is not a discussion of the Federal Reserve System. General condemnation of it would be stupid. But it is bound to come up for discussion one day, and the discussion will become much freer when people understand that it is a system of privately owned banks, to which have been delegated certain extraordinary privileges, and that it has created a class system within the banking world which constitutes a new order.

Mr. Warburg, it will be remembered, wanted only one central bank. But, because of political considerations, as Professor Seligman tells us, twelve were decided upon. An examination of Mr. Warburg's printed discussions of the subject shows that he at one time considered four, then eight. Eventually, twelve were established. The reason was that one central bank, which naturally would be set up in New York, would give a suspicious country the impression that it was only a new scheme to keep the nation's money flowing to New York. As shown by Professor Seligman, quoted in the last number, Mr. Warburg was not averse to granting anything that would allay popular suspicion without vitiating the real plan.

So, while admitting to the Senators who examined him as to his fitness for membership on the Federal Reserve Board—the Board which fixed the policies of the banks of the Federal Reserve System and told them what to do—that he did not like the 12 district banks idea, he said that his objections to it could "be overcome in an administrative way." That is, the 12 banks could be so handled that the effect would be the same as if there were only one central bank, presumably at New York.

And that is about the way it has resulted, and that will be found to be one of the reasons for the present situation of the country.

There is no lack of money in New York today. Motion picture ventures are being financed into the millions. A big grain selling pool, nursed into existence and counseled by Bernard M. Baruch, has no hesitancy whatever in planning for a $100,000,000 corporation. Loew, the Jewish theatrical man, had no difficulty in opening 20 new theaters this year—

But go into the agricultural states, where the real wealth of the country is in the ground and in the granaries, and you cannot find money for the farmer.

It is a situation which none can deny and which few can explain, because the explanation is not to be found along natural lines. Natural conditions are always easiest to explain. Unnatural conditions wear an air of mystery. Here is the United States, the richest country in the world, containing at the present hour the greatest bulk of wealth to be found anywhere on earth —real, ready, available, usable wealth; and yet it is tied up tight, and cannot move in its legitimate channels, because of manipulation which is going on as regards money.

Money is the last mystery for the popular mind to penetrate, and when it succeeds in getting "on the inside" it will discover that the mystery is not in money at all, but in its manipulation, the things which are done "in an administrative way."

The United States has never had a President who gave evidence of understanding this matter at all. Our Presidents have always had to take their views from financiers. Money is the most public quantity in the country; it is the most federalized and governmentalized thing in the country; and yet, in the present situation, the United States Government has hardly anything to do with it, except to use various means to get it, just as the people have to get it, from those who control it.

The Money Question, properly solved, is the end of the Jewish Question and every other question of a mundane nature.

Mr. Warburg is of the opinion that different rates of interest ought to obtain in different parts of the country. That they have always obtained in different parts of the same state we have always known, but the reason for it has not been discovered. The city grocer can get money from his bank at a lower rate than the farmer in the next county can get it from his bank. Why the agricultural rate of interest has been higher than any other (when money is obtainable; it is not obtainable now) is a question to which no literary nor oratorical financier has ever publicly addressed himself. It is like the fact of the private business nature of the Federal Reserve System—very important, but no authority thinks it worth while to state. The agricultural rate of interest is of great importance, but to discuss it would involve first an admission, and that apparently is not desirable.

In comparing the present Federal Reserve Law with the proposed Aldrich Bill, Mr. Warburg said:

Mr. Warburg—" . . . . .I think that this present law has the advantage of dealing with the entire

221

country and giving them different rates of discount, whereas, as Senator Aldrich's bill was drawn, it would have been very difficult to do that, as it provided for one uniform rate for the whole country, which I thought was rather a mistake."

Senator Bristow—"That is, you can charge a higher rate of interest in one section of the country under the present law, than you charge in another section, while under the Aldrich plan it would have been a uniform rate."

Mr. Warburg—"That is correct."

That is a point worth clearing up. If Mr. Warburg, having educated the bankers, will now turn his attention to the people, and make it clear why one class in the country can get money for business that is not productive of real wealth, while another class engaged in the production of real wealth is treated as outside the interest of banking altogether; if he can make it clear also why money is sold to one class or one section of the country at one price, while to another class and in another section it is sold at a different price, he will be adding to the people's grasp of these matters.

This suggestion is seriously intended. Mr. Warburg has the style, the pedagogical patience, the grasp of the subject which would make him an admirable public teacher of these matters.

What he has already done was planned from the point of view of the interest of the professional financier. It is readily granted that Mr. Warburg desired to organize American finances into a more pliable system. Doubtless in some respects he has wrought important improvements. But he had always the banking house in mind, and he dealt with paper. Now, if taking up a position outside those special interests, he would address himself to the wider interests of the people—not assuming that those interests always run through a banking house—he would do still more than he has yet done to justify his feeling that he really had a mission in coming to this country.

Mr. Warburg is not at all shocked by the idea that the Federal Reserve System is really a new kind of private banking control, because in his European experience he saw that all the central banks were private affairs.

In his essay on "American and European Banking Methods and Bank Legislation Compared," Mr. Warburg says: (the italics are ours)

"It may also be interesting to note that *contrary to a widespread idea, the central banks of Europe are, as a rule, not owned by the governments.* As a matter of fact, neither the English, French, nor German Government owns any stock in the central bank of its country. *The Bank of England is run entirely as a private corporation, the* stockholders electing the board of directors, who rotate in holding the presidency. In France the government appoints the governor and some of the directors. In Germany the government appoints the president and a supervisory board of five members, while the stockholders elect the board of directors."

And again, in his discussion of the Owen-Glass Bill, Mr. Warburg ways:

"The Monetary Commission's plan proceeded on the theory of the Bank of England, *which leaves the management entirely in the hands of business men without giving the government any part in the management or control.* The strong argument in favor of this theory is that central banking, like any other banking, is based on 'sound credit,' that the judging of credits is a matter of business which should be left in the hands of business men, *and that the government should be kept out of business.* . . . The Owen-Glass Bill proceeds, in this respect, more on the lines of the Banque de France and the German Reichsbank, the presidents and boards of which are to a certain extent appointed by the government. *These central banks, while legally private corporations,* are semi-governmental organs inasmuch as *they are permitted to issue the notes of the nation*—particularly where there are elastic note issues, as in almost all countries except England—and inasmuch as *they are the custodians of practically the entire metallic reserves of the country and the keepers of the government funds.* Moreover in questions of national policy *the government must rely on the willing and loyal co-operation of these central organs."*

That is a very illuminating passage. It will be well worth the reader's time, especially the reader who has always been puzzled by financial matters, to turn over in his mind the facts here given by a great Jewish financial expert about the central bank idea. Observe the phrases:

(a) "without giving the government any part in the management or control."

(b) "these central banks, while legally private corporations .... are permitted to issue the notes of the nation."

(c) "they are custodians of practically the entire metallic reserves of the nation and the keepers of the government funds."

(d) "in questions of national policy, the government must rely on the willing and loyal co-operation of these central organs."

It is not now a question whether these things are right or wrong; it is merely a question of understanding that they constitute the fact.

It is specially notable that in paragraph (d) it is a fair deduction that in questions of national policy, the government will simply have to depend not only on the patriotism but also to an extent on the permission and counsel of the financial organizations. That is a fair interpretation: questions of national policy are, by this method, rendered dependent upon the financial corporations.

Let that point be clear, quite regardless of the question whether or not this is the way national policies should be determined.

Mr. Warburg said that he believed in a certain amount of government control—but not too much. He said: "In strengthening the government control, the Owen-Glass Bill therefore moved in the right direction; but it went too far and fell into the other and even more dangerous extreme."

The "more dangerous extreme" was, of course, the larger measure of government supervision provided for, and the establishment of a number of Federal Reserve Banks out in the country.

Mr. Warburg had referred to this before; he had agreed to the larger number only because it seemed to be an unavoidable political concession. It has already been shown, by Professor Seligman, that Mr. Warburg was alive to the necessity of veiling a little here and there, and "putting on" a little yonder, for the sake of conciliating a suspicious public. There was also the story of the bartender and the cash register.

Mr. Warburg thinks he understands the psychology of America. In this respect he reminds one of the reports of Mr. von Bernstorff and Captain Boy-Ed of what the Americans were likely to do or not to do. In the Political Science Quarterly of December, 1920, Mr. Warburg tells how, on a then recent visit to Europe, he was asked by men of all countries what the United States was going to do. He assured them that America was a little tired just then, but that she would come round all right. And then, harking back to his efforts of placing his monetary system on the Americans, he said:

"I asked them to be patient with us until after the election, and *I cited to them our experiences with monetary reform.* I reminded them how the Aldrich plan had failed because, at that time, a Republican President had lost control of a Congress ruled by a Democratic majority; how the Democrats in their platform damned this plan and any central banking system; and how, *once in full power, the National Reserve Association was evolved, not to say camouflaged, by them into the Federal Reserve System."*

Remembering this play before the public, and the play behind the scenes, this "camouflaging," as Mr. Warburg says, of one thing into another, he undertook to assure his friends in Europe that regardless of what the political platforms said, the United States would do substantially what Europe hoped it would. Mr. Warburg's basis for that belief was, as he said, his experience with the way the central bank idea went through in spite of the advertised objection of all parties. He believes that with Americans it is possible to get what you want if you just play the game skillfully. His experience with monetary reform seems to have fathered that belief in him.

Politicians may be necessary pawns to play in the game, but as members of the government Mr. Warburg does not want them in banking. They are not bankers, he says; they don't understand; banking is nothing for a government man to meddle with. He may be good enough for the Government of the United States; he is not good enough for banking.

"In our country," says Mr. Warburg, referring to the United States, "with every untrained amateur a candidate for any office, *where friendship or help in a presidential campaign, financial or political, has always given a claim for political preferment,* where the bids for votes and public favor are ever present in the politician's mind, . . . *a direct government management, that is to say, a political management, would prove fatal.* . . . .There can be no doubt but that, as drawn at present (1913), with two cabinet officers members of the Federal Reserve Board, and with the vast powers vested in the latter, the Owen-Glass Bill would bring about direct government management."

And that, of course, in Mr. Warburg's mind, is not only "dangerous," but "fatal."

Mr. Warburg had almost his whole will in the matter. And what is the result?

Turn to the testimony of Bernard M. Baruch, when he was examined with reference to the charge that certain men close to President Wilson had profited to the extent of $60,000,000 on stock market operations which they entered into on the strength of advance information of what the

President was to say in his next war note—the famous "leak" investigation, as it was called; one of the several investigations in which Mr. Baruch was closely questioned.

In that investigation Mr. Baruch was laboring to show that he had not been in telephone communication with Washington, especially with certain men who were supposed to have shared the profits of the deals. The time was December, 1916. Mr. Warburg was then safely settled on the Federal Reserve Board, which he had kept quite safe from Government intrusion.

The Chairman—"Of course the records of the telephone company here, the slips, will show the persons with whom you talked."

Mr. Baruch—"Do you wish me to say, sir? I will state who they are."

The Chairman—"Yes, I think you might."

Mr. Baruch—"I called up two persons; one, Mr. Warburg, whom I did not get, and one, Secretary McAdoo, whom I did get—both in reference to the same matter. Would you like to know the matter?"

The Chairman—"Yes, I think it is fair that you should state it."

Mr. Baruch—"I called up the Secretary, because someone suggested to me—*asked me to suggest an officer for the Federal Reserve Bank,* and I called him up in reference to that, and discussed the matter with him I think *two or three times,* but it was suggested to me that I make the suggestion, and I did so." (pp. 570-571)

Mr. Campbell—"Mr. Baruch, who asked you for a suggestion for an appointee for the Federal Reserve Bank here?"

Mr. Baruch—" Mr. E. M. House."

Mr. Campbell—"Did Mr. House tell you to call Mr. McAdoo up and make the recommendation?"

Mr. Baruch—"I will tell you exactly how it occurred: *Mr. House called me up* and said that there was a vacancy on the

Federal Reserve Board, and he said, 'I don't know anything about those fellows down there, and I would like you to make a suggestion.' *And I suggested the name,* which he thought was a very good one, and he said to me, 'I wish you would call up the Secretary and tell him.' I said, 'I do not see the necessity; I will tell you.' 'No,' he said, 'I would prefer you to call him up.' " (p. 575)

There we have an example of the Federal Reserve "kept out of politics," kept away from government management which would not only be "dangerous," but "fatal."

Barney Baruch, the New York stock plunger, who never owned a bank in his life, was called up by Colonel E. M. House, the arch-politician of the Wilson Administration, and thus the great Federal Reserve Board was supplied another member.

A telephone call kept within a narrow Jewish circle and settled by a word from one Jewish stock dealer—that, in practical operation, was Mr. Warburg's great monetary reform. Mr. Baruch calling up Mr. Warburg to give the name of the next appointee of the Federal Reserve Board, and calling up Mr. McAdoo, secretary of the United States Treasury, and set in motion to do it by Colonel E. M. House— is it any wonder the Jewish mystery in the American war government grows more and more amazing?

But, as Mr. Warburg has written—"friendship or help in *a presidential campaign,* financial or political, has always given a claim to political preferment." And, as Mr. Warburg urges, this is a country "with every untrained amateur a candidate for office," and naturally, with such men comprising the government, they must be kept at a safe distance from monetary affairs.

As if to illustrate the ignorance thus charged, along comes Mr. Baruch, who quotes Colonel House as saying, "I don't know anything about those fellows down there and I would like you to make a suggestion. It is permissible to doubt that Mr. Baruch correctly quotes Colonel House. It is permissible to doubt that all that Colonel House confessed was his ignorance about "those fellows." There was a good understanding between these two men, too good an understanding for the alleged telephone conversation to be taken strictly at its face value. It is possibly quite true that Mr. House is not a financier. Certainly, Mr. Wilson was not. In the long roll of Presidents only a handful have been, and those who have been have been regarded as most drastic in their proposals.

But this whole matter of ignorance, as charged by Mr. Warburg, sounds like an echo of the Protocols:

"The administrators chosen by us from the masses *will not be persons trained for government,* and consequently they will easily become pawns in our game, played by *our learned and talented counsellors, specialists educated form early childhood to administer world affairs."*

In the Twentieth Protocol, wherein the great financial plan of world subversion and control is disclosed, there is another mention of the rulers' ignorance of financial problems.

It is a coincidence that, while he does not use the term "ignorance," Mr. Warburg is quite outspoken concerning the benighted state in which he found this country, and he is also outspoken about the "untrained amateurs" who are candidates for every office. These, he says, are not fitted to take part in the control of monetary affairs. But Mr. Warburg is. He says so. He admits that it was his ambition from the moment he came here an alien Jewish-German banker, to change our financial affairs more to his liking. More than that, he has succeeded; he has succeeded, he himself says, more than most men do in a lifetime; he has succeeded, Professor Selligman says, to such an extent that throughout history the name of Paul M. Warburg and that of the Federal Reserve System shall be united.

Issue of July 2, 1921

LX.

How Jewish International Finance Functions

"Such has been the development of international bankers that they can no longer be regarded in their professional capacity as the nationals of any country, entitled to do business under their own government's supervision exclusively. They are really world citizens, with world-wide interests, and as such ought to be made amenable to some form of supernational control."--George Pattullo, in *Saturday Evening Post.*

N OT only did the Jewish financial firm of Kuhn, Loeb & Company use far-sighted prudence in splitting its political support—one Warburg supporting Wilson, another Warburg supporting Taft and an unnamed member of the firm supporting Roosevelt, all at one time, as Paul M. Warburg testified—but it split its activities in several other ways also.

The international interests of the Jews comprising this firm are worthy of note. The influence which forced the United States to repudiate a commercial treaty with Russia while Russia was a friendly country (1911), and thus to compel all business between the United States and Russia to pass through German-Jewish hands, was generated by Jacob H. Schiff. Russia seems to have been the country on which he chose to focus his activities. The full story is told in THE DEARBORN INDEPENDENT of January 15, 1921, under the title "Taft Once Tried to Resist the Jews—and Failed," and is reprinted in Volume II of the booklet containing this series.

Mr. Schiff's activity consisted in forcing the Congress of the United States to do a thing that was repugnant to the reason and conscience of President Taft, and which he personally refused to do or to recommend. Mr. Schiff left the White House in great anger with the threat, "This means war." It did not mean as much war as it might have, for President Taft acquiesced gracefully in the Jewish victory and has since been extremely laudatory of them on the public platform.

Mr. Schiff's firm also helped finance the Japanese war against Russia, and in return desired Japan as a Jewish ally. The wily Japs, however, saw the game and kept their relations with Mr. Schiff to purely business matters. Which fact is well worth bearing in mind when reading the widespread propaganda for war with Japan. If you will give particular attention, you will observe that the same interests which are just now engaged in most loudly "defending" the Jew, are most active in spreading anti-Japanese sentiments in this country.

The Japanese war with Russia, however, enabled Mr. Schiff to advance his plan to undermine the Russian Empire, as it has now been accomplished by Jewish Bolshevism. With funds provided by him, the basic principles of what is now known as Bolshevism, were sown among the Russian prisoners of war in Japan, who were sent back as apostles of destruction. Then followed the horrible murder of Nicholas Romanoff, Czar of Russia, with his wife, his crippled son, and his young daughters, the full tale of which has now been told by the Jew who managed the crime.

For the part he played in destroying Russia, Mr. Schiff was wildly hailed in New York the night the news came that the Emperor had abdicated.

Meanwhile, the Jew who was "to take the Czar's job" (as the common New York ghetto phrase ran, weeks before the event) had left New York to be in waiting.

This Jew was passed out of the United States at the request of a very high American personage whose subservience to the Jews was one of the marvels of the past seven years.

Halted by the British, this Jew was released from their toils at the request of a very high American personage. And thus, the Jewish Bolshevik Revolution in Russia, the program of which was made in America, was set in operation without a hitch.

This whole firm is German Jewish, its members having originated in Germany. It had German connections. How far it maintained those connections through all subsequent events is a separate question.

Mr. Otto Kahn's allotted portion of the world seems to be Great Britain and France. Mr. Kahn is of German origin, like the rest of the firm, but he has not publicly shown such concern for Germany as have the other members. Mr. Schiff was once very active for the settlement of a peace on the basis of a victorious Germany. Mr. Paul M. Warburg also had interests, discussion of which is postponed for the present. But Mr. Kahn succeeded, though the connivance of American authority and the excessive repression of the newspapers, in conveying the impression that by some species of occult separatism he was not "German-minded."

Therefore Mr. Kahn flits lightly everywhere—except Germany. He is sufficiently French to be able to tell in the first column on the first page of *Le Matin* on what terms America will do business with Europe, and he speaks as one having authority. He is sufficiently British to have thought of standing for the British Parliament, when an unfortunate event made it necessary for him to remain in the United States. Mr. Kahn sometimes flits farther East into the more Jewish portions of Europe, and his comings and goings are marked by certain changes with which his name remains most ostentatiously disconnected.

Mr. Kahn has very recently been telling France on what terms the United States will help her. There apparently being no other spokesman, Mr. Kahn's word is accepted as authority. France is one of the most Judaized countries in the world, the haunt of International Jewish Financiers who exercise their power (thus saving France the trouble of passing laws) to keep the emigrant Jew out of France; so that France presents the spectacle of being Judaized by Jewish finance and not by immigrant Semitic hordes, and is thus a fit platform from which Mr. Otto Herman Kahn may utter his pronouncements.

In his last declaration to France, Mr. Kahn prepares her to expect little by stating that "America is a country of immense resources; but the actual money which the people have at their disposal is comparatively limited." True enough. It was a member of Mr. Kahn's firm who invented a monetary system which was promised to keep *money* in more equal relation to *wealth.*

But as he goes on telling what America will and will not do (The American people knowing nothing about it meanwhile) Mr. Kahn discovers with great enthusiasm a place where he thinks American capital can be placed, namely, *in the development of the vast and immensely rich colonial empire of France."*

And pray where is that? Any Frenchman would tell you now, "In Syria." Syria—ah!—that part of the East where the natives are loudly complaining that the Jews are driving them out contrary to every written and moral law. The Jewish powers have already succeeded in getting French troops over there; bad blood has been caused between France and Great Britain; the Jews on both sides are playing for the middle; and here is Mr. Otto Kahn himself pledging American capital to the development of the French colonial empire! Talk to any Syrian who knows his country's present status, and he will interpret Mr. Kahn's words very vividly.

One of the nicest bits of work Mr. Kahn has done is to denounce "pro-German propaganda" which he says has exasperated Americans in favor of France. Next to committing the United States to an undying admiration for Briand, this is really his finest bit. Especially, with Partner Paul playing the German sympathy string! It is a great international orchestra, this Jewish financial firm; it can play The Star Spangled Banner, Die Wacht am Rhein, the Marseillaise, and God Save the King in one harmonious rendering, paying obsequious attention to the prejudices of each.

Next come the Warburgs. Their interest is, of course, in Germany. Paul stated in his testimony given at the beginning of the World War that he had interests in Hamburg and would dispose of them. The war came on. The Jewish government in the United States was augmented. Mr. Warburg was no mean figure, as precious articles have shown.

The Warburgs are three in number. Felix M. is the other one in America. He appears but slightly in public affairs although he is a member of the American Jewish Committee and of the firm of Kuhn, Loeb & Company. His retiring habit, however, does not argue lack of consequence. He was of sufficient consequence, Jewishly, to have bestowed upon him a sort of honorary rabbinical degree of "Haber" which entitles him to be known as "Haber Rabbi Baruch Ben Moshe." He is the only Jew in America upon whom the title has ever been conferred.

Max Warburg represents the family in its native land, Max Warburg had as much to do with the German war government as his family and financial colleagues in America had to do with the United States war government. As has been recounted in the press the world over, the brother from America and the brothers from Germany both met at Paris as government representatives in determining the peace. There were so many Jews in the German delegation that it was known by the term "Kosher," also as "the Warburg delegation," and there were so many Jews in the American delegation that the delegates from the minor countries of Europe looked upon the United States as a Jewish country which through unheard-of generosity had elected a non-Jew as its President.

Max Warburg is an interesting character also as regards the establishment of Bolshevism in Russia. The Jews had several objectives in the war, and one of them was "get

234

Russia." To this end the German Jews worked very assiduously. Because Russia was a member of the Allies, the work of German Jews was made the easier. But the fact that Russia was an ally made no difference with the Jews who were resident in Allied countries. Win or loose, Russia must be destroyed. It is the testimony of history that it was not so much the German military prowess as the Jewish intrigue that accomplished the downfall of that empire.

In this work Max Warburg was a factor. His bank is noted in a dispatch published by the United States Government as being one whence funds were forwarded to Trotzky for use in destroying Russia. Always against Russia, not for German reasons, but for Jewish reasons, which in this particular instance coincided. Warburg and Trotzky—against Russia!

Poor John Spargo, who ought to know better, denies all this—while every American who comes back from Russia, even those who went over there pro-Bolshevik, yes, and returned Jews themselves, proclaim it.

The crushing fact is that Bolshevism is not only Jewish in Russia, and in America, but it is Jewish in the higher regions of Jewry where better things ought to exist. Take Walter Rathenau, a German Jew on the plane of the Warburgs. Rathenau was the inventor of the Bolshevik system of centralization of industry, material and money. The Soviet Government asked Rathenau directly for the plans, and received them directly from him. Max Warburg's bank held the money; Walter Rathenau's mind held the plans—which makes it a pertinent question: If Bolshevism can be so Jewish outside of Russia, what hinders it being Jewish inside Russia?

It is a most significant fact that, as in Washington, the most constant and privileged visitors to the White House were Jews, so in Berlin the only private telephone wire to the Kaiser was owned by Walter Rathenau. Not even the Crown Prince could reach the Kaiser except through the ordinary telephone connections. It was the same in London. It was the same in Paris. It was the same in Petrograd—in Russia which so "persecuted" the race that controlled it then and controls it now.

Now, this sketchy outline of the internationalism of the firm of Kuhn, Loeb & Company is not offered as the result of keen research, for the facts are found on the very surface of the matter, for anyone to see. What is revealed by research is this: whether Mr. Schiff's interest in Russia had underground features which affected the welfare of the nations; whether Mr. Kahn's flitting missions here and there, which he made with great freedom during the war, were wholly taken up with the business announced in the public notices; and whether Mr. Warburg, whose interest in Germany has not abated, to judge from his recent utterances, was able to retain complete neutrality of mind during the war. These are questions of value. Obviously, they are not easy to answer. But they can be answered.

It was a family enterprise, this international campaign. Jacob Schiff swore to destroy Russia. Paul M. Warburg was his brother-in-law. Max Warburg, of Hamburg, banker of the Bolsheviks, was thus brother-in-law to Jacob Schiff's wife and daughter.

Speaking of the far-sighted manner in which the house of Kuhn, Loeb & Company disposes itself over world affairs, there is also the curious fact that in this Jewish firm is one who goes to a Christian church—a most heinous thing for a Jew to do. Split three ways in American politics and as many ways as international matters require, we find this firm split two says with regard to religion. Mr. Kahn professes—at least he attends—a Christian church and is accounted an adherent of it. Yet he is not ostracized. His name is not taboo. The Jews do not curse him. He is not denounced as a renegade. The Jews have not buried him out of mind, as they do others who desert the faith.

This presents a strange situation when it is considered. Not to recount again the horror and reprehension and active antagonism with which Jews view such a desertion, suffice it to say that there is no greater marvel than that of Jacob H. Schiff retaining in the firm of Kuhn, Loeb & Company a "renegade" Jew. He could not have done it; every fiber of his intensely Jewish nature would have rebelled against it. Yet there it is!

Without going further into this ingenious system of covering all vital points from one center, enough has been said to show one busy Jewish financial firm with which political matters, national and international, is almost a profession. The family of Warburg high in the controlling group of two countries, and enemy countries at that. The family of Warburg high in the negotiations of world peace and the discussions of a League of Nations. The family of Warburg now advising the world from both sides of the earth, what to do next. It was probably with more reason than the general public surmised that a New York paper printed during the Peace Conference an article headed, "Watch the Warburgs!"

The fact seems to be that, as Mr. Pattullo is quoted as saying at the head of this article, the international financiers have been so engrossed in world money that the sense of national responsibility sometimes becomes blurred in their minds. They desire everything—war, negotiations and peace—to be conducted in such a way as to react favorably on the money market. For that is their market: money is what they buy and sell: and because money has no fixed price, it is a market which offers the widest opportunity for the trickster and swindler. One cannot play such tricks with stone or corn or metals, but with money as the commodity everything is possible.

Mr. Warburg is already very much interested about the treatment to be accorded foreign securities in the next war. Readers of the daily newspapers may recall that recently a demand was made for the gold in the Reichsbank, which was resisted on the ground that the Reichsbank, although the central bank of Germany, was really a private concern—just as Paul Warburg said it was and just as he has insisted that our own Federal Reserve System should be, and which it is. There is far-sighted wisdom in that, with a view to possible defeat in war.

Mr. Warburg is apparently quite disapproving of the treatment accorded alien enemy property "by some countries." He quotes a French banker throughout— nationality not stated—and drives home his point. The French banker used as an illustration a possible war between England and France (this was only last year) and said that the bankers in each country would proceed to withdraw their mutual balances and securities, for fear of confiscation, and that such a course would precipitate a panic.

To which Mr. Warburg adds: "I think that our bankers ought carefully to study this very serious question. We have nothing to gain and much to lose by joining in a policy of disregarding the rights of private property. We shall probably, in the course of time, become the largest owners of foreign securities and properties, which would become endangered in case we were drawn into war. To me, however, it is of greater interest that nothing be done that might stand in the way of making the United States the gold reserve country of the world . . . . "

Such talk passes with too little scrutiny. It bears a strong reflection of recent events which should not be overlooked. Moreover, it presents a grandiose vision which is supposed to command instant agreement because of its appeal to superficial national pride and selfish ambition.

If what Mr. Warburg says is an intimation that the International Jews are planning to move their money market to the United States, it is safe to say that the United States does not want it. We have the warning of history as to what this would mean. It has meant that in turn Spain, Venice, Great Britain or Germany received the blame and suspicion of the world for what the Jewish financiers have done. It is a most important consideration that most of the national animosities that exist today arose out of resentment against what the Jewish money power did under the camouflage of national names. "The British did this," the "Germans did this," when it was the International Jew who did it, the nations being but the marked spaces on his checker board.

Today, around the world the blaming word is heard, "The United States did this. If it were not for the United States the world would be in better shape. The Americans are a sordid, greedy, cruel people." Why? Because the Jewish money power is largely centered here and is making money out of both our immunity and Europe's distress, playing one against the other; and because so many of the so-called "American business men" abroad today are not Americans at all—they are Jews, and in many cases as misrepresentative of their own race as they are of the Americans.

The United States does not want the transfer of All-Judaan to this soil. We do not desire to stand as a gold god above the nations. We would serve the nations, and we would protect them, but we would do both in the basis of real values, not in the name or under the sign of gold.

On the one hand Mr. Warburg recites pitiful facts about Germany in order to raise sympathy for her, and on the other hand he stimulates the gold lust of the United States. The plight of Germany is entirely due to the forces from which the United States has only narrowly escaped; and to harken to international Jewish plans for the rehabilitation of Germany is to be in danger of approving plans which will fasten Jewish domination more strongly on that unhappy country than it is now. Germany has paid dearly for her Jews. The Warburg voice that speaks for her would seem indeed to be the voice of Jacob, but the hand that proposes financial dealings is that of Esau.

The internationalism of the Warburgs is no longer in doubt, and cannot be denied. Felix Warburg hung on to the Hamburg connection longer than did Paul, but the breakage of either was probably perfunctory. At the same time that Felix left the Hamburg firm of his brother, Max, a Mr. Stern also left the Frankfort firm of Stern, and both became very active on the Allies side, taking sides against the German nation as lustily as anyone could. "Impossible!" say those who fancy that a German Jew is a German. Not at all impossible; the Jew's loyalty is to the Jewish nation; what the Jew himself refers to as his "cover nationality" may count or not as he himself elects.

This statement is always met with frothing wrath by the Jews' "gentile fronts" in the purchased pro-Jewish press. But here is an example: Do you remember "The Beast of Berlin," that lurid piece of war propaganda? You did not, perhaps, know that its producer was a German Jew, Carl Laemmle. His German birth did not prevent him making money out of his film, and his film does not prevent him annually going back in state to his birthplace. This year he goes accompanied by Abe Stern, his treasurer; Lee Kohlmar, his director; and Harry Reichenbach--a list of names duplicable in any movie group.

Messrs. Stern and Warburg, of Frankfort and Hamburg, respectively, and away from home perhaps only temporarily, were not concerned about the fate of the "Huns," but they were immensely concerned about the fate of Jewish money power in Germany.

To indicate how blind the public has been to the inter-allied Jewish character of much of the world's important international financial activity, note this from the *Living Age* earlier in the year:

"According to the *Svensk Handelstidning,* the recent American loan of $5,000,000 to Norway was really the outcome of an agreement between the Hamburg firm of Warburg & Company and the New York bankers, Kuhn, and Loeb. It is regarded as a significant sign of the times that a German firm should be responsible for an American loan to a neutral country. The conditions subject to which this money was borrowed, are not regarded as very favorable to

Norway, and no marked effect on the rate of exchange between the two countries has followed."

Note, in the light of all the statements made about Kuhn, Loeb & Company, and the Warburgs in particular, the assumption in the above quotation that the transaction was really between a German and an American firm. It was principally an arrangement between the Warburgs themselves in family counsel. But the loan will pass in Norway as *"an American loan,"* and the fact that the terms of the loan *"are not regarded as very favorable to Norway"* will react upon Scandinavian opinion of this country. It goes without saying that *"no marked effect on the rate of exchange between the two countries has followed,"* for that would not be the object of such a loan. The dislocation of exchange is not unprofitable.

It would be most interesting to know in how far Kuhn, Loeb & Company has endeavored to readjust the rate of exchange.

During the war, Kuhn, Loeb & Company made a loan to the city of Paris. Considerable German comment was occasioned by this—naturally. And it is very well worthy of record that in the city of Hamburg, where Max Warburg does business, the chief of police issued this order:

"Further mention in the press of loans made by the firm of Kuhn, Loeb & Company to the city of Paris, and unfavorable comments thereon, are forbidden."

The following story is vouched for as reliable, and if in one or two minor details it does not represent the exact fact, it is a trustworthy illustration of how certain things were done:

"A Jewish international banking corporation bought up the mining and other similar concessions of Jugo-Slavia, and consequently the policy pushed at the Peace Conference was that which was most convenient for that group. An understanding on the Fiume question was in progress between Wilson and Nitti. Certain concessions had been agreed upon and Wilson was willing to negotiate, when Oscar Straus and one of the Warburgs appeared on the scene. Wilson changed his attitude over night and afterward insisted on the Jugo-Slavia solution of the problem. The way in which concessions had been bought through that territory was a disgrace, and observers expected that it would play an important part at the Peace Conference."

The financiers are not the only International Jews in the world. The revolutionary Jews, of all countries and none, are international also. They have seized upon the idea of Christian internationalism, which means amity between nations, and have used it as a weapon with which to weaken nationality. They know as well as anyone that there can be no internationalism except on the basis of strong nationalism, but they count on "cover words" to advance their plan.

Enough transpired between the lower and higher Jewish groups of every large center during the war to render it imperative that Jewry confess, repent and repudiate the madness that has ruled it, or else boldly assert and espouse it before the world.

Certainly enough has transpired to render it desirable that the American people look again into the purposes of those Jews who were instrumental in reorganizing our financial system at a most critical time in the world's history.

Max Warburg was apparently strong enough to suppress German discussion of his brother's activity in America. The Warburgs at present resident in America must suffer it, therefore, that American comment be made as full as need be.

Issue of July 9, 1921.

LXI.

Jewish Power and America's Money Famine

T HE international Jewish banker who has no country but plays them all against one another, and the International Jewish proletariat that roams from land to land in search of a peculiar type of economic opportunity, are not figments of the imagination except to the non-Jew who prefers a lazy laxity of mind.

Of these classes of Jews, one or both are at the heart of the problems that disturb the world today. The immigration problem is Jewish. The money question is Jewish. The tie-up of world politics is Jewish. The terms of the Peace Treaty are Jewish. The diplomacy of the world is Jewish. The moral question in movies and theaters is Jewish. The mystery of the illicit liquor business is Jewish.

These facts are unfortunate as well as unpleasant for the Jew, and it is squarely up to him to deal with the facts, and not waste time in trying to destroy those who define the facts. These facts are interpreted by the Jew and the anti-Semite with strange extremes of blindness. The Jew never gets the world's point of view at all; he always gets the anti-Semite's point of view; and the anti-Semite is equally at fault in always getting the Jew's point of view. What both need is to get society's point of view, which is the one being set forth in this present series of articles.

To say that the immigration problem is Jewish does not mean that Jews must be prohibited entry to any country; it means that they must become rooted to a country in loyal citizenship, as no doubt some are, and as no doubt most are not. To say that the money question is Jewish does not mean that Jews must get out of finance; it means that they must rid finance of the Jewish idea which has always been to use money to get a strangle-hold on men and business concerns, instead of using finance to help general business. To say that the tie-up of world politics is Jewish does not mean that Jews, as human beings, are to be denied a voice in affairs; it means that they must give up trying to make the world revolve around the Jewish nation as its axis. To describe the influence of the Jew on the theater is not to demand that he leave the theater, but it is to demand that he rid the theater of his idea that sensualism is entertaining.

The Jewish Question is first for the Jews to solve; if not, the world will have to solve it for them. They may stay in business, say the theater, for example, if they will cease spoiling the theater; if they do not cease, the theater will be taken away from them just as certainly as that day follows night. The world has been patient and the world will be fair, but the world knows the limit of imposition.

It is not the true Jewishness of the Jew, nor yet the nationalism of the Jew that is on trial, but his anti-national internationalism. A true Mosaic Jew—not a Talmud Jew—would be a good citizen. A nationalist Jew would at least be logical. But an international Jew has proved an abomination, because his internationalism is focused on his own racial nationalism which in turn is founded on this ingrained belief that the rest of humanity is inferior to him and by right his prey. Jewish leaders may indulge in all the platitudes they possess, the fact which they cannot deny is that the Jew has for centuries regarded the "goyim" as beneath him and legitimately his spoil.

The internationalism of the Jew is confessed everywhere by him. Listen to a German banker: imagine the slow, oily voice in which he said:

"We are international bankers. Germany lost the war?—what of it?—that is an affair of the army. We are international bankers."

And that was the attitude of every international Jewish banker during the war. The nations were in strife? What of it? It was like a Dempsey-Carpentier bout in New Jersey, or a baseball game in Chicago—an affair of the fighters--"we are international bankers."

A nation is being hamstrung by artificial exchange rates; another by the sucking of money out of its channels of trade; what of it to the international banker?—he has his own game to play. Hard times bring more plums tumbling off the tree into the baskets of the international bankers than does any other kind of times. Wars and panics are the Jewish international bankers' harvests.

Citizens wake up with a start to find that even the white nations are hardly allowed to see each other nowadays except through Jewish eyes. When the United States supposedly speaks to France, through whom does she speak? All that France sees is Otto H. Kahn! Why must a Jew represent the United States of America to France? When France supposedly speaks to the United States, through whom is it done? Through Viviani, Jewish in every thought and method. Now they are talking of sending Millerand over, another Jew. Britain sends Lord Reading. Germany sent Dr. Dernberg. And to other countries the United States sent Morgenthau, Strauss, Warburg, and lesser Jewlings.

It comes with something of a shock to learn that Foch is coming to the United States. We have not seen a Frenchman since Joffre visited us. It is good to see men of the white race come across the sea as if to reassure us that white men still live in those countries. The business of the Peace Conference was done by Jews—has it come to a point where international diplomacy is to become a Jewish monopoly also? Must the special conversations between France, Britain and the United States be held through Jewish interpreters, while Anglo-

Saxons and true Frenchmen do the routine embassy work--or shall it be possible for the non-Jewish nations to see one another occasionally through non-Jewish representatives?

Internationalism is not a Jewish conviction, but a Jewish business device. It is most profitable. In diplomacy and at the immigrant station, internationalism pays. Jews interpret nation to nation in the high rites of special conversations between governments; Jewish interpreters swarm at the ports of every country also, where the poor swarm in. It was stated in the House of Lords the other day that most of the trouble in Palestine was caused by Jewish interpreters. It was charged that the Jewish administration added an extra language to the official list in order to make Jewish interpreters indispensable.

Go through the government of the United States, where the income tax secrets are kept, where the Federal Reserve secrets are kept, where the State Department secrets are kept—and you will find Jews sitting at the very spot where International Jewry desires them to sit, and where nothing is kept from their knowledge.

Go abroad and come back to your country, and a Jew will open the gate to let you in, or close it to keep you out—as he chooses.

"Will you be going to Detroit while you are here?" asked a Jewish government agent of a gentleman entering the country on a visit a few weeks ago.

"I may go to Detroit," was the reply.

"Well, you go to the damned DEARBORN INDEPENDENT and tell them a Jew let you into this country," said the government agent.

What the visitor replied is known, but had better not be quoted. The American Jewish Committee might shriek that the people were being incited to pogroms.

The incident, however, is but a sample of what is occurring every day. The truth about the Jewish Question in the United States is perhaps the one form of truth that cannot be indiscriminately told.

The international Jewish bankers regard themselves as in similar fashion "letting" the nations do this or that, regarding the nations not as fatherlands but as customers—and as customers in the Jewish sense. If an army wins or loses, if a government succeeds or fails, what of it?—that is their affair— "we are international bankers," and we win, whoever loses.

For international Jewish bankers, the war is not over. The period of actual hostilities and the emergencies of the nations were but the opening of the trade. The ready cash was skimmed in then—all the cash the world had. True, some of it had to be distributed among the people as war wages and bonuses, in order to keep the struggle going, but this was soon recovered through the means of high prices, artificial scarcities and the orgy of extravagance deliberately organized and stimulated among the people. That phase over, and money disappeared.

Is there any more tragic joke than that diligently disseminated in this country—"The United States has more gold than any other country in the world"? Where is it? How long since you have seen a piece of gold? Where is all this gold—is it locked up in the Treasury of the United States Government? Why, that government is in debt, desperately trying to economize, cannot pay a soldier bonus because the finances of the country cannot stand it! Where is that gold? It may be *in* the United States, but it does not belong *to* the United States.

The American farmer, and those American industries which were not "wise" to the tricks of international Jewish bankers, and who were nipped by small loans, are wondering where all this money is. Furthermore, Europe, suffering from every possible lack, is looking to us and wondering where the money is.

The dispatch in a London paper may throw light on the matter: (italics are ours)

"It is learned today that new gold shipments aggregating $2,800,000 are consigned to Kuhn, Loeb &

Company, New York, making nearly $129,000,000 imported by that firm since the movement started. In responsible banking circles the belief is expressed that some of the *German* coin recently imported by the firm is *from Russia, instead of Germany,* as generally supposed."

This dispatch, coupled with one printed in a former article which showed Warburg & Company of Germany arranging with Kuhn, Loeb & Company of New York for a $5,000,000 loan to Norway, is not devoid of light on the question—*Where is the money?*

The Jewish international banking system may be easily described. First, there is the international Jewish headquarters. This was in Germany. It had ramifications in Russia, Italy, France, Great Britain and the South American states. (South American Jewry is very menacing.) Germany and Russia were the two countries scheduled for punishment by the International Jewish bankers because these two countries were most aware of the Jew. They have been punished; that job is done.

Jewish political headquarters, as related to the internal affairs of the Jews, was also located in Germany, but the headquarters dealing with the "goyim" was in France. Statements have been made that the political center of Jewry has been transplanted to the United States. But these statements have been made by American Jews whose wish may have been father to the thought. During the Wilson Administration it was possible for a Jew to think and to hope this, but affairs have slightly changed. The ousting of American Jews from the Zionist movement at the behest of Eastern Jews indicates that if the political center of world Jewry has shifted to the United States, the *power* is still in the hands of *aliens* resident here. The center is still in Jewry; the United States is merely a square on Jewry's world checker-board.

But, wherever the financial and political world centers may be, each country is separately handled. In every country—the United States, Mexico and the republics of South America; in France, England, Italy, Germany, Austria—yes, and in Japan—there is an international Jewish banking firm which stands at the head of the group for that country. Thus, the chief Jewish firm in the United States is Kuhn, Loeb & Company, of which one of the members is Paul M. Warburg brother of M. Warburg & Company, of Hamburg; and another member of which is Otto H. Kahn, resident successively of Germany, Great Britain and the United States, and self-appointed financial spokesman for the United States to France and Great Britain. Great Britain and France seldom see a special American spokesman who is not a Jew. That may be the reason why they reciprocate by sending Jews to us, thinking perhaps that we prefer them.

Paul M. Warburg was the inventor, perfector and director of the Federal Reserve System of the United States. He is not the only Jew in the Federal Reserve System, but he was the chief Jew there. His mind counted for a great deal. There were others in the war government, of course; Bernard M. Baruch; Eugene Meyer, Jr.; Hoover's regiment of Jews; Felix Frankfurter; Julius Rosenwald—hundreds of them, and everywhere; but the financial group alone is receiving our attention just now, and they are not so notably successful in getting the country out of financial difficulty as they were in other lines of effort.

The Federal Reserve System may not be a bad system, in spite of the fact that it yields government monetary functions to private financial corporations, but there are all sorts of testimony that it has been badly manipulated. Mr. Warburg, the reader will remember, spoke about certain things being "overcome in an administrative way," showing that there was a certain amount of "play" or loose motion in the system which could be manipulated either way. The fact remains that the country went swimmingly through the war by reason of the assistance of the System, and is coming very lamely through the Peace, as the result, monetary experts say, of the hindrance of the same System. Mr. Warburg, whose name was so prominently connected with the advertisement of the glory of the System, must also stand being mentioned in connection with the criticism.

Whatever money we are said to have as the per capita in the United States, it is a false statement. The money *per capita* should always be figured on the basis of the money *in circulation*. The statistical "per capita" is not always in circulation. Less than half of it, as a rule. The rest is being juggled.

Whatever the *gold* in the country, the *wealth* is still greater. There is more wealth in the United States than there is gold in the world. One year's products of the farms of the United States exceeds in money value all the gold in the world.

Yet, under our present system, the burgeoning bulk of the country's *wealth* must *pass through the narrow neck of Money*. And the *Money* must pass through the *still narrower neck of Gold*. And the controller of the Gold, under our present system, controls the world. There is more wealth than there is money; there is more money than there is gold; money exists at the pleasure of gold; wealth moves at the pleasure of money. Whoever sits at the neck of money, opening or closing as he will, controls the movement of the world's wealth. And the world's prosperity depends on the movement of that wealth. When wealth stands still and does not pass from hand to hand, the world's circulation has stopped; the world becomes economically sick.

The scarcity of cash in hand has led to Credit. Credit is a form of barter. It is a form of dealing by which many transactions are carried on, only the final one being cleared in money. It is a device which has its dangers, in spite of the efforts of apologists to exploit its advantages. But one thing the system of Credit indubitably does—it allows the money masters to hang on to the *Cash*. When the world is caught, *it is caught with paper,* not with Cash. The Cash is always in the hands of those who extol the advantage of the Credit System. Who holds money holds power, and will hold it, until real barter or *real money* comes in fashion again.

In 1919-1920, according to one of the best monetary authorities in the United States, the total shrinkage in values of the products of our fields, mines, factories, mills and forests represented a sum greater than the total gold supply of the world. It runs as high as the total amount of Liberty Bonds outstanding.

People say, "Well, the prices were too high." Certainly they were too high, but who and what made them too high? It was the generosity with which money was supplied by the private Federal Reserve System. There was plenty of money. People say, "Well, the shrinkage is only in paper values; the real value of the product is still there. " Certainly, but when you live under a system in which "real" value and "money" value are so intimately intertwined that it affects your bread and butter, the tenure of your farm, and the steadiness of your job, it is pretty hard to separate the two. Moreover, when your prosperity was due to the readiness of a group of men to let out money, and your adversity is due to the unwillingness of the same group, and your own welfare and your country's welfare is thus see-sawed up and down without any reference to natural law but solely upon determinations taken in committee rooms, you naturally inquire, "Who is doing this? Where is all the money gone? Who is holding it? Here is the wealth of the country; here is the need of the country; where is the money to transfer the wealth to the need? Every condition remains as it was, except money."

We have a Federal Reserve System, which still is benefiting by the assistance of its perfector and director, Paul M. Warburg. And what is the condition in the United States?

Some of the biggest industrial institutions in the country now in the hands of creditors' committees.

Farmers being sold out by the hundreds, their horses bringing about $3 each.

Cotton and wool enough to clothe the nation, spoiling in the hands of the men who raised it and cannot dispose of it.

Every line of business, railroading, newspaper publishing, store-keeping, manufacturing, agriculture, building, in depression. Why? For lack of money.

Where is the money? This is the country that is supposed to be the financial center of the world—*where is the money?*

It is in New York. The Federal Reserve System, which Mr. Warburg desired to head up in one central bank, has just about turned out that way. *The money is in New York.* Here is the charge made to the governor of the Federal Reserve Board by a responsible public official who knows:

While there is a scarcity of money for the producing sections of the West and Northwest, the South and Southwest, "we find that individual banks in New York City are borrowing from the Reserve System, in a number of cases, more than $100,000,000 each; and sometimes as much as $145,000,000 is loaned there to a single bank—*twice as much* as some of the Reserve Banks have been lending recently to *all* the member banks in their districts."

One bank in New York borrowed $134,00,000 *or* $20,000,000 *more* than the Federal Reserve Bank of Kansas City was advancing to 1,091 member banks in that Reserve District which covers the states of Kansas, Nebraska, Colorado, Wyoming, and parts of Missouri, Oklahoma and New Mexico.

At the same time, another New York bank was borrowing from the Federal Reserve Bank about $40,000,000, which was *more than the aggregate loans which the Federal Reserve Bank of Minneapolis was lending to its 1,000 member banks in the* great states of Minnesota, North and South Dakota, Montana and part of Wisconsin.

Another New York bank borrowed from the Federal Reserve Bank a sum which was *greater by $30,000,000 than the Federal Reserve Bank at Dallas was lending to all the banks in Texas, Louisiana and Oklahoma.*

Still another New York bank got a loan which *equaled the total loans allowed by the Federal Reserve Bank of St. Louis to the 569 member banks* of that very important district, which includes the whole state of Arkansas, parts of Illinois, Indiana, Kentucky, Tennessee and Mississippi, and the larger part of Missouri.

Take the Fifth Federal Reserve District, served by the Federal Reserve Bank at Richmond, Virginia: one New York bank was able to borrow from the New York Reserve Bank *more* than the Richmond Reserve Bank would lend to all its member banks in Maryland, Virginia, North and South Carolina and the larger part of West Virginia.

That is the situation. The twelve regional banks, which were supposed to make money serve all parts of the country equally, have apparently been "overcome in an administrative way" to such an extent that the New York Federal Reserve Bank is to all intents and purposes the Central Bank of the United States, and serves the speculative part of the country with millions, while the productive part of the country is permitted to wilt with paltry thousands.

When it can occur that four New York banks can borrow from the New York Federal Reserve Bank as much money as the banks of 21 states were able to borrow from the five Federal Reserve Banks of St. Louis, Kansas City, Minneapolis, Dallas and Richmond—there would seem to be need of explanation somewhere.

Where did this money loaned in New York come from? It came from those parts of the country where money was scarcest. In May, 1920, the word went out over telephones— "The tie-up will come on the 15th." And it came. Credit was stopped. Payment was pressed. A stream of money, literally

squeezed out of the producing sections of the country, began
to roll toward New York. Otherwise those giant loans just
recorded would have been impossible. It was pressure,
Federal Reserve pressure, politely known as deflation, and
that is the way it worked. The banks of the West were
squeezed dry that the banks of New York might overflow.

*"The money was withdrawn from legitimate business in
various parts of the country to be loaned at fancy rates in Wall
Street"* says the official referred to above.

The speculative banks, it has been discovered, were able
to borrow money at six per cent, which money they loaned at
as high as 20, 25 and 30 per cent.

Federal Reserve deflation created a scarcity which speculative banks utilized. The Federal Reserve policy took the
money out; New York banks borrowed the money thus taken
out, and loaned it at tremendous rates—rates which people
paid to stave off the ruin caused by the moneyless condition
which the ill-measured deflation process brought on.

And all this time the Federal Reserve System was in the
best financial condition of its whole career. In December,
1920, it had 45 per cent of its reserves, which was a higher
reserve than it had in December, 1919. But at this writing
(July, 1921) the reserve has reached 60 per cent.

The money is in New York. Go out through the agricultural states, and you will not find it. Go into the districts of
silent factories and you will not find it. It is in New York. The
Warburg Federal reserve has deflated the country. A System
that was intended to equalize the ups and downs of financial
weather has been used "in an administrative" way to deplete
the country of money.

The Federal Reserve Idea was doubtless right; if it had not
been it could not have been established. But it has been
manipulated. It has not been a "federal" reserve; it has been a
private reserve. It has been operated in the interest of bankers
and not of every one in general. Capable of being used to carry

the country gradually back to a natural flow of business and to a natural level of prices, it was used to bludgeon business at a critical time and to bludgeon it in such a way that money-lenders profited when producers suffered.

If that is the fact, there is no American banker but will say that the method was wrong; economically wrong, logically wrong, commercially wrong, if not criminally wrong.

Today the Federal Reserve boasts of its own reserve as if that were a sign of national economic health. With the country struggling to live, the Federal Reserve ought to be low, not high. The height which the reserve has reached is a measure of the depth of the country's depression.

If the Federal Reserve would let out a part of that flood of money—a high financial authority suggests that less than 10 per cent would do it—it would be like an infusion of blood into the nation's veins.

Kuhn, Loeb & Company, the Speyers and the other Jewish money-lenders have money for Mexico, Norway, Germany, and all sorts of commercial companies being organized to do business overseas, and it is American money. The Warburg Federal Reserve System has been badly misused, badly manipulated, and the country is suffering from it.

Still, the people know not what to do. Money is still a mystery. Banking is still sacrosanct. What would be perfectly apparent if done in ordinary business intercourse with a $5 bill, is exceedingly complicated when the sum is five millions and the parties are (1) country banks, (2) Federal Reserve banks and (3) Wall Street speculative institutions. Yet they are only Tom, Dick and Harry with a $5 bill, after all.

The matter is somewhat affected by the gags that are placed on many men competent to criticize. High officials are more or less tied up, by campaign contributions in which all financial concerns have an interest. Legislative officials are, too many of them, indebted to these same interests. A schedule of the private debts of some of the men who have aspired to the Presidency in the last eight years would be very illuminating—